John Masefield's
England

John Masefield during World War I
(Photo given Fraser Drew by Masefield)

John Masefield's England

A Study of the National Themes in His Work

Fraser Drew

Rutherford • Madison • Teaneck
Fairleigh Dickinson University Press

© 1973 by Associated University Presses, Inc.

Associated University Presses, Inc.
Cranbury, New Jersey 08512

Library of Congress Cataloging in Publication Data
Drew, Fraser Bragg, 1913–

    John Masefield's England.
    Bibliography: p.

    1. Masefield, John, 1878–1967. 2. England in
literature. 3. Characters and characteristics in
literature. I. Title.

PR6025.A77Z6   828′.9′1209   72-415
ISBN 0-8386-1020-X

Printed in the United States of America

to

Hazel Fraser Drew
George Albie Drew
Louise Townsend Nicholl
James Anthony Brophy, Jr.

Contents

7

Preface

For assistance in the preparation of this book I am particularly indebted, in alphabetical order, to Dr. Willard H. Bonner of the State University of New York at Buffalo; Dr. Charles A. Brady of Canisius College; James A. Brophy, Jr., of Kenmore, New York; H. Bacon Collamore of Hartford, Connecticut; Dr. Geoffrey Handley-Taylor of London; Dr. Corliss Lamont of New York City; Miss Louise Townsend Nicholl of New York City; the late President Harry W. Rockwell of State University College, Buffalo; and William Vincent Sieller and J. Robert Sullivan of Norfolk, Connecticut.

This book grew out of a long love for such Masefield poems as "The Everlasting Mercy," "Dauber," "Biography," "Ships," "August, 1914," "The Wanderer," "Reynard the Fox," "The Passing Strange," and "King Cole," and from a correspondence with the Poet Laureate that began in 1948. At that time I started to acquire Masefield first editions and related materials that became eventually a major collection, including A. E. Housman's copy of Masefield's first book, *Salt-Water Ballads*. To this collection, presented to the Guy W. Bailey Memorial Library of my alma mater, the University of Vermont, in 1969, Miss Nicholl added her own Masefield library and her letters from John Masefield. My doctoral dissertation, fifteen articles in British and North American journals, and a list of corrections and additions to the Simmons bibliography of Masefield appeared in the 1950s and 1960s.

The book comes principally from the conviction that John Masefield deserves more critical attention than he has received, that his reputation will reestablish itself, and that "the luck will alter and the star will rise."

Kenmore, New York

11

Acknowledgments

I wish to thank the following publishers for having given me permission to quote from copyrighted material:

Dodd Mead and Company, New York, for permission to quote from John Masefield, *A Tarpaulin Muster*, 1919.

The Macmillan Company, New York, for permission to quote from John Masefield, *The Story of a Round-House and Other Poems*, 1912; *The Everlasting Mercy and The Widow in the Bye Street*, 1912; *Captain Margaret*, 1916; *Gallipoli*, 1916; *Salt-Water Poems and Ballads*, 1916; *The War and the Future*, 1918; *Reynard the Fox*, 1919; *Reynard the Fox*, illustrated edition with introduction by John Masefield, 1920; *Right Royal*, 1920; *Enslaved and Other Poems*, 1920; *King Cole*, 1921; *Midsummer Night and Other Tales in Verse*, 1929; *The Hawbucks*, 1929; *Recent Prose*, revised edition, 1933; *A Letter from Pontus and Other Verse*, 1936; *In the Mill*, 1941; *The Nine Days Wonder*, 1941; *Wonderings*, 1943; *A Generation Risen*, 1943.

Society of Authors, London, for permission to quote from John Masefield, *The Story of a Round-House and Other Poems*, 1912; *The Everlasting Mercy and The Widow in the Bye Street*, 1912; *Captain Margaret*, 1916; *Gallipoli*, 1916; *Salt-Water Poems and Ballads*, 1916; *The War and the Future*, 1918; *Reynard the Fox*, 1919; *Reynard the Fox*, illustrated edition with introduction by John Masefield, 1920; *Right Royal*, 1920; *Enslaved and Other Poems*, 1920; *King Cole*, 1921; *A Sailor's Garland*, selected and edited by John Masefield, 1928; *Midsummer Night and Other Tales in Verse*, 1929; *The Hawbucks*,

1929; *Recent Prose,* revised edition, 1933; *A Letter from Pontus and Other Verse,* 1936; *In the Mill,* 1941; *The Nine Days Wonder,* 1941; *Wonderings,* 1943; *A Generation Risen,* 1943.

Permission for the use of the extract from *A Sailor's Garland* has been granted by the Society of Authors as the literary representative of John Masefield.

Extracts from letters written to me by the late Jack B. Yeats are quoted by permission of Anne and Michael Yeats, for which I thank them.

Finally, I wish to thank my editor, Mrs. Mathilde E. Finch, for her courtesy, patience, and skilled attention to my manuscript.

Introduction

In a public address on St. George's Day in 1918, John Masefield said:

> Understanding is the one thing worth while in this life. Art is nothing but the complete understanding of something. All writers long to understand the spirit of their race.[1]

The spirit of England, Masefield went on to say, is associated with St. George, her patron saint, and is a "manly and beautiful spirit." He finds it in Chaucer and Shakespeare and in the old ballads of Robin Hood, "who stood up for the poor, and was merry walking in the green forest." It is "in the old acts of the English, a shy, gentle, humourous, and most manly soul" that "cared for beauty" and "cared to be just and wise."

In this address, and elsewhere,[2] Masefield deplores the substitution of John Bull for St. George as the symbol of England. Throughout his poetry and prose, from 1902 to 1967, he persistently seeks evidence of the St. George in Englishmen and English life. His chief dedication is to what he feels is the English spirit and to the interpretation to the world of that spirit, the land and the heritage from which it springs, and the men and words and deeds that it inspires.

This study proposes to examine these interpretations, to see what phases of English life Masefield's work presents, to note how Masefield further defines and pictures English life, to detect what "English spirit" Masefield's work exhibits, and to show the relationship between the dedication described above and Masefield's appointment to the Poet Laureateship and his work as Poet Laureate.

15

Although Masefield's work has been scrutinized and criticized frequently in reviews and short essays, only three book-length studies of his work, those of W. H. Hamilton, Gilbert Thomas, and Muriel Spark, have been published. Four other studies, those of Cecil Biggane (1924), L. A. G. Strong (1953), Yu Da-Yuen (1934), and J. E. Mason (1938), are but brief appraisals, and the two latter are elementary and superficial. None of these has followed the suggestion that Masefield himself gave regarding his extraordinary interest in the "spirit of the race."

W. H. Hamilton's *John Masefield: A Critical Study*, published in 1922 and revised in 1925, and Gilbert Thomas's *John Masefield* (1933) are, of course, incomplete, written as they were in the middle years of Masefield's career. Both are general studies, treating no Masefield work in detail except *The Everlasting Mercy;* they are pleasant and objective introductions to their subject but lacking in scholarly apparatus. Muriel Spark's *John Masefield* (1953) shows that novelist Spark is "strongly attracted by Masefield's narrative art"; she approaches her subject as a story-teller and centers her study on *The Everlasting Mercy, Dauber, Reynard the Fox,* and some of the narrative prose.

The theme of this book is anticipated only in the title of Hamilton's ninth chapter, "The Sense and Spirit of England," which is brief and sketchy and fails to develop the theme suggested by the chapter title. Spark's only comments relevant to this book are that when Masefield writes, "as in the war histories, of national events on the grand scale, there are times when he seems to interpret fully the function of laureate"; and that *"Gallipoli, The Nine Days' Wonder,* and *Reynard the Fox* are primarily the work of a national-minded poet."[3]

Louise Townsend Nicholl's unpublished essay, *John Masefield: English Poet,* written in 1919, contains much valuable information obtained directly from Masefield, but it is concerned largely with Masefield's American experience, his wartime activities and war books, and his dramas.

No extensive and detailed examination of the entire body of Masefield's work has yet been attempted. It is hoped that this study may do something to fill this need and to clarify Masefield's role as national poet. Of the various types of work produced by Masefield, the poetry, fiction, and miscellaneous prose have been most useful in this study; the stories for children and the dramas have been of little importance.

Chapter 1 considers Masefield's interest in England's past, particularly in Roman Britain and the Arthurian cycle, his interest in the literary tradition, and his relationships with Chaucer and Shakespeare, the "poets of the race."

Chapter 2 explores Masefield's love for England, particularly for the actual earth and landscape of the homeland, and shows that he equates love of country with love of the countryside.

Chapter 3 concerns Masefield and the English people and emphasizes the galleries of English portraits in *Reynard the Fox* and *The Hawbucks*. Masefield's dedication to the common man and the "beaten man" is examined in this chapter.

English games and pastimes occupy chapter 4, with emphasis upon the traditionally English fox-hunt, point-to-point race, traveling circus, and fair, as they appear especially in *Reynard the Fox, Right Royal, The Widow in the Bye Street, King Cole,* and several of the novels.

The major Masefield theme of the sea is the subject of chapters 5 and 6. Masefield's concern with English ships and English sailors, both past and present, fills the large body of sea prose and sea poetry from *Salt-Water Ballads* and *A Mainsail Haul* down to *The Bluebells and Other Verse* and *Old Raiger and Other Verse.* Special attention is given to the marine novels, to *Dauber,* and to the saga of the ship *Wanderer.*

Chapter 7 presents Masefield's war work and his treatment of the English soldier. Chapter 8 discusses his appointment to the Poet Laureateship and his varied service to literature and the nation as Poet Laureate.

In all this work one perceives the unifying thread of Masefield's progress from his initial "consecration" to the common man, through his growing preoccupation with England and the English common man, to his most recent work as England's official poet. The dominant themes in Masefield's work are seen to be his interpretation of English life and the English spirit and his portrayal of English landscape and Englishmen.

Several limited contributions to Masefield bibliography have been made from time to time,[4] and in 1930 the Columbia University Press published Charles H. Simmons's *A Bibliography of*

John Masefield, a list of Masefield's writings and of critical mate-
riel concerning Masefield through 1929. In 1959 my own *Some
Contributions to the Bibliography of John Masefield* added 318
book reviews in the *Manchester Guardian* and fifty items of other
addenda and errata to the Simmons listings, and a year later
Geoffrey Handley-Taylor's *John Masefield, O. M., the Queen's
Poet Laureate* brought the canon of Masefield's own work along
from 1930 to 1960. There is need for an exhaustive bibliography
to incorporate the work of Simmons, Drew, and Handley-Taylor
and include the post-1960 writings of Masefield and his critics.

The Masefield biography is yet to be written. Corliss Lamont's
1971 *Remembering John Masefield,* with its introduction by the
late poet's daughter Judith, is a useful beginning. The publication
of additional letters and a full-length biography must follow.

Notes to Introduction

1. "St. George and the Dragon: A Speech for St. George's Day,
April 23rd, 1918," *The War and the Future* (New York: The Macmillan Co., 1918), p. 4.

2. See "On England," *The Country Scene* (London: Collins, 1937),
pp. 9–10; introductory sonnets in E. Gordon Craig, *Scene* (London:
Oxford University Press, 1923), pp. x–xi; "Dame Myra Hess Playing
to the Troops," *A Generation Risen* (London: Collins, 1942), p. 54;
John Ruskin (Bembridge: Yellowsands Press, 1920), pp. 4–8.

3. Muriel Spark, *John Masefield* (London: Peter Nevill, 1953),
pp. xi and 59.

4. Iolo A. Williams, *Bibliographies of Modern Authors, No. 2,
John Masefield* (London: Leslie Chaundy, 1921); H. S. Boutell,
"Modern English Firsts: John Masefield," *Publishers' Weekly* (June
21, 1930), pp. 3030–34; Clarence E. Sherman, "John Masefield: A
Contribution Toward a Bibliography," *Bulletin of Bibliography* 8
(1915): 158–60.

*John Masefield's
England*

1

The English Heritage

Masefield and England's Past

"A nation's past is the poet's pasture," wrote England's then Poet Laureate in "The Joy of Story-Telling," an essay published in 1951.[1] The early history of his country always interested John Masefield and found expression in one of his novels, several of his essays, and many of his poems. The story-teller Masefield often urged English artists to make greater use of

> Our English stories, in themselves a joy
> Deep and undying as the tale of Troy,
> But not yet consecrated to our use.[2]

In "An Art Worker," among the "ten tales that still / Have living power to thrill," he lists "four old tales of ours,/ English as Berkshire flowers." Three of them are from the early history of Britain: the Shropshire tale of Sabrina, Arthur's last fight on the Camlan Sands and his passing, and the Tristan and Isolt legend of the "fruit, Eternal Life."[3]

Again in 1944, Masefield urged the cause of the early English tales, asking that postwar England strengthen herself for the future and refresh herself in a revival of interest in such good things of her earlier days as his own favorite art of story-telling. Great bodies of fable lie untouched, an opportunity for every brooding imagination. The Arthur stories, the tales and half-memories of our pre-history and of our history; the legends of our standing stones, the ghosts and the highwaymen, the great who stood up against the wicked, and the wicked who stood up against life. We have a wealth and a wonder there, not yet touched with undying life such as brought Macbeth and Lear from the dull lines in Holinshed.[4]

Many of these tales Masefield has retold in his Roman British poems, his Arthurian poems, and his novel, *Badon Parchments*.

The Roman Britain Poems

From *Salt-Water Ballads* (1902) to *Grace Before Ploughing* (1966), there is frequent evidence of the poet's interest in the early years of Britain. In several poems he combines historical reminiscence with his favorite theme of the persistence of human influence in those places where human existence has been especially violent or tragic or beautiful, a theme that will be discussed in detail in chapter 2. The earliest of these poems is "On Malvern Hill," from Masefield's first volume. The poet describes the wind, which once "awakened into chorus/ The heartstrings in the ranks of Rome" and which now blows "the poising kestrel over/ The crumbling ramparts of the Caer." The lines recall details of the ancient battle and then close gently with "Quiet are clan and chief, and quiet/ Centurion and signifer."

This theme of persistence, only hinted at in the poem above, is strong in several poems from the 1912–1921 volumes.[5] The "Haunted Gate" sonnet from *Good Friday* (1916) tells of an evil place where a Roman soldier, burying stolen coins, had "stamped his anguish on that place's soul."

In "The Downland," from *Sonnets and Poems* (1916), the mood is elegiac rather than foreboding when Masefield writes of the "wind-barren lonely," once host to the Roman "from the palace by the Tiber" but now only to the moorland fowl.

The mood of "Here the Legion Halted" in *Lollingdon Downs* (1917) is similar, with its reconstruction of a Roman camp-site and its sentry, sick with longing for his home by a southern sea.

The longest Roman/Britain poem of Masefield's middle years

is the little drama from *Lollingdon Downs* called "The Frontier." Its persons are two soldiers, Lucius and Cotta, and their chief. Their speeches are short and clipped, and they talk, like any soldiers, of their distance from home, the dangers and boredoms and changing fortunes of service in a foreign land, and their foe, Old Foxfoot. Through their talk runs an undercurrent of the dissolution of Roman power in Britain, and in the closing lines the trumpets bray and the legionaries burn camp and march, seeing "the end of things."

Exclusive of the Arthurian poems to be discussed later, there are three poems, all narratives, from later collections, in which Masefield's interest in the legends or the relics of early Britain appears. In "The Wild Swan" from *Minnie Maylow's Story* (1931), Masefield retells the legend of the arrival of the Trojan Brutus in the islands that are to take their name, Britain, from him. Thus the poet is able at one point to link two bodies of story particularly dear to him—the Trojan and the early British. Much of the poem is devoted to a retelling of Troy's fall by her exiled prince, but the chariot race of princes for the hand of King Berroc's daughter gives Masefield an opportunity to read a roll of Old British and Celtic names: black-haired Erbin, ruler from Snowdon to the Dee; Howell of Bredon, "hearty as a horse"; pale Cradoc of Cornwall, "Fatal as the adder or the sea"; merry Prince Math of Kent; the boor Llywarch from the Wye; bald, coarse Conan of Eire, "swift-footed as a stag." It is a good race, but as in *Right Royal* (1920), supernatural "Helpers," this time the spirits of the royal Trojan dead, enter the race to help Prince Brutus to victory. An epilogue reveals that King Brutus governed so well, exhibiting the virtues, often recommended by the poet, of kindness to women and the weak, and of encouragement to the arts, that "this most blessed England then was named/ Britain from him (or so it has been claimed)."

Two narrative poems, "Simkin, Tomkin and Jack" from the same 1931 volume, and "Jouncer's Tump" from *On the Hill* (1949), reveal Masefield's interest in the physical survivals of the past. In the first poem, three modern youths break into an ancient barrow near the Roman Way and disclose a skeleton, still "Kingly, tho' fifteen centuries in the grave." The poet then proceeds to satirize contemporary blindness to certain permanent values, and contemporary preoccupation with science and business, by having two of the brothers clothe the skeleton in synthetic flesh and animate it with "Synthetic Spirit," while the third brother plans to sell the golden armor to collectors, to "have in the Press and Moving-Picture men," and to charge admission at the gates. The fantastic experiment is temporarily successful, as the ancient giant stirs, then strides out into the sunlight and summons "Spirits of the Morning" and Arthur from the dead. The spirits of the past answer the call and throng to the side of Arthur's comrade, "Beauties and powers wearing aureoles." The warrior's body drops into dust and the brothers hear a cry, "Open your doors and let the new life in." Once again, in this poem, Masefield has voiced his belief, stated in one of his American lectures, that the brave and the beautiful deeds of the past "build up a soul, which never dies, but lingers about the land for ever." It is this soul which in time of national danger "kindles and quickens and is alive"[6] and enters into Englishmen to strengthen and support them. Increasingly, through the later decades, Masefield revealed his fear for England's future and his anxiety lest Englishmen fail to recognize and cherish this spirit which alone may save them and recreate from "the dead England of our discontent" a land in which "our sign will again become the Rose."[7]

In "Jouncer's Tump" another barrow is robbed by a returned soldier and one of his cronies. Their motive is uncomplicated by any desire for scientific research; they seek only gold buried there for "twice a thousand year, or very near." In several stanzas of the poem the poet's love of the past shines through the story, as when one robber meditates over one small piece of his loot that the law has failed to confiscate, "a coin, or link, or flake/ Stamped with an ear of corn."

The Roman occupation of Britain and its survivals have less interest for Masefield, however, than the great body of Arthurian legend.

The Arthurian Poems and the Arthurian Novel

None of Masefield's accounts of his earliest reading, even "Early Reading" from *Grace Before Ploughing* (1966), includes any mention of the Arthurian tales of Malory or of any other

Arthurian story-teller except Tennyson. Writing from the view-point of 1895 in *In the Mill* (1941), he records that he had tried to read some of the *Idylls of the King* years before but "had never read one right through." While working in New York, in the bar of Luke O'Connor's Columbian Hotel, the young Masefield bought from a Sixth Avenue bookseller named Pratt "the first volume of a *Morte d'Arthur* issued in the Camelot classics."[8] This purchase is described in "My Library: Volume One":

> So it fell
> That summer morning on Sixth Avenue.
> I had gone shopping better than I knew,
> Returning friend to Bors and Lionel,
> Cousin to Tristan and Romance's Son.[9]

At the end of "In a New York Saloon," one of the prose sketches of *A Mainsail Haul* (1905), Masefield tells us that his work in the bar ended about 2:00 or 2:30 A.M., when he would go to his garret and read from "the 'Morte d'Arthur,' my only book, until I fell asleep." The poet reaffirms in *In the Mill* that for some of the year it was his only book and continues:

> I took a great deal of pleasure in it. Though I did not know it, I was born into a decade certain to be much moved by Malory and the sentimental view of the Middle Ages. . . . I was much moved by Malory's preface, and supposed that he was right, that Arthur had lived, and that relics of him might be seen in England, at Winchester, Dover and elsewhere. . . . The book seemed to me genuine, and Tennyson's poems seemed lifeless when set beside it.

Later in the same book Masefield writes of his discovery in a magazine, when he had been working in Yonkers for a few weeks, of an illustrated article on the Arthurian legend, containing an account of Glastonbury and of several villages that claimed to have been built on the site of Camelot. The article delighted the young man and fired his interest in Arthur.

Hoping to master the subject, he wrote a firm of New York booksellers for information on available books. The reply, with a bibliography of two hundred titles in stock and the promise of more, amazed Masefield, but he bought a complete Malory and read it "straight through." Thirty years were to pass before Masefield published, in 1927, a verse play, *Tristan and Isolt,* and, in 1928, *Midsummer Night and Other Tales in Verse,* a book of Arthurian poems, but there are occasional references to the matter of Malory before the appearance of these books.

In "The Joy of Story-Telling" (1951) Masefield writes again of the book that is "a foundation . . . for the imagination to work upon, for the story-teller to invent upon, for the romantic dancer to make enchanting and the musician to bring into the heart," a book which from French and British origins "passed into the imagination of the world" and became "our nearest approach to a holy book."

The first poem of the 1903 volume, *Ballads,* is called "The Ballad of Sir Bors." Although Sir Bors is the speaker of the lines and there is reference to the Quest of the Holy Grail, the poem is full of Celtic twilight and owes more to the early William Butler Yeats than to any Arthurian story-teller.

In 1913 Masefield wrote an introduction to a slim volume of poems by R. C. Phillimore, which includes "Sir Breuse sans Pitie" and "The Betraying of Guinever."[10] In his introductory essay Masefield comments on the "interesting metrical retelling of some of the Arthurian story" and continues:

> Against the Arthurian story it may be objected that Malory has told it finally in a fitting form, and that since we have it in prose we should therewith be content. Similar objections were raised, no doubt, when Shakespeare made free with Holinshed. The two or three great English stories should be a quarrying ground for the imaginations of our poets. . . .

Fourteen years later Masefield turned aside from several years of preoccupation with romantic adventure in Latin America and with the retelling of stories of Troy, Palestine, and Rome,[11] to write the first of his tales of Tristan and Isolt, a subject to which he was to return in two subsequent volumes.[12]

Although Malory includes many of the adventures of Sir Tristram in his *Morte d'Arthur,* Masefield adheres to the original independence of the Tristan story and the Arthurian body of legend. His collection of Arthurian poems, *Midsummer Night and Other Tales in Verse* (1928), contains no mention of Tristan, and in *I Want! I Want!* (1944) he lists "the tale of Tristan" and "the Arthur stories" as separate entities. Both are to him English, although the French Lancelot plays a major role in *Midsummer Night;* the Tristan legend he calls Cornish in origin.

In his retelling of the tales of Tristan and of Arthur, Masefield does not follow Malory or any other Arthurian story-teller completely. He even adds new details, new motives, new characterizations of his own, borrowing and inventing freely in the medieval tradition.

The Tristan of Masefield's verse play, *Tristan and Isolt* (1927), wins the gratitude of his uncle, Marc of Cornwall, by killing the pirate Kolbein, not Sir Marhaus, the Irish envoy of Malory's Book Eight, and it is by the dying Kolbein's will that Tristan takes the pirate's body to Ireland and claims his step-daughter Isolt for Marc. Malory's Irish queen hates Tristram for killing her brother Marhaus, but Thurid in the Masefield play thanks Tristan for freeing her from Kolbein's tyranny.

As in other versions of the story, Tristan and Isolt fall in love and unwittingly seal their love forever by drinking a magic wine. Here, as in his later poem, "The Love Gift," from *Minnie Maylow's Story* (1931), Masefield has Brangwen play the Queen on the wedding night and drink the wine that makes her forever love King Marc. As the drama increases in intensity, the modern poet seeks to relieve the tension by a rollicking incident in which Arthur tricks the meddlesome Kai and Bedwyr at the king's pig-pens and makes ridiculous these knights who are trying to trap Tristan and Isolt in their illicit love. However, Marc learns the truth and exiles Tristan. Isolt escapes with her lover and lives in the forest with him until Marc's generosity in sparing their lives, when he finds them asleep and unarmed, leads her to give up her guilty love and return to the court. Tristan, as in Malory's legend, from sorrow, not from petty jealousy, runs mad in the forest; coming to the castle in Marc's absence, he is repulsed by Isolt, flogged, and flung out of the court. Too late Isolt repents and goes to Tristan, finds him dying, and stabs herself. The conclusion seems melodramatic after Malory's bare statement in Book Nine that Marc, that traitor king slew the noble knight Sir Tristram, as he sat harping afore his lady La Beale Isoud, with a trenchant glaive, for whose death was much bewailing of every knight that ever were in Arthur's days;

and that Isolt died "swooning upon the corse of Sir Tristram, whereof was great pity." It is, however, as satisfactory an ending as the happy outcome of "Tristan's Singing" in the *Minnie Maylow* volume, in which the lovers are reunited in the forest when Isolt is drawn there irresistibly by Tristan's singing of the songs taught him by Nature. In this later poem, Isolt and Tristan are translated into spirits "Laughing aloft and singing and away/ Into some summer knowing no decay," while their fallen rags and robes become relics at a shrine where lovers go to pray to the "God of Love."

"Tristan's Singing," with its tapestry-like pictures, its Goddess Nature and its shrine to the God of Love, has more of the early and middle-period Chaucer,[13] when Chaucer is least English, than of Malory and the Tristan stories.

"The Love Gift" tells the story named by Masefield in "An Art Worker" as one of the four finest English tales. A forest-goddess like the Nature of *The Parliament of Fowls* and of "Tristan's Singing" gives Marc, who is never in Masefield the sly, despicable traitor-king of Malory, a gift of the fruit of immortality, whose "Eater cannot taste of Death." The gift may be given again but cannot be shared. Marc gives it to Isolt, and eventually from Brangwen it returns to Marc, who gives it to a child for his sick mother.

In the poem, "Tristan and Isolt," from *On the Hill* (1949), Masefield turns again to his favorite tale and retells it in irregular couplets. Here the story is simplified into a love affair between Tristan and Isolt, whose parents favor the suit of King Marc. The poet then mingles with the Tristan story the devices of a Herculean labor calculated to rid the parents of Tristan, a talking messenger-chaffinch called Mimi, a death-crystal stratagem reminiscent of Friar Laurence and Juliet, and finally an elopement like that of Paris and his stolen queen in "The Taking of Helen." The result is entertaining, but "Tristan and Isolt" ceases to be the tale from

John Masefield in Yonkers, 1896
(Photo given Fraser Drew by Louise Townsend Nicholl)

First Editions from the Fraser Drew Masefield Collection
(Courtesy J. Robert Sullivan)

Cornwall, "English as Berkshire flowers." Masefield's several treatments of the Tristan story well illustrate his liking for collecting, and for retelling in new versions "stories gather'd about many fires," some Asian and some from English shires.

In *Midsummer Night and Other Tales in Verse* (1928), twenty of the twenty-two poems are concerned chiefly with the legends of Arthur's birth, his coming to his kingship, and his death, with the intervening matter of Gwenivere and Lancelot and Modred and their part in the "breaking of the links." Although Masefield told us earlier of his particular fondness for the stories of Merlin and of Balin and Balan,[14] the brothers make no appearance in the *Midsummer Night* volume, and Merlin is only a minor character. The Grail cycle, with Bors, Percival, and Galahad, is missing, as are Tristan and Palomides, while Gareth, also important in Malory[15] and one of his most attractive figures, is allotted but a few lines in two poems.

Masefield's alterations and innovations are too numerous to cite in this study. Some have the imaginative qualities that Vida D. Scudder calls[16] the "coveted gift" and that "startle and waylay."[17] The most effective retellings are those, like "The Fight on the Wall" and "The Fight on the Beach," which are spare and terse and have an epic quality. This is the "touch of the Viking North" which Scudder commends; it comes when the poet is faithful to the English "genius, which is of the North."[18]

Effective in a very different way, and perhaps more characteristic of Masefield, are such lines as the closing stanzas of "Gwenivere Tells." The queen has retired to a cloister to do good and to break her beauty "with dule and dole." One day a pilgrim, unrecognizable in his hood, thrusts a package toward her through the bars of the convent.

> Within, on scarlet ivory, there lay
> A withered branchlet, having leaves of gray.
> A writing said: "This is an olive spray
>
> Picked for your blessing from a deathless tree
> That shades the garden of Gethsemane;
> May it give peace, as it has given me."

Did it give peace? Alas, a woman knows
The rind without may deaden under blows;
But who has peace when all within's a rose?

Among the battles in Arthurian story, Badon Hill especially
interested Masefield, and it is the central event in his only novel
of Ancient Britain.

In *I Want! I Want!*, a National Book Council Lecture in 1944,
urging research in the field of Britain's "Dark Ages," Masefield
cites the problems of the Wansdyke, Bokerley Dyke, Offa's Dyke,
and of the identification of Badon Hill "beyond any possibility of
error." He has twice told the story of the battle, once in the poem
"Badon Hill" in the *Midsummer Night* volume, once as the
central incident of his last novel, *Badon Parchments* (1947).

The novel is described on its jacket as "a work of fiction, based
upon the normal darkness of the Dark Ages, but speculating on
what MAY have been, for all that we know." The narrator is John
of Cos, a "servant" of the Emperor Justinian and the Empress
Theodora, subjects of two earlier Masefield novels *Basilissa* (1940)
and *Conquer* (1941); the narrator gives account of "events in
Britain," culminating in the battle of Badon Hill. In this novel
Masefield chooses to follow Nennius[19] and those other chroniclers
who assign Badon Hill to Arthur's long list of victories, rather
than the Welsh Gildas,[20] who omits Arthur from his story of the
battle, or the twentieth-century scholar, Wade-Evans,[21] who dates
the battle two centuries after Arthur's time.

Much more interesting than the question of sources is Masefield's
reconstruction of civilian life and of political and military tactics
in Ancient Britain. Although he shows corruption in medieval
government in a manner that constantly suggests modern parallels,
Masefield's picture of Arthurian Britain and its people is generally
a stirring and attractive one. Arthur, the old King Aurelian, King
Ocvran, and Prince Cador of Cornwall are memorable and admirable figures, and the narrator's report to his sovereigns is full
of praise for Britain, from the musical and impassioned speech
of its people to their virtues as "steadfast friends . . . valiant in a
cause . . . hopeful in a time of despair . . . generous to an enemy."
These, the reader of Masefield will find, are virtues of Masefield's
English heroes from Arthur down through Highworth Ridden of

ODTAA (1926) and Cyril Trewsbury of *The Bird of Dawning* (1933) to the anonymous soldiers and sailors of *A Generation Risen* (1943).

In a description of the training of British youths for war against the Heathen, Masefield casually explains the origin of Arthur's Round Table. The narrator writes of the youth of Caer Ocvran, each fifty of whom called themselves tables because they ate together. They were named "The Square, The Pentagon, The Triangle, The Nine-Sides, The Green Earth, The Bright Broom, and our guide's own Table, the best of them, The Round." The tale of the battle is carefully and excitingly told, differing in many respects from the poetic account in *Midsummer Night and Other Tales in Verse*. Names vary, and the earlier exploit of Arthur and Lancelot in firing the pirate fleet is not retold. Lancelot, perhaps because he is, after all, a French intruder into the English tale, does not appear in the novel.

The belief that Arthur will come again, that his exile in Avalon is but temporary, appears frequently in English folklore. It is a tradition that Malory reports and that is particularly pleasing to Masefield, as it was to Tennyson and Chesterton.[22] In a *Midsummer Night* poem, Masefield has Gwenivere say that the country folk believe in Arthur's return and watch for him each Midsummer Eve. In the brief lines of "On the Coming of Arthur," Masefield expresses the belief of literal-minded Gwenivere's "country-folk," such English country-folk as he often celebrates in verse and prose. Here is the Arthur whose spirit Masefield invokes for England-in-need, as he invokes the "great soul" of all the English dead and the "manly and beautiful spirit" of Saint George.[23]

> By ways unknown, unseen,
> The summer makes things green,
> The pastures and the boughs
> Wherein birds house.
>
> Summer will come again,
> For sick things become sane,
> And dead things fat the root
> That brings forth fruit.

Arthur, like summer, waits,
For Wit and Will are gates,
Like those the summers pass
To green earth's grass.

Arthur will come like June,
Full meadow and full moon
With roses up above
As red as love.

And may-bloom down below,
As white as fallen snow,
And no least linnet dumb;
O Arthur, come.

Although Masefield refers briefly to Malory and to the Arthuriad at various times, from 1903 to 1951, only three complete books, *Tristan and Isolt* (1927), *Midsummer Night and Other Tales in Verse* (1928), and *Badon Parchments* (1947), are devoted to Arthurian material. Masefield's active interest is apparently limited to the 1927–1931 and 1947–1951 periods of his writing. Thus the early enthusiasm which he records that he felt for Malory provides a recurring topic, but not a major theme, in Masefield's work.

Later English History and English Folklore

The long course of English history between Arthurian times and the great events of his own time holds less interest for Masefield than these extremes of the prehistory and the twentieth century. One exception is the story of England's development as a naval power; Masefield's interest in the great sea-captains and their battles and explorations will be discussed in chapter 6 in connection with his treatment of the sea and the English sailor.

There are, however, several poems and plays that deal with English historical figures neither very early nor modern. One of these is the poem "Dust to Dust" in the *Midsummer Night* volume. Henry Plantagenet and "Fair Rosamond" hear that "monkish picks" have disclosed the burial place of Arthur and his Queen. They come to look upon

> . . . those great ones placid under pyx;
> Arthur enswathed as by a burning wing
> Or wave of Gwenivere's undying hair,
> Which lit the vaulty darkness with its gold.

As King Henry and Rosamond kneel, a petal from "the crimson rose in Rosamunda's belt" drops on the dead, and the bodies crumble to powder within lead.

In "The Rose of the World" in the *Minnie Maylow's Story* collection, the poet retells the oft-told tale of Rosamond and the little house where Henry visited her, the jealous Queen's discovery of the secret, and Rosamond's death at Eleanor's hands.

Two of Masefield's plays deal with later periods of English history. "The Hour Strikes" is a poetic drama from the same volume as "The Rose of the World." "The Seeker," against the warning of shepherds, climbs a hill on Midsummer Night where, he is told, the Kings of the past go by, with Arthur at their head, and speak "of Times past and things to come." "Destiny" appears and, with her, veiled figures who reveal themselves in turn as Katharine of Aragon, Thomas Wolsey, Anne Bullen, and finally Henry VIII. Before the hour of midnight strikes, each tells his story.

Katharine speaks of sorrows that ensued "not singly but brood upon brood" until she died. Wolsey, the butcher's son who became "Bishop, then Lord Chancellor, Archbishop . . . more, Legate and Cardinal," records his glories and then his ruin when he was "stricken to the dust" and all his schemes became "Dust too, forgotten as men's dreams."

Anne introduces her tale by naming herself "Anne Bullen, whom men still remember with pity." Henry addresses Wolsey and the two Queens as three "pawns in a game." He then reviews his achievement as king in a proud summary, concluding that he had ruled "to greater purpose/ Than any English king since Arthur's time."

End and Beginning (1934) takes its name from its heroine's words, "In my End is my Beginning," which furnished a title for Maurice Baring and lines for T. S. Eliot as well. Mary Stuart is the only major character in the play; Elizabeth, Bothwell, Darnley, and the other actors in the drama of Mary's life are merely mentioned in the speeches of the Queen and of the minor characters. Mary is a prisoner when the play begins, and its action is brief. She is carefully and sympathetically presented, and her death is described at length by a nobleman who had been required to attend her. His concluding words praise her courtesy and announce the beginning of her true reign as "beautiful in the world's heart." The reader familiar with Masefield's dislike for John Bull as the symbol of his country will note with interest that Masefield gives this name to the Queen's executioner, the "brute" who snatched Mary's gold rosary from her hands and thrust it in his shoe.

At least two of the closing books of Masefield's career reveal his continued interest in English history. References in *Grace Before Ploughing* (1966) and *In Glad Thanksgiving* (1967) are few, but three poems of the 1961 *The Bluebells and Other Verse* have English historical subjects alongside Trojan, Mexican, and Biblical tales. "King Edward the Second Tells His Story" is an unusual account of the king's escape from Berkeley Castle to the life of a religious recluse in Italy. "Question and Answer: A Tale of Sutton Walls" returns to St. Guthlac, King Ethelred, Elfrida, and Offa for its characters. The third poem is an attractive ballad of an English saint-and-king's devotion to the Apostle John; its title is "King Edward the Confessor and His Ring."

Much of Masefield's work, particularly the two early collections of short stories and several later books of verse, shows evidence of his interest in folklore as well as in his nation's history and her heroic legends. The folklore material that Masefield uses in his prose or poetic retellings is often, but not always, English. Many of the yarns and sketches of *A Mainsail Haul* (1905) and *A Tarpaulin Muster* (1907) involve superstitions and survivals, but some of these are specifically nautical and some belong to Ireland[24] and other countries rather than to England. There are frequent ballad imitations in Masefield's volumes of verse; some of these, as in *On the Hill* (1949), are apparently French or Spanish in origin, or at least in locale, but the most powerful of the ballads are British.

The strongest evidence of Masefield's interest in English folklore lies in his long narrative poem, *King Cole* (1921); the ballads, "Cap on Head" and "The Hounds of Hell" from *Enslaved and Other Poems* (1920); and two pieces about Richard Whittington, one a verse play from *Minnie Maylow's Story* (1931) called by the hero's name, the other a narrative poem, "The Boy from Pauntley," from *A Letter from Pontus and Other Verse* (1936). Several poems from much later collections evidence a continuing attraction to folklore themes. *The Bluebells and Other Verse* (1961) includes "The Buried Bride or True Love Finds a Way," a Romeo and Julietish story that takes us through the vaults of death and charges of witchcraft to a happy ending. In *Old Raiger and Other Verse* (1965), the poem "Ryemeadows" is filled with fairy rings and night fears, while "Jane" delightfully records the title character's glimpse, one evening in June, of "THEM, many as snow snowing," dancing and singing for their fairy queen.

Perhaps Masefield's best poem of middle length is "The Hounds of Hell." John Gould Fletcher calls it "decidedly a fine ballad,"[25] worthy of a place beside *The Rime of the Ancient Mariner,* and much more akin to the old ballads than Swinburne's work or Wilde's *The Ballad of Reading Gaol*. It begins with chilling weirdness:

> About the crowing of the cock,
>   When the shepherds feel the cold,
> A horse's hoofs went clip-a-clock
>   Along the hangman's wold.

> The horse-hoofs trotted on the stone,
>   The hoof-sparks glittered by,
> And then a hunting horn was blown
>   And hounds broke into cry.

Suggesting the Saint Withold fragment from *King Lear,* III, 4, the ballad tells the story of St. Withiel's initial terror before the hooded huntsman, Death, a black horse "whose flecking foam was flame," and nine black hell-hounds. When finally he receives spiritual assistance through "a cool, green dream of paradise" and faces the nightriders,

> The baying of the hounds fell still,
>   Their jaws' salt fire died.
> The wind of morning struck in chill
>   Along that countryside.
>
> The blackness of the horse was shrunk,
>   His sides seemed ribbed and old.
> The rider, hooded like a monk,
>   Was trembling with the cold.

The huntsman is only a sickly hag who whimpers when faced with courage and the sign of the cross, and at cockcrow dwindles away with her pack to nothing. In addition to its genuine ballad-like quality, the poem also achieves what Gilbert Thomas calls "one of Masefield's most splendidly sustained lyrical expressions of that spiritual vision which alone enables man to rise above the brute."[26]

In the same volume with "The Hounds of Hell" appears "Cap on Head," a ballad retelling of a prose tale that had previously been published with the title, "In a Castle Ruin," in *A Mainsail Haul*. This tale is clearly of the British Isles, but it is difficult to localize it more specifically. Its hero bears the Irish name of O'Neill, but he serves a Scottish king, and the superstitions and other folklore elements involved are characteristic of a number of English and Scottish popular ballads.

It is hard to decide whether to assign King Cole to history, to heroic legend, or to folklore. In the Masefield poem, which will be discussed at length in chapters 2 and 4, he appears as the spirit of the old English king, privileged now to walk modern English roads in disguise and to bring comfort and happiness to deserving mortals.

Richard Whittington actually existed and was thrice Lord Mayor of London, but his story has long been combined with various versions of the favorite European folktale-motif of the gifted cat. Of Masefield's two tellings of the story, the second is by far the better. The first tricks out the legend as a verse play, in which Richard, his love Alice, and the cruel Mistress Mercer are joined as characters by Fortune, a Messenger, and Mapongo, grateful ruler of the fabulously wealthy land so well served by Dick's sea-going cat and her kittens. The story supports all the dignity of speech and scene with difficulty, especially at the end, when Richard and Alice vie with one another in suggesting marvelous philanthropic enterprises as beneficiaries of their newly acquired wealth.

Much more in keeping with the subject is the later narrative poem, "The Boy from Pauntley." This time the story does not lag or suffer from stilted dialogue, an unconvincing romantic situation, or an excess of philanthropic ardor at the end. Dick's cat is a cat right for story, and the Grocer and the Sea Captain, missing in "Richard Whittington," are welcome additions here. Richard Whittington's is just the sort of tale to appeal to Masefield's story-telling instinct (in fact, he tells us in "The Joy of Story-Telling" that a poem about Dick Whittington and his cat was one of his earliest favorites), and Dick is a typical Masefield boy, with the English pluck and self-reliance and decency to be found in such boy-heroes of Masefield's juvenile tales as Martin Hyde, Charles Harding, Jim Davis, and Kay Harker.[27] And Masefield's men are Masefield's boys grown older. Martin, Kay, and Jim grow into youths like Dauber, Dick Pomfret, and Hi Ridden,[28] and then into young men like Ned Mansell, Sard Harker, and Charles Cothill.[29] The folk story of Dick Whittington, then, had more than its Englishness of origin and detail to commend it to Masefield.

Masefield and Other English Writers

It is to be expected that a writer as much interested as Masefield in the history and the legends of his country would also admire many of the earlier writers who had established her literary tradition. A number of his critical essays and lectures and some less formal utterances offer the reader Masefield's opinions of his predecessors; internal evidence in his work, as well as several acknowledgments on his part, assists in an evaluation of his indebtedness to them.

In 1950 Masefield published *My Favourite English Poems,* a personal anthology of poems and lines from poems that he has "loved or admired for fifty years." The terminal limit of the anthology, 1849, excludes all Masefield's contemporaries, and he further limits the selection to poems written by Englishmen. At the end of a long introduction, Masefield offers his book in thanks especially to "seven among them" from whom "all that has been glad to me has come." Immediately the reader asks: Which seven? The poet does not tell. Perhaps his "seven" is the indeterminate, indefinite, magical seven of the popular ballads. But if he does mean seven, are they the seven of the forty-five poets in the anthology to whom the most space is allotted? The first six in order are: Shakespeare (58 pages), Milton (31), Chaucer (27), Shelley (21), Keats (18), and Wordsworth (17). Then after a long gap, come those from whom to choose the seventh: Beaumont and Fletcher (9), Donne (8), Coleridge (8), Browning (8), Spenser (7), Marlowe (7), Blake (6), Gray (6), Tennyson (6), Arnold (6), Herrick (5), Rossetti (4), and so forth.

This is not a fair way of selecting the seven, especially since many of the better poems of Tennyson, Browning, Arnold, and Rossetti were written after 1849.[30]

A survey of Masefield's bibliography in search of clues to his favorites reveals three studies of Shakespeare, and one each of Chaucer, Rossetti, and the later Yeats and Synge, as well as another that Shakespeare shares with Homer, Aeschylus, and Dante.[31] There are also editions of Marlowe, Keats, Jonson, Beaumont and Fletcher, Restoration Lyricists, Herrick, Defoe, Ruskin, and Du Maurier, which Masefield has edited, or for which he has written prefaces or notes.

In the preface to his *Collected Poems* (1918), Masefield writes of his early reading and of the influence of this reading on his work. Then, looking ahead to the years after the war, he writes of his hope of knowing

in fuller measure what the poets of my race have known, about that world and those people existing forever in England, the images of what England and the English may become, or spiritually are. Chaucer and Shakespeare, some lines of Gray, of Keats, of Wordsworth and of William Morris, the depth, force, beauty and tenderness of the English mind, are inspiration enough, and school enough and star enough to urge and guide in any night of the soul, however wayless from our blindness or black from our passions and our follies.

Clearly, no compilation of comments by the poet will make possible the absolute identification of his seven giants. A likely list would comprise Chaucer, Shakespeare, Milton, Wordsworth, Keats, Shelley, and either Morris or Rossetti.[32] Of these, Chaucer and Shakespeare are of greatest importance to Masefield, and in the passage just quoted he states clearly that his major indebtedness is to them: "Some lines" he cites from other writers, but the whole body of Chaucer and Shakespeare.

Chaucer and Shakespeare

Masefield's relationships to Chaucer and to Shakespeare are particularly interesting. The story of Masefield's conversion from work in a carpet factory and interest in the study of medicine is well known and is told by the poet in *In the Mill* (1941), as well as in the preface to the 1918 *Collected Poems*. One Friday afternoon in William Palmer East's Yonkers, New York, book shop, he bought a copy of Chaucer's *The Parliament of Fowls*, "price 75 cents, in a dull red binding." A glance into the book revealed that the old poet was "a lively spirit," and that very Sunday afternoon young Masefield stretched out on his bed and began to read, entering into "a world of poetry until then unknown."[33] In the preface to the 1918 *Collected Poems*, Masefield writes that Chaucer was the poet of his conversion and the *Parliament of Fowls* the poem.

Chaucer's influence upon Masefield is most to be noted in the long narrative poems, particularly in *Reynard the Fox* (1919); there are Chaucerian echoes in *The Everlasting Mercy* (1911), *The Widow in the Bye Street* (1912), and *Right Royal* (1920), as well as in such shorter pieces as "The Passing Strange" from

Enslaved (1920), and "The Love Gift," "Tristan's Singing," and one poem written in Chaucerian English, "Adamas and Eva" from *Minnie Maylow's Story and Other Tales and Scenes* (1931). The rime royal, the seven-line stanza form that Chaucer borrowed from Machaut and brought to perfection in *The Parliament of Fowls, Troilus and Criseyde,* and some of the *Canterbury Tales,* Masefield used to startling advantage in *The Widow in the Bye Street, Dauber, The Daffodil Fields,* parts of *King Cole, The Dream,* "Adamas and Eva," "Natalie Maisie," and "Pavilastukay," and with variations in rhyme pattern in "The Love Gift," "Tristan's Singing," and *South and East.* This form, used by Chaucer's immediate followers and by Shakespeare in *The Rape of Lucrece,* but for the most part neglected, Masefield calls "Chaucer's great contribution to our ways of writing" and "one of the most useful and beautiful of common English verse forms."[34]

Masefield's most important inheritance from Chaucer, however, is not the rime royal. Gilbert Thomas says that Masefield is in the tradition of great poets from Chaucer on down "who have taken the whole full-blooded life of man for their domain."[35] Henry A. Beers, reviewing *The Tragedy of Nan* and Masefield's first three long narrative poems for the *Yale Review,*[36] calls Masefield "a new poet of the true old English breed: like Chaucer . . . ," and points out that like Chaucer Masefield touches all kinds of life. "It has taken English poetry five hundred years to recover Chaucer's freedom and impartiality." Masefield's debt to the medieval poet in *Reynard the Fox* will be discussed at length in chapter 3.

Masefield's major statement on Chaucer is the Leslie Stephen Lecture at Cambridge University, later printed in book form as *Chaucer* (1931). It is an unpretentious hour's talk about "the first of the three great English poets." Story-teller Masefield speaks of Chaucer as "one fond of stories and interested in all ways of telling them and in all systems of arranging them when told." His words apply as well to himself. The Chaucer lecture closes with a fine tribute from pupil to master:

> . . . Chaucer was the first of our three great poets, the creator of a method and of a system. No other English poet, except Milton, added so much to the armoury of the art: no other,

except Shakespeare, has been so true, gentle, wise and merry in his statement of what is significant in life.

Although Masefield owes much to Chaucer and has frequently avowed and demonstrated his love for his master, he has never hesitated to grant Shakespeare first place among English writers and among all Englishmen. "The greatest English mind," and "England's chief contribution to the world"[37] he calls him; elsewhere he writes, "No other man born in these islands compares with him," and again, ". . . the plays are the greatest things ever made by the English mind."[38] In a third essay Masefield comments that Shakespeare's matchless sense of right and wrong has been felt by every age since his time—a distinction shared by no other English writer.[39]

It is a commonplace that the critic reveals himself in his criticism of others. Gilbert Thomas remarks that Masefield, writing of Shakespeare,

> has indirectly given us a reflection of the spirit that inspires himself . . . it is impossible to study the whole mass of Masefield's work without realising that there is behind it "a quick and noble nature," earnest with the passion for spiritual values, and undaunted in the belief, despite a far more than normal experience of humanity in its grossest aspects, of the divinity and high destiny of man. . . . "Poets," he says, "are great or little according to the nobleness of their endeavour to build a mansion for the soul." In that endeavour, at least, he has never flagged.

In *Shakespeare and the Spiritual Life* (1924), Masefield lists the shaping influence of Shakespeare's life and some of his personal qualities and "aptitudes." Many of these have striking parallels in Masefield's own experience and character.

"Orthodox religion, whether as ritual or as dogma, seems to have meant almost nothing to him," Masefield writes of Shakespeare. There is no evidence that Masefield adhered to any church or sect, although his essentially religious nature is obvious to any careful reader of his work, particularly in "The Passing Strange," *The Everlasting Mercy,* and the last pages of the lecture called *Poetry.*

Shakespeare's formal education was not extensive. Masefield's own schooling was brief, limited to his early years at the King's School, Warwick, and the specialized naval training aboard the ship *Conway*.[40] He attended no university and was largely self-educated through his wide reading and study. Masefield never scorns formal education, however, and has frequently praised the institution of the university. At Sheffield University he once said, "Wherever a University stands, it stands and shines; wherever it exists, the free minds of men, urged on to full and fair enquiry, may still bring wisdom into human affairs."[41]

The "old wives' tale side" of Masefield's training was important to him, as it was to Shakespeare, especially as we find evidence of it in the tales told him by Wallace Blair and other seamen during the *Conway* years and the sailing and wandering years. He pays tribute to Wally Blair, "a yarn-spinner of the old dog-watch kind," in *New Chum* (1944), *The Conway* (1933), and the dedication of *A Mainsail Haul* (1905), and more recently in "The Joy of Story-Telling" (1951). The "memory of the country-side" and "the tradition of the great events of the past" are interests common to Masefield and Shakespeare and material for much of their writing.

The "aptitudes within himself" that Masefield lists for Shakespeare include

> an intense delight in the beauty of natural objects; a love of flowers, of effects of light, of the flights and cries and songs of birds, of the colours, joys, and changes of the seasons; of the flavour that these things give to life, and of the intensity of joy that comes from being at one with such mysteries.

These are special delights and joys for Masefield, too; they will be discussed at length later, particularly in connection with *King Cole* and its catalogues of birds, flowers, and animals.

Masefield goes on to list Shakespeare's robustness and energy, his love of fun and of excitement such as that of hunting, and the "zest" of sex that "ran in him like a sea." For the existence of most of these aptitudes and characteristics in Masefield, there is ample evidence. His youthful love poems are none the less passionate for their tenderness and grace. His love of fun is evident particularly in the juvenile novels like *The Midnight Folk* (1927).

Robustness, energy, and excitement are major characteristics of the Masefield narrative poems and adventure novels, and, even if Masefield's attitude toward the hunt is not completely clear, *Reynard the Fox* and "Fox Hunting"[42] are certainly among the classics of the English fox-hunt. "These things," Masefield writes of Shakespeare, referring to the qualities and aptitudes mentioned above, "made up his equipment for the craft and mystery of poetry." Their parallels in the modern poet's life largely provide his own equipment for his work.

Masefield frequently speaks of Shakespeare in his writing: four of his books are largely concerned with the earlier writer. The first, *William Shakespeare* (1911), praised by W. H. Hamilton as "a unique primer and a masterpiece of its kind,"[43] requires longer comment below. *Shakespeare and Spiritual Life* was first presented as the Romanes lecture at Oxford in 1924. It is a brief examination of Shakespeare's England, the formative influences upon Shakespeare's life and work, and the greatness of the plays, particularly of *Julius Caesar, Hamlet, The Tempest,* and *Macbeth. Poetry,* also a lecture, is a consideration of "four supreme poets: . . . Homer, Aeschylus, Dante, and our own Shakespeare." Shakespeare is represented by *Macbeth,* in which occur "the most intensely felt lines he ever wrote or that were ever written in English." Masefield's most recent book about Shakespeare is *A Macbeth Production* (1945), his thoughts about the play and its production recorded for a band of young men who had asked his advice.[44]

William Shakespeare was published in 1911, as a volume in the *Home University Library of Modern Knowledge,* and in a revised and expanded edition in 1954. Its chief virtue and chief deficiency are cited by Hamilton in his comment that "nothing fresher has been written of the plays, although the compass of the little essays is necessarily narrow." For the student of Masefield rather than of Shakespeare, the book's main interest lies in its emphasis upon those Shakespearean qualities which are also characteristic of Masefield, particularly Shakespeare's love for his native countryside and for England as a nation. Shakespeare's love of country is also discussed at some length in chapter 2. Masefield speaks of it here in his essays on *Love's Labour's Lost, A Midsummer Night's Dream, King Richard II, The Taming of the Shrew, II King Henry IV, King Henry V,* and *The Winter's Tale.* The lyric at the end of *Love's Labour's Lost* he calls "the loveliest thing ever said about England," and of *King Henry V* he writes that in the epilogue to this play Shakespeare had "done more than any other English writer to make England sacred in the imaginations of her sons."[45] It is this quality in Shakespeare, as much as his supreme poetry and dramatic excellence, which gives him first rank in Masefield's mind and heart. Masefield felt that England's theaters had not given Shakespeare enough attention, and he complained about this neglect as early as 1911, in *William Shakespeare,* and as recently as 1950, in the introduction to *My Favourite English Poems.*[46] He must have been gratified, however, by the opening of the Shakespeare Memorial Theatre, "given to us by many hundred hands, American and British," on the great poet's birthday anniversary in 1932. For this occasion he wrote an ode dedicated to the new theater and to the "blackened shell" of the old theater built by Flower "lest English love of Shakespeare grow cold."[47]

Two other comments of Masefield add to an understanding of his relationship to Chaucer and Shakespeare. In 1916 the poet said that the English poets were not so much "masters of men's brains" as they were "companions of their hearts."[48] So, to John Masefield, are Chaucer and Shakespeare. And so, too, for those who read him, is John Masefield.

In his 1924 lecture, *With the Living Voice,* Masefield spoke of the added assistance a poet has when he speaks or sings his poem. The excitement of his hearers urges him on, and he becomes "one with the race and speaks from his race's heart like Chaucer, like Shakespeare."

His nation's past was indeed Masefield's pasture. His frequent concern in much of his work—with Roman Britain, with the legends of Tristan and Arthur, with English history and folklore, and with the literary tradition made by his masters, Chaucer and Shakespeare—serves as example to those artists whom he has urged to make use of "our English stories."

When critics like Gilbert Thomas and Henry A. Beers place Masefield in the succession of the great English poets, from Chaucer and Shakespeare downwards, and call Masefield a "new poet of the true English breed," it is because they find in his work that spirit of the race which Masefield found expressed in Chaucer and Shakespeare who were "at one with the race" and spoke from its heart.

Notes to Chapter 1

1. Part II, *Atlantic* (April 1951), p. 67, later included in *So Long to Learn* (London: William Heinemann, 1952).

2. *Wonderings* (London: William Heinemann, 1943), p. 56.

3. *Gautama the Enlightened and Other Verse* (London: William Heinemann, 1941), pp. 37–62.

4. *I Want! I Want!* (The Second Annual Lecture of the National Book Council) (London: National Book Council, 1944), p. 20.

5. In a review of Hilaire Belloc's "Hills and the Sea," *Manchester Guardian* (Oct. 19, 1906), Masefield writes of Belloc's "sense of that spirit of the past brooding over each landscape" and of his "very wonderful" treatment of the Roman occupation of the land.

6. "St. George and the Dragon," *The War and the Future* (New York: The Macmillan Co., 1918), p. 3.

7. *Wonderings*, p. 63; *A Generation Risen* (London: Collins, 1943), p. 7.

8. "The Joy of Story-Telling," Part II, p. 61.

9. *Saturday Review* (May 20, 1950), p. 16.

10. *Poems* (London: Sidgwick and Jackson, 1913), pp. 19–20.

11. *Sard Harker* (1924) and *ODTAA* (1926); *The Taking of Helen* (1923); *The Trial of Jesus* (1925), *Esther* (1922), and *A King's Daughter* (1923); *Berenice* (1922).

12. *Minnie Maylow's Story and Other Tales and Scenes* (1931) and *On the Hill* (1949).

13. E.g., *The Book of the Duchess, The House of Fame, The Parliament of Fowls,* and *The Legend of Good Women.*

14. *In the Mill* (London: William Heinemann, 1941), p. 44.

15. *Le Morte d'Arthur* (Everyman's Library, New York: E. P. Dutton and Co., 1906), references for Sir Gareth: I, 17; II, 11; VII, *passim;* X, 21, 55, 58, 60, 63, 67, 69, 76; XIII, 15–16; XVIII, 3, 18, 22–24; XIX, 11; XX, 1, 8–10, 16; XXI, 8.

16. "Masefield's Arthurian Tales," *Yale Review* (Spring 1929), p. 592.

17. Other innovations, such as the favorite Masefield motif of the "Helpers," add little to the tales and may even detract from their

essential Englishness, *e.g.*, "The Birth of Arthur," pp. 16–23, "The Sailing of Hell Race," pp. 50–64.

18. *Chaucer* (Cambridge: University Press, 1931), p. 28.

19. *Historia Britonum* 56, cited by Lucy Allen Paton, introd. to *Histories of the Kings of Britain by Geoffrey of Monmouth* (Everyman's Library, London: J. M. Dent and Co., 1911), pp. viii–ix.

20. *De Excidio et Conquestu Britanniae* 26, cited by Paton, p. x.

21. *Y Cymmrodor* 22 (1910): 125ff., cited by Paton, p. x.

22. *Le Morte d'Arthur* 21: 7: "But many men say that there is written upon his tomb this verse: Hic Jacet Arturus Quondam Rexque Futurus." See also Chesterton, "The Grave of Arthur" (1930), and Tennyson, "The Passing of Arthur," *Idylls of the King*.

23. "St. George and the Dragon," pp. 3, 4.

24. For Masefield's Irish relationships and influences, see Fraser Drew, "The Irish Allegiances of an English Laureate: John Masefield and Ireland," *Eire-Ireland* 3, no. 4 (Winter 1968): 24–34.

25. "John Masefield: A Study," *North American Review* (Oct. 1920), pp. 548–51.

26. Gilbert Thomas, *John Masefield* (London: Thornton Butterworth, 1932), p. 103.

27. In *Martin Hyde* (1910); *Lost Endeavour* (1910); *Jim Davis* (1911); and *The Midnight Folk* (1927).

28. In *Dauber* (1913); *Victorious Troy* (1935); and *ODTAA* (1926).

29. In *Dead Ned* (1938); *Live and Kicking Ned* (1939); *Sard Harker* (1924); and for Charles in *Reynard the Fox* (1919); *Right Royal* (1920); and *The Hawbucks* (1929).

30. For Masefield's attitudes toward his contemporaries, of whom he especially admired Hardy, Housman, Yeats, and Synge, see "The Joy of Story-Telling," Part II, pp. 64–67; John Cournos, "A Visit to John Masefield," *Independent* (Sept. 1912), pp. 533–38; Louise T. Nicholl, *John Masefield*, unpublished MS, pp. 6–7; Fraser Drew, "The Irish Allegiances of an English Laureate," pp. 24–34; and Judith Masefield, Introduction to Corliss Lamont, *Remembering John Masefield* (Rutherford: Fairleigh Dickinson University Press, 1971), p. 14.

31. *William Shakespeare* (1911), *Shakespeare and Spiritual Life* (1924), and *A Macbeth Production* (1945); *Chaucer* (1931), *Thanks Before Going* (1946), *Some Memories of W. B. Yeats* (1940), and *John M. Synge* (1915); *Poetry* (1931).

32. In the Introduction to *My Favourite English Poems* (London: William Heinemann, 1950), p. xxvi, Masefield writes: "I end this book with poems by Rossetti. What thanks Man can render to the

dead I offer here to him." See also sonnets at the beginning and end of *Thanks Before Going*.

33. *In the Mill*, pp. 96–97.

34. *Chaucer*, p. 19.

35. *John Masefield* (1932), p. 39.

36. (April, 1913), pp. 560–63.

37. *William Shakespeare* (London: Williams and Norgate, 1911), p. 175, and *Poetry* (London: William Heinemann, 1931), p. 12.

38. "On Shakespeare," *The Spear* (June 31 [sic], 1922), and *William Shakespeare*, p. v.

39. *Shakespeare and Spiritual Life* (Oxford: Clarendon Press, 1924), p. 12.

40. See *The Conway*, 1933, and *New Chum*, 1944, *passim*.

41. The University of Sheffield, "Speech by John Masefield, O. M., Poet Laureate, in reply to the Toast of the Honorary Graduands proposed by the Chancellor, 25th June, 1946," p. 2.

42. First printed as introduction to first illustrated edition of *Reynard the Fox* (New York: The Macmillan Co., 1920).

43. *John Masefield: A Critical Study* (London: George Allen and Unwin, 1922), p. 57.

44. See also *Manchester Guardian* reviews: "Shakespeare's Sea Terms Explained" (Jan. 5, 1911), and "Shakespeare as Playwright" (Jan. 26, 1914).

45. *William Shakespeare*, p. 33.

46. See also untitled sonnet, *Selected Poems* (1923), pp. 264–65, and "On Shakespeare," *The Spear* (June 31 [sic], 1922).

47. "Mr. Masefield's Ode," *Manchester Guardian* (Apr. 23, 1932).

48. Interview in *The Outlook* (Jan. 26, 1916), p. 173.

2

The English Countryside

Patriotism and Love of the Land

Love of country has always been a favorite subject for poetry, as frequent a subject as the seasons, death, love, war, and the passing of beauty, and England has had her share of patriotic poets. A list of them would include among others such diverse figures as Milton and Rupert Brooke, Shakespeare and Siegfried Sassoon. It would range from the rural muse of John Clare, rarely looking beyond the Northamptonshire fields, to the voice of Rudyard Kipling, unofficial laureate of a worldwide British empire.

John Masefield would grant few of these poets the complete "understanding of the spirit of their race" for which he believes all writers should long and strive. They may express with passion certain emotional attitudes toward England, or they may faithfully reproduce certain aspects of England and English life, but only a few does he find possessed of the spirit of Saint George. In *William Shakespeare* (1911) he writes:

> It is a strange and sad thing that the English poets have cared little for England; or, caring for England, have had little sense of the spirit of the English. . . . Only two or three show the mettle of their pasture in such a way that he who reads them can be sure that the indefinable soul of England has given their words something sacred and of the land.

Shakespeare is an exception. Masefield hails him as the possessor of "all the spiritual powers of the English" and as the maker of "a map of the English character" of which "we have not yet passed the frontiers."

In this essay, as elsewhere in his work, Masefield equates or identifies patriotism, the love of country, with love of *the country,* the actual earth of the homeland.

> It is one of his (Shakespeare's) humanities that the English country, which made him, always meant much to him, so that, now, wherever his works go, something of the soul of that country goes too, to comfort exiles over the sea. . . . Shakespeare's heart always turned for quiet happiness to the country where he lived as a boy.

Earlier in *William Shakespeare,* Masefield describes the placid charm of the country about Stratford and the bolder beauty of the Cotswold hills, a few miles away, "where country life was at its best and the beauty of England at its bravest," and in another essay, *Shakespeare and Spiritual Life* (1924), he records the earlier writer's "intense delight in the beauty of natural objects."

In Masefield's own poem "Biography,"[1] he is thankful for two gifts above all others received at "life's hands": the gift of being near ships, and that other, granted to both Shakespeare and Wordsworth, "the gift of country life." In the same poem the poet records among his "golden instants" that English dusk when once more he beheld the shores and the streets of his country. The commonplace but always real happiness of the man come home is also described in the novel *The Hawbucks* (1929), when George Childrey returns to "something stable in his life, a piece of England that had been among his forbears for more than two hundred years." His first night home he goes out into the mild winter night to hear the "triple bark of the vixen" and looks forward to hearing "the other English cries" of the rabbit, the stormcock, and the lark.

The equally commonplace and equally real homesickness of the wanderer and the exile also finds expression in Masefield's work. In *The Daffodil Fields* (1913), Michael and Lion meet in the Argentine, where "the Shropshire name/ Rang trebly dear in that outlandish spot." They recall partridge shooting, "the old Shropshire mountain and the fair," and in quieter moments think

> . . . of English fields which that moon saw,
> Fields full of quiet beauty lying hushed
> At midnight in the moment full of awe,
> When the red fox comes creeping, dewy-brushed.

There is a record, too, of Masefield's own thoughts of home in *In the Mill* (1950), when he is writing of the beauty of autumn days along the Hudson, where he walked during his stay in Yonkers. Even in the midst of this beauty, the young Masefield is thinking of England.

> At the time, I used to say to myself, that the sun was going down on his way to England, and that before I saw him again he would have roused the cocks in the English roosts, and risen over England and then come floating across the gray sea to where I was. Many a time I watched the sun going down behind these cliffs; and bade him take my love there.

Perhaps Masefield's equation of patriotism and love of the earth shows to best advantage in his only war poem of the First World War, one of his finest utterances, "August, 1914."[2] The form and the mood of this poem recall Gray's famous *Elegy*, which Masefield much admires and has called "a burst of religious feeling for England."[3] Masefield's patriotism, shown in "August, 1914," is not of the popular variety. In his play, *The Tragedy of Pompey the Great* (1910), Cato tells Metellus that the Rome he serves is not a Rome of bricks but one which "glimmers in the uplifted heart." In "August, 1914" the poet serves both the physical and the spiritual England. First he describes the English countryside near nightfall, praising with warmth of love the beauty of "these English fields/ Touched by the twilight's coming into awe." The lines recall one of Masefield's addresses given in America in 1918, "St. George and the Dragon," when he speaks of the last week before the outbreak of the war. He had been in an eight-hundred-year-old Berkshire house with "a little company of lovely friends," including Rupert Brooke. He had never seen England so beautiful as then, and the friends had read poems "in that old haunt of beauty, and wandered on the Downs."

Looking out over the valley, the poet sees the familiar country-side of "heartfelt things, past-speaking dear/ To unknown genera-tions of dead men" in centuries past. These men too had faced war, with its threatened loss of home, of family and friends, the cessation of well-loved work at home, and the promise of death "for some idea but dimly understood/ . . . which love of England prompted and made good."

Masefield's Theme of the Persistence of Beauty on the English Land

In the second part of "August, 1914," Masefield turns to a theme that has a particular fascination for him, a theme that recurs frequently in his poetry and his prose, the concept of immortality "near the men and things we love," of the persistence of the beautiful and the good near the original scene of that beauty and that goodness, a place "inestimably dear." "August, 1914" closes with the original twilight scene now in darkness, a darkness "that makes the meadows holier still." Silence broods with the darkness, and moonlight runs over the grass of the ancient road, built and traveled by the Romans and now rutted by the passing guns on their way to battle.

One of Masefield's clearest statements of his belief in this sort of immortality and persistence of spirit is made in "St. George and the Dragon." Prefacing his explanation of England's position in the First World War and his appeal for American aid, the poet said:

> I believe that the people of a country build up a spirit of that country, build up a soul, which never dies, but lingers about the land for ever. I believe that every manly and beautiful and generous and kindling act is eternal, and makes that soul still greater and more living, till in the land where manly and kindling souls have lived, there is everywhere about the earth, present like beauty, like inspiration, this living gift of the dead, this soul.

Masefield believes that a nation can be great only when it is true to this soul, and that in time of national danger "the soul behind a nation kindles and quickens and is alive and enters into men" to strengthen them. This is the English spirit descended from the ancient Britons, Robin Hood and the ballads, the *Canterbury Tales,* and the plays of Shakespeare, which will continue to support Englishmen and bring them "out of the land of Egypt into their pleasant heritage."

An interest in the history of the land itself and in the immemorial associations that cling to the land appears early in Masefield's work. In his first volume, *Salt-Water Ballads* (1902), the poem "On Malvern Hill" describes fields that had once heard Latin and the shrilling of Roman trumpets, there "where the cattle/ Are lowing home." But now clan and chief are quiet, and "quiet/ Centurion and signifer." "Biography," published ten years later, evidences the same interest, quickened now into a feeling that the land is haunted by the "not dead memory of the Roman men." In his catalogue of "bright days," the poet lists a June day among old Roman ruins where he felt the eagerness of "souls unseen"

> That man alive should understand men dead
> So many centuries since the blood was shed,
> And quickened with strange hush because this comer
> Sensed a strange soul alive behind the summer.

This interest in the old English past, which led eventually to the novel, *Badon Parchments* (1947), and to the many Arthurian poems, runs through the *Lollingdon Downs* volume (1917) with the concomitant themes of mutability and the persistent influence of the human spirit upon the land. The land receives the impress of all that has passed upon it. Sometimes that heritage is evil, as in the sonnet from *Good Friday* (1916) on a haunted gate and a chest of Roman coins. It is evil, too, in the 1917 poem called "The Cold Cotswolds." Here is a farm where murder has been done:

> No man takes it,
> Nothing grows there,

Blood straiks it,
A ghost goes there.

Two of the finest poems in *Lollingdon Downs* are written with
this theme of the persistence of influence. "The Downland,"
where "the Roman lived on the wind-barren lonely," ends in a
night "full of the past." The poem called "On the Downs" presents the timeless picture, like Hardy's "In Time of 'the Breaking
of Nations,'" of men at work on the downs, burning gorse, followed by these lines which Robinson Jeffers, the creator of Tamar
Cauldwell, must have liked:

And today on the downs, in the wind, the hawks, the grasses,
In blood and air,
Something passes me and cries as it passes,
On the chalk downland bare.

More often the ghosts that haunt the land are spirits of beauty
and goodness and strength, as in "August, 1914." There are
suggestions of these spirits in *King Cole* (1921) and *Right Royal*
(1920), as well as in shorter poems.

In the generally unsuccessful novel, *The Street of Today* (1911),
are several descriptions of rural England. The lovers, Rhoda and
Lionel, wandering near an old quarry in April, give the writer
occasion to ask what lies beyond life and to urge residence in
places haunted by good spirits, for "a place expresses the quality
of the spirits which seek life there." A few pages later the novelist
again withdraws from the story and touches upon the favorite
subject. "The landscape was a heritage displayed," he writes, and
suggests again that "men of strong passions" have lived in this
place, hallowing the land by the intense moments of their own
life, "wherever love, or hate, or joy has been."[4] This is the
thought several times expressed in Masefield sonnets, notably in
the thirty-fifth sonnet in the 1916 *Good Friday* collection, where
we read that "wherever beauty has been quick in clay/ Some
effluence of it lives, a spirit dwells," and in the twentieth sonnet
of the same volume, with its reminiscence of *The Rubaiyat:*

I never see the red rose crown the year,

Nor feel the young grass underneath my tread,
Without the thought "This living beauty here
Is earth's remembrance of a beauty dead.

One passage of *The Street of Today* continues the thought to an expression of belief in a personal immortality, for "our lives are creating spirits which will haunt the ways we have trodden." This is the conclusion, too, of "The Passing Strange," in which man is granted

Only a beauty, only a power
Sad in the fruit, bright in the flower,
Endlessly erring for its hour

But gathering, as we stray, a sense
Of life, so lovely and intense,
It lingers when we wander hence.

That those who follow feel behind
Their backs, when all before is blind,
Our joy, a rampart to the mind.[5]

The years did not alter Masefield's faith in a personal immortality of this sort. *On the Hill* (1949) has a dedication, "For L, from C and J," which we may assume is for the son, Lewis Crommelin Masefield (1910–1942), killed in action in the Second World War, from the parents, Constance[6] and John. The touching but serene lines of this dedication are:

You who knew this,
You who walked this hill and drew
Thoughts of what the truth is
From the Earth's remembered sweet,
Now are here, on hill and in the flower
In the whole vast valley of the wheat,
In its beauty, in its life and in its power.

The "Gift of Country Life"

Masefield's love of the land and his gratitude for the "gift of country life" have already been noted. In several of his earliest poems, his preference for the country is clear. Most of these poems were written when he was living in London "and thinking it a dark, dismal, and oppressive city." In the preface to a 1935 collected edition of his poems, he writes of his longing for the open spaces and freedom of his earlier years. "My first book of verses . . . consisted chiefly of ballads expressing a longing for fresh air." The swinging rhythm of "London Town,"[7] reminiscent of Henley's "Falmouth" and the old Bell-Bottom Trousers song, and at the same time of Housman, praises London's sights, her girls, and her ale, but asks for "Bredon Hill before me and Malvern Hill beyond." The lines have that charm so frequently lent by parochial reference, to "Tewksbury inns, and Malvern roofs, . . . and Ledbury church's spire," and the poet concludes by asking for "the hearty land, where I was bred, my land of heart's desire."

The first Masefield volume, *Salt-Water Ballads,* includes "Tewkesbury Road," a poem that celebrates the joy of travel, not at sea or in distant lands, but "through meadow and village." Though the language has the somewhat precious quality frequently to be observed in early Masefield verse and prose, the sincerity of the emotion is not to be questioned. One of the poet's most frequently anthologized poems is "The West Wind," with its moving plea to the wanderer to come home to the "west lands, the old brown hills" where "April's in the west wind, and daffodils."

Masefield's clearest statement of preference for the country occurs in his foreword to the A. J. Munnings exhibition catalogue, "Pictures of the Belvoir Hunt" (1921), where he praises the artist's scenes for their freshness and sincerity, "the records of his enjoyments in English country life." To Masefield the beauty of the earth is an enduring beauty. "Country things," he writes, in the Munnings foreword, "abide while the fever passes." This sense of the continuity of life and landscape lightens temporary human griefs and burdens. The thought of "men going on long after we are dead" comforts the old widow and her condemned son in

The Widow in the Bye Street (1912) and Joe's father in *Dauber* (1912). It is the underlying theme of *The Daffodil Fields* (1913), in which a human tragedy is framed by two pictures of the brook that, in the first stanza of the poem, bubbles up from a spring near Ryemeadows Farmhouse, and runs out to sea, a river, at the poem's end. The river goes on, a symbol of life's continuity, from generation to generation, while the sad small story of Mary and Michael and Lion becomes a sea chanty for men of later days. This is the poet's comfort in one of his 1949 poems, "The Hill," as he looks at

> . . . what is man's foundation, the enduring scene that stands,
> Comforted by sun and water, glad of either in their season,
> Something that outlasts our minute, and has majesty for reason,
> While its granites wear to sands.

Masefield's knowledge of the landscape and the land is intimate and reveals itself over and over again in his poetry and in the descriptive passages of his novels and essays. One need look only at the last pages of *The Everlasting Mercy* (1911) or at *Reynard the Fox* (1919) or *The Country Scene* (1937) to find striking evidence of this detailed and sympathetic knowledge.

In the little volume called *Wonderings* (1943), a record of memories recalled from the first six years of his life, the poet lists his earliest recollections as water and a cataract; rooks making their cradles, "high in the elms . . . in sunlight, in an April sky"; and a trackway through an orchard to a boat "wherein my pilgrim self first went afloat."

From the longer passages that follow, it is easy to see that the sights of country life made early and vivid impression on the boy. The first memories of flowers, to be described again and again in *King Cole, The Daffodil Fields,* and other poems, are of dim white clover and pale blue chicory. Masefield's native town, "a little town of ancient grace," appears in this poem, with the old canal, and the "daily western view" in which the boy delighted. The fields are described for their terrors, such as the bull, gypsies, and a weird and straggly fir, and their joys—"Three oaks together; three/ Like islands in the sea," a ring on the grass where the fairies must have danced, pools and brooks, the colors of flowers and birds, and a spring that was "blackbird-wet-and-green-and-mauve." Spring, high June day, harvest-time are all presented as the poet first experienced them, and the genesis of the poet of *The Everlasting Mercy, Reynard the Fox,* and the sonnets is clearer to the reader from an examination of *Wonderings.*

In October of 1950 at Hereford, Masefield received the "Freedom of the City" and paid tribute to that city, its county, and England in the following words:

> I am linked to this County by subtle ties, deeper than I can explain: they are ties of beauty. Whenever I think of Paradise, I think of parts of this County. Whenever I think of a perfect Human State, I think of parts of this County. Whenever I think of the bounty and beauty of God, I think of parts of this County.

> I know no land more full of beauty and bounty than this red land, so good for corn and hops and roses. I am glad to have lived in a country where nearly everyone lived on and by the land, singing as they carried the harvest home, and taking such pride in the horses, and in the great cattle, and in the cider trees. It will be a happy day for England when she realises that those things and the men who care for them are the real wealth of a land: the beauty and bounty of Earth being the shadow of Heaven.

> Formerly, when men lived in the beauty and bounty of Earth, the reality of Heaven was very near; every brook and grove and hill was holy, and men out of their beauty and bounty built shrines so lovely that the spirits which inhabit Heaven came down and dwelt in them and were companions to men and women, and men listened to divine speech. All up and down this County are those lovely shrines, all of the old time.

> I was born in this County where there are so many of these shrines, the still living evidence that men here can enter Paradise. I passed my childhood looking out on these red ploughlands and woodland and pasture and lovely brooks, knowing that Paradise is just behind them. I have passed long years thinking on them, hoping that by the miracle of poetry the thought of them would get me into Paradise, so that I might tell the people of Paradise, in the words learned there, and that people would then know and be happy. I have not done that,

of course, nor begun to, but in giving me this freedom you recognise that I have tried, and I therefore thank you.[8]

One of Masefield's later books is an essay called *The Ledbury Scene As I Have Used It in My Verse* (1951). Hearing that the bells of Ledbury Church, "the church so fair" of *The Everlasting Mercy,* "had to be silenced for a time of costly and difficult repair, and that much money would be needed to do this work, strengthen the tower, and then rehang the peal," Masefield wrote the essay and contributed to the restoration fund his part of the proceeds of the sale of a limited, autographed edition. In his essay the poet traces the part played by Ledbury and Herefordshire in his verse; on every page he reveals his love for his native region, rich, as the Spanish proverb suggests, in "the three good things of life, 'good air, good water and good bells.' " His hope in much of his writing has been "to make some familiar place . . . more dear, by filling it with an imagined passion," as Thomas Hardy had done for "Wessex" in Southern England. Yet, with characteristic modesty, Masefield concludes his essay thus:

> Let it not be thought that I think my verse important. What merit may be in the pieces quoted from is due to the power of the Ledbury Scene upon the wax of youth and to the voice of the scene from the church tower.

English Landscape in the Novels

Five of Masefield's twenty novels, not counting the juvenile tales, *Martin Hyde, Lost Endeavour, Jim Davis,* and *The Midnight Folk,* have a nineteenth-century or twentieth-century English locale.[9] In one of these five, *Eggs and Baker* (1936), the action takes place in the towns of "Tatchester," "Condicote," and "Stanchester." The reader sees nothing of the English countryside. Most of the action of *Dead Ned* (1938) is confined to London and Cholsington, and, except for a glimpse of the October Fair at Cholsington, one learns little of country life. *The Street of Today* (1911), *The Square Peg* (1937), and *The Hawbucks* (1929) are the only Masefield novels that show, to any extent, their writer's interest in the English countryside.

In *The Street of Today,* the countryside near Pudsey and Drow-cester creates an idyllic background for the courtship of Lionel and Rhoda and initiates some philosophical digressions on the part of the novelist. Masefield writes much more convincingly about the English April than about the love affair of the chief characters, who are stilted, unreal figures with strange conversations and marionette-like behavior. Often only the descriptive passages redeem the book from dullness.

All of *The Square Peg* takes place in the countryside near Tatchester, and much of it on Frampton Mansell's property, "The Mullples," at the edge of Spirr Wood. There are some outdoor scenes and some hunts, but the land actually plays only an indirect part in the novel. Its use is the subject of contention between Mansell, who wishes to make a bird and animal sanctuary, and the local fox-hunting gentry, who wish to hunt Spirr Wood as they have always done before Mansell's purchase of the property. The reader is left with the feeling that neither party really loves the land and that the writer does not support either party. Mansell's attachment to the land is in sentimental memory of his dead fiancée, who really loved it, while the fox-hunters, with the exception of Sir Peter Bynd, are actuated by their affection for the merely social and traditional aspects of their sport. They do not love the open air and the country, as do the men and women of *The Hawbucks* and *Reynard the Fox.*

In *The Hawbucks* the country atmosphere is comparable to that in many Masefield poems. The action of the novel never leaves the country, and the reader meets all the rural English folk from the squire, the doctor, and the canon to the servants, the gypsies, and the poachers. The fox-hunt, the hiring-fair, and the point-to-point race are all pictured, and the landscape varies from a blinding winter snowstorm on the downs, an eighteen-page incident, to the perfect early spring weather of the twenty-eight-page Cock-and-Pye hunt.

The novel's story is trivial, the often ridiculous rivalry of a dozen men for the hand of a beautiful girl, who unerringly chooses the one villain of the lot, but Gilbert Thomas praises the "lovely little cameos of the English countryside." English critical opinion united in pronouncing the detail correct, the atmosphere authentic. One reviewer wrote:

There are glimpses of country life in these pages which have rarely been surpassed in the language. They capture its very spirit just as Mr. Masefield has before now captured the very spirit of the sea.

and another journal commented that it could think of "no other novel one would more gladly place in the hands of a visitor from abroad with the recommendation, This is England."[10]

From this brief survey of the country element in Masefield's novels, it is evident that he makes little use of the English landscape in his prose narratives. His most successful attempts at fiction, *Sard Harker* and *The Bird of Dawning*, have employed either the sea or a foreign locale.

English Landscape as Background in the Narrative Poems

An examination of the narrative poetry of Masefield yields a far different conclusion. Of the major narrative poems, only *Enslaved* (1920) and *Rosas* (1918) have exotic backgrounds, one African, one Argentine, while *Dauber*, a sea poem, has one long English episode in flashback. The other six are completely English, except for one Argentine sequence in *The Daffodil Fields*, and many of the shorter narratives have English settings.

The English episode in *Dauber* occurs when the ship's painter has an opportunity to tell the reefer Si about the days before he came to sea. Dauber had been a farm boy near Pauntley. His father and sister loved the farm, but the boy and his mother had hated it; after the mother's death he had gone to sea. But in recollection of the farm, even Dauber admits that he loved "the beasts, the apple trees, and going haying." In Dauber's words, however, the landscape never comes alive, and the incident has little importance in the poem except to tell the story of the chief character's earlier years.

The English country scene is the background of six major narrative poems, *The Everlasting Mercy, The Widow in the Bye Street, The Daffodil Fields, Reynard the Fox, Right Royal,* and

King Cole. Its role never assumes the proportions of that of Egdon Heath and the Wessex country of Thomas Hardy, but it is often more than a pleasant backdrop for the action of the narrative. At times the land, its weather, and its plant and animal life reflect and intensify the moods of the characters in the poems; again, the landscape is often in contrast to the action, as Masefield employs his favorite device of the juxtaposition of ugliness and beauty, or of the contrast of peace in nature, tumult in man.

The scene of *The Everlasting Mercy* and *The Widow in the Bye Street* is definitely established as Ledbury, in Herefordshire. The identification is not made positive in the poems, but there is evidence in a later statement of the poet and in postcards sent to this writer by Masefield and annotated to show the relationship of the postcard scenes to the action and the characters of the two poems. Still more recently, in the 1951 essay described earlier in this chapter, Masefield established the scene of the two poems, and of other passages in his verse, as Ledbury and the surrounding countryside. This is the country of Masefield's childhood, no doubt frequently revisited, and he knew it well. Henry A. Beers, commenting on the reality of the background of these poems, writes that Crabbe, "Nature's sternest painter, yet the best," according to Byron,[11] does not come "so close to the harsh actuality as do these Shropshire pastorals."[12]

In a prefatory essay to the 1935 "complete" edition of his poems, Masefield tells how he came to write *The Everlasting Mercy.* One of the essay's most interesting revelations is the fact that the English countryside not only affords him a background for his narratives but was, in at least one instance, the specific inspiration for the writing of the poem. Masefield tells of beginning, in 1911, a new way of writing in which he continued for several years:

Towards the end of May in that most beautiful sunny year, it chanced that I went for a lonely evening walk in lonely country. I had walked for some miles; I cannot now recollect where; but was certainly returning home on a northerly course through a beech-wood. As I thrust through the hedge which parted the beech-wood from a stretch of common land, I said to myself, "Now I will write a poem about a blackguard who becomes converted." Immediately as I broke into the common land, the beginning of the poem floated up into my mind and

I began to compose it. When I reached home I wrote down what I had composed, and wrote on with great eagerness until nearly midnight.

Gilbert Thomas, commenting on this experience, suggests that "the contrast between the darkness of the wood and the light of the common brought one of those visions, those 'glimpses,' by which his best inspiration is always kindled. A more fundamental emergence from darkness into light was suggested."[13]

Certainly the contrast between light and dark is vivid in *The Everlasting Mercy;* there are few subtle or intermediate shades in the landscape or in the characters. Night and sin are black; dawn, and the new path that opens before the converted Saul, are a blinding white.

The poem is the story of the conversion of a drunken blackguard, appropriately named Saul Kane, to a decent Christian life. Saul tells his own story, beginning with an account of his fight with another poacher on Wood Top field one moonlit autumn night. The poet sketches a dark picture of the haunted quarry-pit near the field where the fight is to be held, a fitting landscape for the resolution of a sordid quarrel. After Saul's victory, his backers go with him to the local pub; on the way, Saul breaks the story to comment on the beauty of the night, a beauty that contrasts violently with the brutal tavern scene to follow.

After two drunken escapades in which he rouses the town by ringing the fire bell and is bested in an argument by the village parson, Saul wanders into the country and watches a stormy sunset. The beauty of the scene is one of the several agents in Saul's change of heart. After his later encounter with Miss Bourne, the Quaker, the poem rises in intensity and beauty to the climax of Saul's conversion. The countryside no longer opposes the ugliness of the tavern, but complements the change in Saul, as he wanders in mounting ecstasy through a dawn that changes from rain to bright sunlight.

> The waters rushing from the rain
> Were singing Christ has risen again.
> I thought all earthly creatures knelt
> From rapture of the joy I felt.

The narrow station-wall's brick ledge,
The wild hop withering in the hedge,
The lights in huntsman's upper storey
Were parts of an eternal glory,
Were God's eternal garden flowers.
I stood in bliss at this for hours.

. . . .
It's dawn, and I must wander north
Along the road Christ led me forth.

Saul passes a gypsy camp and comes to Callow's Lane, where "two great fields" rise against the sky. There he sees old Callow at his autumn plowing, silhouetted against the sky. This episode also results directly from an experience that Masefield has recorded.

I had risen very early and had gone out into the morning with a friend who had to ride to catch a train some miles away. On our way down a lane in the freshness and brightness of the dew we saw coming towards us, up a slope in a field close to us, a plough team of noble horses followed by the advancing breaking wave of red clay thrust aside by the share. The ploughman was like Piers Plowman or Chaucer's ploughman, a staid, elderly, honest, and most kindly man whom we had long known and respected. The beauty and nobility of this sight moved me profoundly all day long.[14]

Saul watches "Old Callow at the task of God . . . turning a stubborn clay to fruit," and sees his own work there, "in the muddy fallow." He crosses the hedge, hitches his "boxer's belt a strap," jumps the ditch and takes the hales from farmer Callow. In a sort of epilogue, in which John Masefield rather than Saul Kane may be speaking, the poem resolves the realism of the country scene and the rapture of the conversion.

How swift the summer goes,
Forget-me-not, pink, rose.
The young grass when I started
And now the hay is carted,
And now my song is ended,
And all the summer splended.

. . . .
> O lovely lily clean,
> O lily springing green,
> O lily bursting white,
> Dear lily of delight,
> Spring in my heart agen
> That I may flower to men.

The Widow in the Bye Street presents more of a country pageant than does *The Everlasting Mercy*. Not only is the reader admitted to the cottage of a poor laborer and his widowed mother, where he shares their conversation, their troubles, and their simple pleasures, but he also attends the October Fair and a session of the Assize, and he consorts with railway workers, shepherds, blacksmiths, and gypsies.

The landscape is painted much less frequently in this poem than in its predecessor, but it is always in the background. When Jimmy stays up all night in anger and pain over his discovery of Anna's faithlessness, the poet describes the night's noises and the coming of the dawn. When Jimmy is imprisoned, awaiting execution for his murder of Anna's lover, the English countryside in April is presented at length. Its peace contrasts with the tumult in man's existence, and the coming of Spring to Jimmy's country is set against his own approaching death.

Anna, bringer of death to many men, leaves the scene of the murder and the trial, and goes away into the "pleasant pastured hills . . . sweet with thyme." There the quiet and loveliness of April are a contrast to the ugliness and unrest in her soul, although outwardly she too is serene and beautiful. The poor old widow loses her reason with grief for her son's death. Her wasted figure becomes a familiar sight as she wanders, mad and seemingly happy in her madness, through the countryside. In her singing are echoes of Proud Maisie, of Ophelia, and of the "solitary Highland lass."

> Singing her crazy song the mother goes,
> Singing as though her heart were full of peace,
> Moths knock the petals from the dropping rose,
> Stars make the glimmering pool a golden fleece,
> The moon droops west, but still she does not cease,

The little mice peep out to hear her sing,
Until the inn-man's cockerel shakes his wing.

And in the sunny dawns of hot Julys,
The labourers going to meadow see her there.
Rubbing the sleep out of their heavy eyes,
They lean upon the parapet to stare;
They see her plaiting basil in her hair,
Basil, the dark red wound-wort, cops of clover,
The blue self-heal and golden Jacks of Dover.

Dully they watch her, then they turn to go
To that high Shropshire upland of late hay;
Her singing lingers with them as they mow,
And many times they try it, now grave, now gay,
Till, with full throat, over the hills away,
They lift it clear; oh, very clear it towers
Mixed with the swish of many falling flowers.

Like *Dauber* and *The Daffodil Fields,* this narrative is a tragedy, and like them it ends peacefully.[15] The poor widow is reconciled with her son before his execution, and after his death she is spared the keenest of suffering by the loss of her reason. The poet leaves her at peace, singing and straying among the flowers. The tragedy is resolved into a final beauty, a beauty achieved partly, at least, through the poet's knowledge and love of English landscape.

The very title of *The Daffodil Fields* indicates the importance of the English countryside in this poem. Reference has already been made to the descriptive passages that frame the narrative at its beginning and its end. The story is of two men and a girl who grow up together on adjacent farms. Mary Keir is loved by quiet Lion Occleve, but gives her love to the more attractive but unstable Michael Gray. Deserted by Michael, Mary finally marries Lion, but when Michael returns at the news of her marriage, she runs away with him. After a time they decide to part, and Michael goes to tell Lion of the decision. The outraged husband attacks Michael, and in a bloody fray they kill each other.

This sordid tale of adultery and murder is narrated against the background of the well-loved Shropshire countryside. At first the landscape, lovely as it is, seems purely decorative and incidental to the story. The reader rejoices in it, as he cannot always rejoice in Masefield's characterizations and his dialogue, but the integration of action and description is not always successful here. The opening picture of the three farms, Ryemeadows, the Roughs, and the Foxholes, first presents the fields of daffodils, dancing and shivering beside the brook in early spring. The daffodil theme persists throughout the poem. The flowers glimmer in the moonlight on the windy night when Lion and Mary go to meet Michael at his first homecoming from France; when Michael leaves Mary to seek his fortune in South America, she flings herself down to cry among the withered daffodils. Their recurrence marks the passing of a year of Michael's absence, and when Lion goes to the Argentine to seek Michael, the strange land is characterized as "Far from the daffodil fields and friends." Mary waits another year for her lover's return, as once more March brings the daffodils. When he does come back, he debates his course of action, swayed finally by his recollection of "her ways,/ There in the daffodils in those old April days," and when they do meet again, in passionate embrace, it is in the fields, "While the brown brook ran on by buried daffodils."

Thirty times in the course of the poem the daffodils appear,[16] with increasingly dramatic significance as the action rises. At the last, Michael and Lion lie dying among the flowers spattered with their blood, and Mary, left alone with her dead lovers, strews their bodies with "primroses, daffodils, and cuckoo flowers." The symbolic flower is the last word in each of the seven cantos and the final word in the poem.

Landscape does more than mark the passing of the seasons and underline the horror of the climactic struggle in the fields. When Mary and Michael swear eternal love, by night, in the wood near the daffodil fields, there is no contrast of mood, but rather an integration. The lovers and the night become one in a breathless and beautiful hour, and Masefield, usually an unconvincing portrayer of human love, is here eminently successful. It is the magic of the wood, however, not of the lovers.

The wood's conspiracy of occult powers

Drew all about them, and for hours on hours
No murmur shook the oaks, the stars did house
Their lights like lamps upon those never-moving
    boughs.

. . . .

No word profaned the peace of that glad giving,
But the warm dimness of the night stood still,
Drawing all beauty to the point of living,
There in the beech-tree's shadow on the hill.

At the close of this often melodramatic poem, the tragedy is
resolved, as in *Dauber* and *The Widow in the Bye Street,* in a
scene of peace and beauty. The river of the daffodil fields finds its
way into a mightier water, where all the ocean opens to a ship
and the crew sings "this old tale of woe among the daffodils."

The atmosphere of *Reynard the Fox* and *Right Royal* is a change
from the horror and tragedy and danger of the four earlier narrative poems. In these two there is no cruelty or crime of passion,
no madness or heartbreaking grief. They are poems of the open
air, of swift, joyous activity and good health and spirits. They
will receive consideration later as paeans in praise of the horse
race and the fox-hunt; here they will be reviewed as glorifications
of the English countryside.

Reynard the Fox opens with a detailed picture of the activity
at the Cock and Pye inn on the morning of the hunt. The stables,
harness room, and inn yard all reflect the poet's microscopic
observation and descriptive power. As the day advances, the
hunters begin to arrive, and each is presented to the reader in
turn. There is a glimpse of the landscape in the picture of Charles
Cothill, who is later to appear in both *Right Royal* and *The
Hawbucks,*

He loved to hurry like a swallow
For miles on miles of short-grassed, sweet
Blue-harebelled downs, where dewy feet
Of pure winds hurry ceaselessly.
He loved the downland like a sea,
The downland where the kestrels hover,
The downland had him for a lover.

and another glimpse when Tom Dansey, the "first whip," is
described.

> He loved the English countryside;
> The wine-leaved bramble in the ride,
> The lichen on the apple-trees,
> The poultry ranging on the lees,
> The farms, the moist earth-smelling cover,
> His wife's green grave at Mitcheldover,
> Where snowdrops pushed at the first thaw.
> Under his hide his heart was raw
> With joy and pity of these things.

These are among the lines to which Middleton Murry objects in
his criticism of the "nostalgia of Mr. Masefield." Murry finds the
last two lines uncharacteristic of a first whip and a betrayal of
the "outsider" in Masefield. "In his fervour to grasp at that which
for all his love is still alien to him," writes the critic, "Masefield
seems almost to shovel English mud into his pages; he cannot
persuade himself that the scent of the mud will be there otherwise."
Murry appears to be alone in detecting in Masefield a straining
for the realism of landscape and of character, overemphasizing detail and betraying a hint of decadence and the "desperate bergerie
of the Georgian era."[17] Other critics and the general reader seem
to find the open-air quality of the poem, especially in its description
of the English landscape, one of its finest achievements. Theodore
Maynard finds *Reynard the Fox* "the most English of all Mr.
Masefield's poems."[18] Coulson Kernahan calls *Reynard the Fox*
Masefield's best poem because "it sings the England we all love"
and because Masefield obviously loved writing it.[19]

The second part of the poem concerns the hunt itself, and here
the reader meets for the first time the hero, Reynard. In the section
on fox-hunting in chapter 4, Reynard will be described in detail.
His haunts are pictured:

> On old Cold Crendon's windy tops
> Grows wintrily Blown Hilcote Copse,
> Wind-bitten beech with badger barrows,

Where brocks eat wasp-grubs with their marrows,
And foxes lie on short-grassed turf,
Nose between paws, to hear the surf
Of wind in the beeches drowsily.
There was our fox bred lustily . . .

As later the hunt gets under way, the reader follows it, now
with the riders, now with the fox, and there are frequent views of
the country. The pageant of the hunt, which Masefield praises as
one of England loveliest sights, along with the ships in her harbors
and the ploughmen moving against her skylines,[20] appears with
its swiftness and its color. Place after place, town, orchard, farm,
brook, crossing, is called by name as men pause in their work to
watch the hunt go by, and Mourne End Wood, in which Reynard
takes refuge, is as vividly described as the fields. After Reynard
finally escapes, the reader relaxes in the peace of the closing
picture—moonlight over the quiet countryside:

Then the moon came quiet and flooded full
Light and beauty on clouds like wool,
On a feasted fox at rest from hunting,
In the beech wood grey where the brocks were grunting.

The beech wood grey rose dim in the night
With moonlight fallen in pools of light,
The long dead leaves on the ground were rimed.
A clock struck twelve and the church-bells chimed.

Masefield once told an American reporter, several years before
the publication of *Reynard the Fox:*

To him (the English poet) each bit of the landscape has its
warm, personal meaning. Your hills and rivers and fields are
not your intimates. Your wide stretches of country seem raw;
the green of your foliage is more metallic, dusty, compared to
the rich green of our roadsides. Nature has a wide place in
our poetry.[21]

Right Royal has much the same energy and vigor and color as

Reynard the Fox, but its confinement to the race course gives its poet less scope for his landscape painting. Perhaps the freshest lines in the poem are those describing Emmy Crowthorne in the opening stanzas. Fit mate for Charles Cothill (the "tall, black, bright-eyed handsome lad" of *Reynard the Fox*), Emmy is "as dear as sunshine after rain" and loves the land as deeply as Charles does.

The exciting race finally won by Right Royal is filled with quick flashes of landscape description and similes drawn from the weather and the creatures of the countryside. Most of Masefield's similes are drawn from England, but now and then an occasional memory of the Argentine or of North America serves him.[22]

Once again the poet ends a narrative poem with a country picture, this time with evidence again of that interest in the historical heritage of the land which is so prominent in *Lollingdon Downs* and other volumes. Charles marries his lady and lives on the downland, where "he and Right Royal can canter for hours."

> There the Roman pitcht camp, there the Saxon kept sheep,
> There he lives out this living that no man can keep,
> That is manful but a moment before it must pass,
> Like the stars sweeping westward, like the wind on the grass.

Before considering the last major narrative poem, *King Cole,* one might notice briefly some of the shorter narratives published between 1920 and 1938. In many of these the English landscape also plays a significant part. The twelve-sonnet sequence, *Animula* (1920), tells a story of a love-triangle and its unhappy consequences. The setting is a house beside the sea and "two fields, all green with summer." Throughout, the sea and the shore reflect the moods of the characters and their story-teller.

A similar use of natural description and of similes from the landscape and its denizens may be observed in the ballad called "The Hounds of Hell" (1920).[23] When St. Withiel is in fear of the hellhounds and the spectre who unleashes them, rain, wind, darkness and a desolate land add to the effect of terror. But when the saint triumphs and unmasks the Death-spectre, there is sunlight and birdsong and a sound of church bells "over the sunny wold." In the ballad, "Cap on Head" (1920),[24] short stanzas of seasonal description serve to mark the passing of time in the story.

In *Midsummer's Night* (1928), as Arthur and his queen, Lance-lot, and the other figures come alive for Masefield, they are blended with the English countryside and the seasons. Here is the poet's picture of the coming of spring, which is also the coming of the west wind and of Arthur:

> Then the rooks call from elm-tops,
> And lambs from the fold;
> And the larks joy in heaven
> For death of the cold;
>
> And the blackbird calls clearest
> Of sweet birds that sing,
> And the dear becomes dearest
> Because it is Spring;
>
> And a joy of rejoicing
> Springs green in the corn;
> Such a joy was Ygerna's
> When Arthur was born.

The beauty of June fills the lines of the title poem, "Midsummer Night," and summer is invoked in the brief lyric, "On the Coming of Arthur." Even when the setting of the poem's action is not English, as in "The Sailing of Hell Race," and "South and East," the closing stanzas return to an English landscape. The returning Arthur, "as the haze blew seaward," sees "The hills of home, the country green with corn," and "South and East" ends with the stanza:

> Then, sometimes, in the hush, a glimmering glows
> Into a brightness in that Berkshire grass.
> Those lovers come where their first meeting was
> Beside the spring, within the holy close.
> They dance there through the night,
> Treading adown in patterns of delight
> Moon-daisy, vetch, and fallen hawthorn blows.

Minnie Maylow's Story (1931) is another collection of tales gathered, as the pilgrim of the Prologue says, from both Asian sands and English shires. "The Love Gift" and "Tristan's Singing," from this volume, are both stories of the lovers, Tristan and Isolt. Both have to do with visions of Midsummer Eve, in which there are extended pictures of the English landscape. These passages do not have the reality of the descriptions in the earlier narrative poems. They have a tapestry-like quality, like the pictures in a Chaucerian dream-vision, and the figures of Nature and her attendant creatures have beauty and color, but not life. Such, too, with its elaborate personifications of fruits and flowers, is the wondrous landscape of "Naia and Edward," the longest poem in *Tribute to Ballet* (1938), one of Masefield's collaborations with the artist Edward Seago.

One narrative from the collection, called *A Letter from Pontus* (1936), has highly realistic country scenery. "The Long Drive" is the poet's story of a motor trip of a night and a day from Edinburgh to his home at Boar's Hill. The poem is a running commentary on the country seen from the speeding car. Night in Scotland gives way to dawn over Lancaster and Preston; Shropshire is seen in daylight, and twilight falls on Bromsgrove. The drive ends at night again at Boar's Hill near Oxford. Of particular interest is the description of Carlyle's "granite-strown moors," and the lakes of the Wordsworth district appear at greater length as the poet recalls

. . . that those waters had mirrored the faces
Of a brother and sister, most dear to us still,
He, stern as the crags and as deep as their bases,
She, calm with a love that no evil can kill.

They lived with those mountains and lakes till the brother
Was one with their spirit and spoke with their voice,
And April herself laid her hand on the other
And gave her her power to bless and rejoice.

The water that mirrored their faces, the grasses
They trod on, have gone, as their bodies have gone,
But power vouchsafed to a soul never passes,
And beauty once given forever lives on.

Of the long verse narratives by Masefield, the quietest and most serene is *King Cole* (1921). It is as free from the rush and excitement of *Reynard the Fox* and *Right Royal* as it is from the danger and violence of *Rosas* and *Enslaved,* the pathos of *Dauber* and *The Widow in the Bye Street,* and the mixture of beauty and brutality that characterizes *The Everlasting Mercy* and *The Daffodil Fields.* The realism of *King Cole* is softened and sweetened by an extraordinary atmosphere of fairyland, which pervades the whole poem. It is as if King Cole's magic touched not only the town of Wallingford and the miserable circus troupe, but also the very pages of the book itself.

The English countryside is here, but it is touched with the supernatural and shines with the spirit. This is no photograph in black and white or in colors, nor yet is it the tapestry of landscape to be found in some of the minor narratives; this is water color, painted by a versatile artist who may be at his very best in this medium.

When King Cole, for his goodness, is permitted to return to the earth, he wanders England, "shore and shire," to help "distressful folk to their desire/ By power of spirit that within him lies." He wanders in the guise of an old and penniless traveler and "sees the great green world go floating by." When dusk begins, men hear him "piping a wooden flute to music old," as he walks on the downs or stops in a lonely inn, haunting the Downs and Chilterns and the "beech-tree-pasturing chalk."

Among the most appealing lines in the poem are those which catalogue the English flowers and list the birds and butterflies and creatures of the forest that follow the piping of the spirit-King. Masefield's poetry is thronged with descriptions of animals and flowers and with similes that employ them, attesting to his love for all life. When the spirit of Cole leads the circus through Wallingford in all the glory that his magic can command, all the English animals and birds join the procession. Such is the poet's sincerity and skill, that the result has nothing of the quality of ark, zoo, or natural history textbook, but becomes a fairyland parade.

> . . . walking by the vans, there came
> The wild things from the woodland and the mead,
> The red stag, with his tender-stepping dame,

> Branched, and high-tongued and ever taking heed.
> Nose-wrinkling rabbits nibbling at the weed,
> The hares that box by moonlight on the hill,
> The bright trout's death, the otter from the mill.
>
> There, with his mask made virtuous, came the fox,
> Talking of landscape while he thought of meat;
> Blood-loving weasels, honey-harrying brocks,
> Stoats, and the mice that build among the wheat,
> Dormice, and moles with little hands for feet,
> The water-rat that gnaws the yellow flag,
> Toads from the stone and merrows from the quag.

The poet's love for the English flowers is evident to the reader of his sonnets, *The Daffodil Fields,* or the Arthurian poems, and flowers are present in *King Cole,* especially

> Moist poppies scarlet from the Hilcote sheaves,
> Green-fingered bine that runs the barley-rows,
> Pale candylips, and those intense blue blows
> That trail the porches in the autumn dusk,
> Tempting the noiseless moth to tongue their musk.

The children of Wallingford, coming to the circus, walk before the royal patrons, scattering flowers along the way:

> Rust-spotted bracken green they scattered down,
> Blue cornflowers and withering poppies red,
> Gold charlock, thrift, the purple hardihead
> Harebells, the milfoil white, September clover,
> And boughs that berry red when summer's over,
> All autumn flowers, with yellow ears of wheat.

For the lover of forest and meadow creatures, as well as the lover of man's animal friends, there is delight almost everywhere in Masefield. His tenderness toward horse, dog, and deer is evident in scores of poems,[25] and his feeling for the fox in *Reynard* only escapes the ridiculous because it carries the reader along to the same point of view.

Masefield is aware of English weather and season and is sensitive to every change and token. He praises midsummer nights,[26] autumn,[27] and winter snow,[28] but most of all he loves April. A concordance to Masefield's poetry would reveal April as one of his favorite words. Not only does he describe springtime beauty and joy, but he uses April as a symbol for all that is fresh and lovely and bright. "Some April of a woman," he writes in *Lollingdon Downs,* and "Beauty herself, the universal mind, Eternal April, wandering alone," in one of the *Good Friday* sonnets. "April's in the west wind, and daffodils," is the promise in "The West Wind," and "Death brings another April to the soul," in "Waste." "I have seen the lady April bringing the daffodils," he writes in "Beauty,"[29] and "April was quick in Nature like green flame," in *The Daffodil Fields.* In *A Play of St. George,* the loveliest maidens are named Sea Wave and April Morning, while perhaps the best known of all are the lines from "On Growing Old":

> Beauty, have pity, for the strong have power
> The rich their wealth, the beautiful their grace,
> Summer of man its sunlight and its flower,
> Spring-time of man all April in a face.[30]

One of the last books, *Old Raiger and Other Verse* (1964), includes among its twelve poems "When April Comes" and "Mornings and Aprils."

As early as 1910, in *William Shakespeare,* Masefield complained that the English poets had "cared little for England," or, at least, had "had little sense of the spirit of the English"; to the poetry of only a few, including Shakespeare, had "the indefinable soul of England" given "something sacred and of the land." It is clear from the examples cited in this chapter from his prose and his poetry that Masefield's own love of the English earth and the beauty of the English landscape is a major theme throughout much of his work. His patriotic feeling for his country is evident in his varied service in France and in the Gallipoli campaign, his lecture tours of the United States and his work as war historian, as well as in his later books of World War II. However, Masefield's love of England is most clearly and most eloquently expressed in *William Shakespeare,* "August, 1914," "St. George and the Dragon," and "The Hereford Speech," in those passages in which he combines and equates love of country and love of the English land itself.

Notes to Chapter 2

1. *The Story of a Round-House and Other Poems* (New York: The Macmillan Co., 1912), pp. 187–209.

2. *Philip the King and Other Poems* (London: William Heinemann, 1914), pp. 72–75. One dissenting voice from the chorus of praise for "August, 1914" is that of O. W. Firkins, "Mr. Masefield's Poetry," *Nation* (Mar. 15, 1919), pp. 389–90: "Even in the partly beautiful but over-lauded 'August, 1914' war itself at that crucial date is treated almost like an historic memory, adding its distant smoke-wreath to the half tints of a fading English sky. The point of view is undoubtedly poetic, but neither contemporary nor martial nor English."

3. Quoted from "John Masefield," *Outlook* (Jan. 26, 1916), p. 173.

4. Pp. 191, 215.

5. *Enslaved and Other Poems* (London: William Heinemann, 1920), p. 108.

6. Constance de la Cherois Crommelin married John Masefield in 1903, died in 1960.

7. *Ballads* (London: Elkin Mathews, 1903), pp. 27–30.

8. *Recent Prose,* rev. ed. (London: William Heinemann, 1932), pp. 208–10.

9. Of the other 11 novels, two (*Basilissa* [1940] and *Conquer* [1941]) are laid in Byzantium in the time of Justinian; three (*Sard Harker* [1924], *ODTAA* [1926], and *The Taking of the Gry* [1934]) in Latin America; three (*Captain Margaret* [1908], *The Bird of Dawning* [1933], and *Victorious Troy* [1935]) at sea; and one (*Badon Parchments* [1947]) in ancient Britain. Two others (*Multitude and Solitude* [1909] and *Live and Kicking Ned* [1939]) divide their time between England and Africa.

10. *John O'London* and *Daily Chronicle,* quoted in advertisement on p. 308 of *The Square Peg.*

11. Byron, *English Bards and Scotch Reviewers,* l. 389.

12. *The Yale Review* (April 1913), pp. 560–63.

13. *John Masefield* (London: Thornton Butterworth, 1932), p. 117.

14. Quoted in *John Masefield,* pamphlet (New York: The Macmillan Co., c. 1927), p. 8.

15. Dauber, after victory over fear and the scorn of his fellow-seamen, dies with his hope of artistic victory unrealized. The poem ends in description, as Dauber's ship sails into the safe and beautiful harbor of Valparaiso. Thomas, p. 184, writes of this last scene that its beauty "heightens the tragedy of Dauber's loss. And yet, while there is no jarring note of explicit moralizing, the resolving spiritual chord is struck; and we feel that Dauber, after his buffetings of body and soul, cannot have found less fair anchorage than the earthly port he has failed to reach."

16. *The Daffodil Fields* (New York: The Macmillan Co., 1913), pp. 2, 3, 4, 7, 16, 22, 31, 32, 41, 43, 49, 56, 65, 68, 73, 81, 83, 87, 90, 110, 112, 113, 115, 122, 124.

17. "The Nostalgia of Mr. Masefield," *Aspects of Literature* (London: Cape, 1934), p. 156.

18. "John Masefield," *Catholic World* (April 1922), pp. 64–71.

19. *Six Living Poets* (London: Thornton Butterworth, 1922), p. 29.

20. "Fox-Hunting" (introd. to *Reynard the Fox* New York: The Macmillan Co., 1920), p. vi.

21. *Survey* (April 1, 1916), pp. 40–42.

22. *E.g.,* "Like leaves blown on Hudson when maples turn gold" and "As a snow in Wisconsin when the darkness comes down." Effective as these figures often are, there is danger in their repeated use of distraction from the narrative; they slow the action in a poem where swift movement is a major objective.

23. *Enslaved and Other Poems* (London: William Heinemann, 1920), pp. 69–81.

24. *Ibid.,* pp. 91–100.

25. For a partial list, see *The Everlasting Mercy, The Widow in the Bye Street, The Daffodil Fields, Lollingdon Downs, Reynard the Fox, Right Royal,* "Cap on Head," "The Hounds of Hell," *Midsummer Night and Other Tales in Verse, The Country Scene, The Hawbucks, The Midnight Folk, The Square Peg,* "Joseph Hodges and the Corn," *Wonderings,* "Land Workers."

26. For a partial list, see "The Love Gift," "Tristan's Singing," *The Everlasting Mercy,* various sonnets, *Wonderings, On the Hill.*

27. For a partial list, see *Right Royal, The Country Scene,* "Tristan's Singing," "Autumn."

28. For a partial list, see *Right Royal, The Country Scene,* "Wild Geese," "Candlemas," "The Boy from Pauntley."

29. *Salt-Water Ballads* (London: Grant Richards, 1902), p. 79; *Ballads and Poems* (London: Elkin Mathews, 1910), p. 91; *Ballads* (London: Elkin Mathews, 1903), p. 36.

30. *Enslaved and Other Poems* (1920), p. 124.

3

The English People

Masefield and the English Character

The two English writers most admired by Masefield have both excelled at portraiture of the English character. Of Shakespeare Masefield writes, as noted above, that he "made a map of the English character" and that "we have not yet passed the frontiers of it."[1] Of Chaucer he writes:

> He set down a scheme or image of the England he knew, simplified to its elements. He displayed the significant figures of the time in their habits and their natures, with their jealousies, franknesses, and generosities, in a way of his own.[2]

Masefield has not approached, of course, the genius of his two predecessors at characterization. At times his characters fail miserably, as individuals and even as types, and he is particularly inept in his portrayal of women. He does show great skill at other times in his presentation of the men he knows best—the English sailor and the English countryman.

A survey of Masefield's fiction and narrative poetry reveals that his favorite characters are countrymen, sailors, and sportsmen. The sailors and the followers of English sports and pastimes, because of Masefield's frequent concern with them, will be discussed separately in chapters 4 and 6 below; the people of the English countryside, which has just been considered, are the subject of this chapter.

78

The English Countryman: Baldy Hill

Among the earliest childhood recollections of the poet, as revealed in *Wonderings* (1943), are three men who represent "England's constant elements": a carpenter, an "old goat-toothed Briton," slow but steadfast, quiet, tender, "one with the earth," and Old Joseph, whom the boy Masefield used to see sitting in the sun outside his cottage and whose one delight was looking at the cornfields he had worked "when he was hale." The goat-toothed Briton and Old Joseph display certain characteristics that are to be found in countrymen in many of Masefield's books—characteristics of dress, age, livelihood, and attitude. The poem "Joseph Hodges, or the Corn"[3] is a glorification of country life that begins with the portrait of such a man. His name and his description suggest that he is the same "Old Joseph" of the poet's boyhood. He too wears the "smock-frock of the country's past" and looks out over the fields he can no longer plough and harvest.

In *The Square Peg* (1937), Frampton Mansell hires an old man, Zine, to do fencing on the estate that he has bought. The old man is one of the few surviving land-workers who take pride in their work, one of the men who really "had cared for England." Old Zine finds Mansell a stranger who asks peculiar questions about the values of fox-hunting, but he is willing to talk to him about older days and to sing him the ballad of Spirr Wood.

Men like Zine and Joseph Hodges are those recalled in "Land Workers," a poem in which Masefield compares the husbandry of the 1880s, and before, with that of the 1940s. The hoppers, bull-men, horsemen, farm-carters, and ploughmen are all here, men whose pastoral had been "piped beneath no beech-tree shade." The poet describes them as "unlike us, clothing, gait and face,/ That uncouth, ancient British race."[4] These are the countrymen whose spirit has not only fed their race but has turned back England's enemies and been the reason why "all seas have felt the ploughs/ Of England's island-builded bows."

Masefield has described the ploughman and his team, "bowing forward on a skyline," as one of the three most stirring sights to be seen in England, "beautiful unspeakably."[5] It is not surprising that in *The Everlasting Mercy* (1911) he uses the ploughman Callow as one of the final agents of Saul Kane's conversion.

Perhaps the most extensive of Masefield's countryman portraits is that of Baldy Hill, who appears in one narrative poem, one long essay, and two of the novels. Baldy appears first in *Reynard the Fox* (1919), where, as an earth-stopper (whose function is to close with stakes the holes in which a fox might take refuge), he advises Sir Peter Bynd, the Master of the Hunt, "to draw Heath Wood." In *The Hawbucks* (1929), ". . . old Purton and old Baldy Hill, carrying guns and nets, followed by two lads, each carrying a bag of ferrets, came round the corner." Baldy is not described and fulfills only the function of interrupting a tense situation between two other characters.

One incident in *Eggs and Baker* (1936) also presents Baldy. It is his gun with which murderers have shot Mr. Okle, and Baldy is a witness at the trial "to do what he could for his friends, but also to put himself right with the world: it was his gun." He is called "one of the hardest-headed old knaves that even Condicote could produce," but it also said that his appearance was in his favor, for he was spotlessly clean and "a very fine old man to look at."

In the essay "Fox-Hunting" (1920), written in response to many inquiries about *Reynard the Fox,* there is a long description, part prose, part verse, of "old Baldy Hill the earth-stopper." This is probably the source of the picture of Baldy in the later *Eggs and Baker,* for here are to be noted the same clear blue eye, white hair, smock, and spindle-fruit. It is Baldy who "in the darkness of the early morning gads about on a pony, to 'stop' or 'put-to' all earths, in which a hard-pressed fox might hide."

> He dates from the beginning of man. I have seen many a Baldy Hill in my life; he never fails to give me the feeling, that he is Primitive Man survived. Primitive man lived like that, in the darkness, outwitting the wild things, while the rain dripped, and the owl cried, and the ghost came out of the grave. Baldy Hill stole the last litter of the last she-wolf, to cross them with the King's hounds. Perhaps when all the other forms of English life are gone, the Baldy Hill form, the stock form, will abide, still striding, head bent, with an ashen stake, after some wild thing, that has meat, or fur, or is difficult, or dangerous, to tackle.

The poet concludes the discussion of the Baldy Hill type with a four-stanza picture in verse of the old man who used to wear flowers in his smock and, in hunting season, the spindle-fruit. "I hope," concludes the poet, "that he may continue to wear spindle-fruit for many seasons to come."

The English Community
in Reynard the Fox and Chaucer's Prologue

It is not to be assumed that Masefield's country people are all ploughmen and earth-stoppers. In *The Hawbucks* and in *Reynard the Fox* he offers the reader a whole gallery of country portraits, from the gentry to those lowest in the social scale.

Reynard the Fox is a long poem that comprises a picture of the typical English rural community at a fox-hunt and the story of that hunt. Part Two of the poem, the tale of the hunt itself, is treated elsewhere in this study, in the chapters on the English landscape and the English games. Part One is the richest single source for a consideration of Masefield's characterization of English country people. The triple purpose of the poem, in its glorification of country, countryman, and sport, is evident in the explanatory essay, "Fox-Hunting."

In "Fox-Hunting" Masefield writes:

As a man grows older, life becomes more interesting but less easy to know; for, late in life, even the strongest yields to the habit of his compartment. When he cannot range through all society, from the court to the gutter, a man must go where all society meets.

In Chaucer's time, the pilgrimage gathered many representatives of English society; in Masefield's, people met at the English games, especially at the fox-hunt, a sport "in which all who come may take a part, whether rich or poor, mounted or on foot."

At a fox-hunt, and nowhere else in England, except perhaps at a funeral, can you see the whole of the land's society brought together, focussed for the observer, as the Canterbury pilgrims were for Chaucer.

In his essay on Chaucer, Masefield discusses the professional complexion of the group of Canterbury pilgrims and cites the changes
likely in a contemporary group going on a pilgrimage to "Saint
Ski." Not only does Masefield derive the general idea of Part One
of *Reynard the Fox* from the Prologue to the *Canterbury Tales;*
he borrows some of the people from Chaucer. Several are Nineteenth Century reincarnations of Fourteenth Century pilgrims,
while others are reminiscent, in a phrase or an epithet, of a Chaucerian figure.

Critics disagree as to the extent of Masefield's success in his
characterization. W. H. Hamilton believes that no one since
Chaucer has "sketched with such lightning artistry, English types
and English character."[6] Gilbert Thomas finds Masefield's portraits "varied and . . . thoroughly English,"[7] but effigies when
compared with the Canterbury pilgrims. Although the modern
poet does not have Chaucer's "life-imbuing subtlety," Thomas
praises his "real insight into human nature," his "quick eye for
essentials," and "the gift of summing up the fundamental qualities
of a character in a single phrase." On the whole, *Reynard the Fox*
met with general critical approval in England and has become
possibly its writer's most popular poem. In America Amy Lowell
praised the poem as "a work of high art, a vivid picture of a
place and time," but she did not praise the array of characters in
Part One, whom she found a "stupid" lot, "superficially sketched":

> Here is no such . . . carefully worked psychology, drawing on
> the threads of innumerable contacts to weave its figures, as
> Chaucer displayed. These followers of the hunt are very much
> in the rough, and I think the reason is not far to seek. Mr.
> Masefield can depict men when he chooses, he has abundantly
> proved so much; this time, consciously or unconsciously, he
> did not choose. His hunt is not a character study, it is a sym-
> bolical treatment of "home."[8]

Miss Lowell doubts that Masefield ever hobnobbed with people at
a hunt. Therefore his people are typical, not individual—well-
chosen samples of the rural English population; the "real actor of
the drama is the land itself."

Any comparison of Chaucer and Masefield in this regard must
be prefaced by a consideration of the purposes of the writers of

Reynard the Fox and the *Canterbury Tales*. Chaucer wished to tell a group of stories. Masefield wished to glorify the English countryside and the English sport of fox-hunting by telling the story of a typical hunt; the third purpose, the presentation of an English community, "made the subject attractive." Throughout the *Canterbury Tales* the pilgrims, as story-tellers, are important figures. They are frequently reintroduced to the reader in the links between the tales and often increase in vividness and familiarity as he meets them again and again; the reader of Chaucer forms his impression of the pilgrims generally from the whole body of the tales rather than from the Prologue alone. Masefield's people, once introduced, play only a small part in the fox-hunt that follows; interest in them flags as interest in Reynard grows. They are part of the background of the poem, of the many-colored setting of the fox-hunt. Although they are modeled on the Canterbury pilgrims, their creator probably did not strive to make them as real and as distinct as Chaucer's people; they have life enough for the section of the poem that, as Thomas points out, "aims almost exclusively at pictorial effect." Interesting as the parallel is, these men and women of Masefield and Chaucer are not to be judged by exactly the same criteria.

The following pages will show in some detail parallels in phrasing and characterization from the *Canterbury Tales* and *Reynard the Fox;* occasional references will be made to other poems of Masefield and Chaucer.

Reynard the Fox opens abruptly with a description of the starting point, a modern Tabard conducted by a modern Harry Bailly and his wife; they are not, however, the vivid innkeeper and his virago, Goodelief. The modern poet makes no use of the Enderbys beyond an opening description of the busy innyard, where Martha flings grain to a "spangled cock" that might be a direct descendant of Chauntecleer.

It is the day of the hunt, and soon the company gathers. Among the first is the round-bellied clergyman from Condicote. The reader immediately recalls the Monk, who was "a lord full fat and in good poynt." He learns about the clergyman's "mighty voice to preach," for, like Chaucer, whose Somonour sang "a stif burdoun" ("was nevere trompe of half so greet a soun"), Masefield is much interested in the voices of his characters. Old Steven

from Scratch Steven Place comes next, on his "string-halty grey."
He has "a white beard and a rosy face" like Chaucer's Frankeleyn's, whose beard was as white "as is the dayseye" and who was
"sangwyn of his complexioun."

Next, three men come riding in a row. All of them have some-
ing in common with the Miller of the *Tales*. John Pym is "a bull-
man, . . . yet sweet-voiced as a piping flute." Tom See is "red,"
a color that we associate with the Miller, for "His berd as any
sowe or fox was reed." Tom's mouth is "twitched upward out of
place," while the Miller's mouth is also mentioned, but only for
its size: "His mouth as greet was as a greet forneys." Stone is
a man

> . . . whose bulk of flesh and bone
> Made people call him Twenty Stone.
> He was the man who stood a pull
> At Tencombe with the Jersey bull
> And brought the bull back to his stall.

We recall that the Miller was

> . . . a stout carl for the nones;
> Ful byg he was of brawn, and eek of bones.
> That proved wel, for over al ther he cam,
> At wrastlynge he wolde have alwey the ram.
> He was short-sholdred, brood, a thikke knarre

Molly Wolvesey is drawn briefly but unforgettably. She is "red
as a rose, with eyes like sparks," and Masefield uses the same
simile to describe Doxy Jane in *The Everlasting Mercy*. The figure
is like Chaucer's in the description of the Frere, whose eyes
"twinkled in his heed aryght,/ As doon the sterres in the frosty
nyght." Molly is "bright," like so many Masefield characters.
J. C. Squire chides the poet for his overuse of this word, which
was also one of Chaucer's favorite words.[9]

The parson's son is a famous runner, with little in common
with any of the Prologue group. The last two lines of his sketch
are reminiscent, in language but not in content, of the Shipman,
who "knew all the havenes . . . fro Gootland to the cape of

Fynystere." Masefield says of the parson's son that the otter-hounds and harriers "from Godstow to the Wye all knew him."

The parson's wife is a reincarnation of the Wyf of Bath. She deserves a full quotation:

> She was a stout one, full of life
> With red, quick, kindly, manly face.
> She held the knave, queen, king, and ace,
> In every hand she played with men.
> She was no sister to the hen,
> But fierce and minded to be queen.
> She wore a coat and skirt of green,
> A waistcoat cut of hunting red,
> Her tie pin was a fox's head.

The second line recalls "Boolde was hir face, and fair and reed of hewe." The third and fourth lines suggest Chaucer's Wyf in her successful dealings with men. She recounts her successes with her five husbands in the Prologue to her Tale, and in the general Prologue it is said that "Of remedies of Love she knew per chaunce,/ For she koude of that art the olde daunce." The attire of the parson's wife is described, as is that of the Wyf in the earlier poem. Red was a favorite of both women; the Wyf's "hosen were of fyn scarlet reed."

Masefield's parson is a composite character, with attributes and characteristics of the Monk, the Frere, and the Persoun. "The Parson was a manly one" is a direct echo of the Monk's "A manly man, to been an abbot able." Later in the description, the parson "kept no Lent to make him meagre." The Monk, similarly, was not pale and kept no Lent, for he loved a fat swan "best of any roost." Like the Frere, the parson "loved the sound of his own voice," but his voice was far different. The parson's talk "was like a charge of horse," while the Frere, "for his wantownesse," lisped somewhat "to make his English sweete upon his tonge." Masefield's parson is worldly, like the Monk and the Frere, although their worldliness varies. The Frere justifies his worldliness on religious grounds; not so the Monk and Masefield's churchman. There is no implication of wantonness or dishonesty in this man, as there is abundantly in the description of the Frere. On the other hand, the parson is more worldly than Chaucer's Persoun in the description of his probable future.

> Some grey cathedral in a town
> Where drowsy bells toll out the time
> To shaven closes sweet with lime,
> And wall-flower roots drive out the mortar
> All summer on the Norman Dortar,
> Was certain some day to be his.
> Nor would a mitre go amiss
> To him, because he governed well.

With the Persoun, however, he does have some characteristics in common. The Persoun was a "lerned man," and Masefield's parson "had read in many a tongue." Like the Persoun, he "loved his God . . . and man," but he loves "himself" as well. The parson's worldliness is chiefly to be seen in his jolly nature and his practical approach to the trials and troubles of human kind.

> He did not talk of churchyard worms,
> But of our privilege as dust
> To box a lively bout with lust
> Ere going to heaven to rejoice.

Jill and Joan are thoroughly modern young women, but several of their lines are modern Chaucerian. "Bright" is applied to their eyes, teeth, and hair; "Like spring, they brought the thought of pairing" and "They were as bright as fresh sweet peas."

Charles Copse is one of the most attractive of Masefield's hunters.

> . . . In face and limb
> The beauty and the grace of him
> Were like the golden age returned.
> His grey eyes steadily discerned
> The good in men and what was wise.
> He had deep blue, mild-coloured eyes,
> And shocks of harvest-coloured hair,
> Still beautiful with youth. An air

> Or power of kindness went about him;
> No heart of youth could ever doubt him
> Or fail to follow where he led.
> He was a genius, simply bred,
> And quite unconscious of his power.
> He was the very red rose flower
> Of all that coloured countryside.

In the last two lines are four of Chaucer's favorite words—red, rose, flower, coloured. Perhaps, however, the word that contributes most to the Chaucerian quality of the lines is "very." This is not the intensifying adverb of modern usage, but Chaucer's adjective, "verray."[10] One recalls "O verrey lord, O love, O god, allas." and "He was a verray, parfit, gentil knyght."[11]

"Flower of all that coloured countryside" has many partial parallels in Chaucer. Arcite is called "flour of chivalrie," and in the *Monk's Tale* are "flour of moralitee," "flour of strengthe," "flour of knyghthood," and "flour of freedom." Phoebus in the *Manciple's Tale* is "flour of bachelrie." In the *ABC* the Blessed Virgin is addressed as "Glorious virgine, of alle floures flour," while elsewhere Alceste is called "of all floures flour,"[12] and Troilus addresses Criseyde in a letter as "right fresshe flour." Masefield's two lines

> He was the very red rose flower
> Of all that coloured countryside.

are among his best, and Chaucer might have written them.

The terrible Squire Harridew, "fierce, hot, hard, old, stupid squire," has three daughters, Carrie, Jane, and Lu. His son, a "ne'er-do-weel," like the "good-for-little son" of John and Pity Hankerton, reminds one of the Frankeleyn's son, whose failings his father describes to the Squyer directly after the tale told by that exemplary young man. Carrie, youngest of the Squire's three daughters, is a lovely, golden-haired girl. Both Masefield and Chaucer often show their love for beautiful hair, especially if it is blonde. It has been suggested, however, that Chaucer's interest in physical characteristics is not simple aesthetic pleasure; he may be portraying character through a detailing of physical features recognized in his day as signs of temperament and character types.[13] Her hair is the only good feature of the Miller's daughter in the *Reeve's Tale:* "But right fair was hire heer, I wel not lye." Of Virginia in the *Physician's Tale* Chaucer writes that Phoebus himself had dyed her tresses. In *The Book of the Duchess,* Blanche's hair is praised, among her other comely features, as being "most lyk gold." Chaucer also notes the hair of his men. The Squyer has "lokkes crulle as they were leyd in presse," while Absolon's hair is not only curly but golden. Even the unpleasant Pardoner "hadde heer as yelow as wax." Masefield's Carrie, Sal, Polly, Charles, Jill and Joan, Hattie, and Jane are all described for their hair, as is yellow-haired Menelaus in "The Taking of Helen."[14] "Miss Hattie Dyce from Baydon Dean" has "golden hair piled coil on coil/ Too beautiful for time to spoil," while Sal Ridden is "loud, bold, blonde, abundant," with "stooks of hair like polished brass."

Carrie is not an intellectual girl, but "A rosebud need not have a mind./ A lily is not sweet from learning." She is no healthy young animal like Chaucer's Alison but more akin, perhaps, to Emelye, who was fairer to see than the "lylie on his stalke grene" and whose complexion vied with the rose.[15] Chaucer frequently employs the rose and the lily together for the description of lovely ladies; however, he may be as conscious of the significance of the flowers as symbols of love and purity as he is of their appropriateness for simile and metaphor. The maid Virginia, for instance, is a masterpiece of nature's artistry.

> For right as she kan peynte a lilie whit,
> And reed a rose, right with swick peynture
> She peynted hath this noble creature.[16]

In the *Second Nun's Tale* of Saint Cecilia, the lily and the rose appear together four times and Beauty in *The Romaunt of the Rose* is likened to both flowers.

Like Emelye and Alison and her own sister Lu, Carrie sings. She sings "mild, pretty, senseless songs," while Lu prefers songs composed "before the German King/ Made England German in her mind," like "those sweet things/ Which Thomas Campion set to strings." Emelye also sings, but "as an aungel hevenysshly." Alison's song "was as loud and yerne/ As any swalwe sittynge on a berne."[17] Again one finds evidence of the importance of the voice to both Chaucer and Masefield in their characterizations.

Carrie's sister Lu is somewhat more akin to Alison. She is described by similes from nature, but while Alison's character is pure country, Lu's has a less simple, almost suburban flavor. Lu is "round, sweet and little like a cherry," and her laughter is "like a robin's singing." The robin and the cherry, which should have been attractive to Chaucer because of his interest in birds and trees and because of his love of red, actually appear but once each in his pages.

When the reader meets Dr. Frome of Quickemshow, he expects a modern version of the Doctor of Phisik. However, the two have nothing in common; if anything, the Doctor is like the Persoun in his love for humanity.

The Squyer is represented at the hunt by Dr. Frome's son, Richard, a jolly youth as "merry as a yearling is/ In Maytime in a clover patch." His age would seem to be near the Squyer's "twenty yeer of age," and there are echoes in these lines of "a lovyere and a lusty bacheler," and "as fressh as is the month of May." Like the Squyer, Richard is "curteis, lowly, servysable," with his "gallant" and "blithe and kind." As the Squyer was like his father in some respects, so is Richard, who had "all his father's love of mind/ And greater force to give it act." Richard's athletic ability is a modern parallel of the Squyer's medieval "chivachie." The reader remembers that the Squyer was "wonderly delyvere and of greet strengthe" when he reads

> To see him when the scrum was packt,
> Heave, playing forward, was a sight.
> His tackling was the crowd's delight
> In many a danger close to goal.
> The pride in the three quarter's soul
> Dropped, like a wet rag, when he collared.
> He was as steady as a bollard,
> And gallant as a skysail yard.

When Masefield writes that he was the "crown imperial of all the scholars of his year," one recalls the social graces and the artistic accomplishments of the Squyer at singing, fluting, riding, dancing, drawing, and writing. Richard, along with Bell Ridden, the parson and his wife, the Gurneys, and Sir Peter Bynd, is one of the happiest of Masefield's reincarnations of the Canterbury pilgrims.

Polly Colway's brother John is "lean, puckered, tight-skinned from the sea." His ship is named, as is his counterpart's in the Prologue; John's ship is not the *Maudelayne,* but she does have a Chaucerian name, the *Canacee.*[18] Like the Shipman, John is forceful and relentless, "able to drive a horse, or ship or crew of men, as long as they could go." John "looked ahead as though his craft/ Were with him still, in dangerous channels." These lines recall the skill and knowledge and alertness of the sailor from Dertemouthe, from whose description Masefield repeats the exact phrase, "his craft." Polly's brother rides better than the Shipman, who "rood upon a rouncy, as he kouthe." John can "drive a horse" as well as a ship, although his horsemanship is not described so fully as that of Polly's husband, Hugh.

Bell, daughter of Sal and Bill Ridden, is a lovely girl, as good as blowing air

> But shy and difficult to know;
> The kittens in the barley-mow,
> The setter's toothless puppies sprawling,
> The blackbird in the apple calling,
> All knew her spirit more than we
> So delicate these maidens be
> In loving lovely, helpless things.

Though younger and simpler than the Prioress, Bell has in common with Madame Eglantyne a love for the small and the helpless. Chaucer's Nun was also "charitable and pitous." These are two figures which Middleton Murry cites in his essay, "The Nostalgia of Mr. Masefield," discussed in greater detail in chapter 2. Murry censures Masefield for his lack of the naturalness of Chaucer; he feels that Masefield emphasizes, underlines, and demonstrates too much. This writer agrees with Murry only when he reads the last two lines of Bell's picture; the other lines are charming and natural.

Charles Cothill is one of Masefield's most attractive men, and the poet liked him so thoroughly that he made him the hero of his next long narrative, *Right Royal*. Cothill has no prototype in Chaucer, but in four of the lines describing him, there is something Chaucerian, something more than the repetition of "April" and of "bright."

> So beautiful he was, so bright,
> He looked to men like young delight
> Gone courting April maidenhood,
> That has the primrose in her blood.

Four pages of *Reynard the Fox* are allotted to Ock Gurney and Old Pete, his uncle. They are lusty, good-tempered countrymen, with cheeks "brown as any brew." At once one thinks of the "broun visage" of the Yeman and the Shipman's "hewe al broun," as well as of the Monk's palfrey, "broun as is a berye." The Gurney humor is broad and rustic like the American Vermontese.

Ock's words to his hunter have the same combination of hearty cursing and real love for his animal that the carter shows for his mired team in the *Friar's Tale*. Ock

> . . . cursed his hunter like a lover,
> "Now blast your soul, my dear, give over.
> Woa, now, my pretty, damn your eyes."

He also has two qualities in common with the Frere, who was "strong as a champioun" and "certainly had a merry note."

> He had a back for pitching hay,
> His singing voice was like a bay.

Tom Dansey, the whip, is delineated at some length. There are echoes of the Monk in his description. "His 'gone away' when foxes broke,/ Was like a bell" reminds one of the jingling bridle of the Monk in the whistling wind, "as loude as dooth the chapel belle" and also of Masefield's parson, whose "voice was like the tenor bell/ When services were said and sung." A little later, when reading of Robin Dawe, the huntsman, one finds that he had a voice "clear tenor, full and mellow." Of Tom, Masefield writes that hunting was his "chief delight." So, too, the Monk, a

far different man, but one who also "loved venerye" and had "ful
many a deyntee hors in stable" and "was a prickasour aright."
Tom's second whip, Kitty Myngs, is also fond of the hunt and
"longed to be a horseman bold," one who could "charge full
tilt/ Blackthorns that made the gentry wilt." Once more the
Monk comes to mind, and the fact that "of prikyng and hunting
for the hare/ Was al his lust."

The Master is the admirable and lovable Sir Peter Bynd, the
reincarnation of Chaucer's knyght. The reader recalls that the
knyght "At mortal batailles hadde been fiftene," when he learns
that Sir Peter "had fought/ Five wars for us." Here is Masefield's
picture of the Master, "past sixty now":

> An old, grave soldier, sweet and kind,
> A courtier with a knightly mind,
> Who felt whatever thing he thought.
> . . . Within his face
> Courage and power had their place,
> Rough energy, decision, force.
> He smiled about him from his horse.
> He had a welcome and salute
> For all, on horse or wheel or foot,
> Whatever kind of life each followed.
> His tanned, drawn cheeks looked old and hallowed,
> But still his bright blue eyes were young.

Here are many of the knyght's qualities—his love for "chivalrie,/
Trouthe and honour, fredom and curteisie," his worthiness and
wisdom, his "port as meeke as is a mayde." Sir Peter's welcome
for all, "whatever kind of life each followed," shows that he has
the same regard for men of all classes that Chaucer attributes to
the Knyght in the lines:

> He never yet no vileynye ne sayde
> In al his lyf unto no maner wight.
> He was a verray, parfit gentil knyght.

Reynard the Fox *Characters in Later Poems and Novels*

When Masefield wrote *Reynard the Fox,* he painted into the backdrop of the fox-hunt, along with English woods and streams and meadows, a bright array of some seventy English men and women. Although he did not develop these characters during the second part of the poem, he apparently liked them and could not abandon them entirely. One becomes the hero of the narrative poem, *Right Royal* (1920), and another is described at length in the essay, "Fox-Hunting." A third appears briefly in the novel, *Eggs and Baker;* two more reappear in *The Square Peg,* one as a fairly prominent character. The hero of *ODTAA* (1926) is a boy whose parents and sister participate in the hunt in *Reynard the Fox. The Hawbucks,* however, is the novel in which *Reynard the Fox* people reappear almost en masse. All its chief characters and many minor figures, to the number of thirty-two, as well as several of their relatives, derive directly from *Reynard the Fox.* Place names recur, and one of the meets described in *The Hawbucks* is similar to the Ghost Heath Run of the poem. The inn called "The Cock and Pye" is again the assembling point for the hunt, and even three of the hounds, Arrogant, Daffodil, and Queenie, reappear!

A study of these repeated characters reveals that, in general, Masefield does not alter them drastically when he transfers them from the poem to another poem or novel. Of the *Reynard the Fox* characters transferred to other works, twenty-two are of some importance in the poem and are allotted a considerable amount of descriptive space. Eleven of these twenty-two assume corresponding positions of importance in their later appearances, while the other eleven become minor characters. Ten of the transferred characters played very minor roles in *Reynard the Fox;* six of these are restricted to minor roles, while four are raised to some importance in the later tales. In general, characterization is more effective in the compression of the verse than in the expanded prose of the novel, with the exceptions of the colorful Manor family and, of course, of those minor characters in *Reynard the Fox* who become major elsewhere.

Only ten of the hunting crowd in *Reynard the Fox* who are

described in any detail fail to appear again in Masefield fiction, abandoned along with a score of minor figures who are names only. Conversely, there are only five characters of any importance in *The Hawbucks* (Maid Margaret, Catlington, Tom Clench, Sandy, and "Ethelberta") who do not derive from the poem.

All the characters transferred to *Right Royal* and the novels keep their original ages except Dr. Frome, who in *The Hawbucks* is an older man, and Richard Frome, who advances from boyhood to young manhood and becomes a physician like his father. Many of the *Reynard the Fox* people, however, do develop family connections in their later appearances; a mother, a sister, three wives, four sons, four daughters (three legitimate and one illegitimate), and five deceased relatives enter the picture, all unmentioned in *Reynard the Fox!*

Only one *Reynard the Fox* character, Charles Cothill, since he is Masefield's ideal young Englishman and is therefore of special significance to this study, will be discussed here. Perhaps Charles Cothill is Masefield's favorite creation. Appearing originally as one of the most attractive hunters in *Reynard the Fox,* he becomes the hero of *Right Royal* and his name is used subsequently in the essay "Fox-Hunting." Nine years later in *The Hawbucks* he is again presented as the ideal young Englishman. In addition to the first presentation of Charles in *Reynard the Fox,* described above, there are also three brief glimpses of him in Part Two, during the hunt. In "Fox-Hunting," Masefield describes the ideal run of 1750 and the typical hunt of "today." In the former meet a catalogue of hunters includes no name from *Reynard the Fox,* but the account of the run is signed by "Charles Cothill," perhaps an ancestor of the contemporary Charles.

In *Right Royal,* Charles has staked everything on a dream that his horse, a cast-off that he has regenerated, will win. The poem is a vivid description of the runners and their race, which Charles and Right Royal win by a half-length. This poem is discussed in some detail in the chapter on Sports below. From a brief description at the start of the poem, it is obvious that this is the same Charles:

> He was from Sleins, that manor up the Lithe.
> Riding the Downs had made his body blithe;

Stalwart he was, and springy, hardened, swift,
Able for perfect speed with perfect thrift,
Man to the core, yet moving like a lad.
Dark honest eyes with merry gaze he had.

Throughout *The Hawbucks,* Charles Cothill seems the most promising of the suitors of Carrie Harridew. The first glimpse of him is at the Harridew manor, where he is presented as "a dark lad with keen eyes, who looked as though he had a good deal in him," and later as "a singularly good-looking man, black and comely, wind-tanned and fine, as well as rich." At one point in the novel, Carrie's eldest sister praises Cothill as having "all the qualities which could make a woman happy, and no serious blemish."

In *The Hawbucks* there is a delightful description of the Sleins, "old, beautiful and comfortable," with lime trees and "a noise of waters where the Sleins brook, cunningly led, splashed down its fall to fill the pools in front of the house." Here the reader is introduced to Charles's sister, Topsy, and meets his exquisite mother, neither of whom appears elsewhere in Masefield narrative. The writer's picture of Mrs. Cothill is curiously fashioned, like one of the tapestries she loves to weave. Here at the Sleins, a neighbor named Emmy Crowthorne is "vetting" an injured mare in Charles's stables. Emmy has the same name as the "golden lady" of *Right Royal,* but she is much more practical and "horsey" than the girl who is characterized in the poem as "the very may-time that comes in/ When hawthorns bud and nightingales begin." Charles Cothill appears at several other times in the novel, once when in a thrilling photo-finish of a point-to-point race he and his beautiful black lose to George Childrey and finish just ahead of Bunny Manor. It is soon after this that both Charles and George learn that they have lost the race for Carrie's hand. Even a favorite character, presented so attractively, is not allowed always to win.

Not all Masefield's interesting characterizations of Englishmen are to be found in *Reynard the Fox* and in later work employing the characters from that poem. The early narratives are also well worth study. Dauber, in the poem bearing his name, will be discussed in a later chapter. Lion and Michael of *The Daffodil*

Fields, Jimmy in *The Widow in the Bye Street,* and Saul Kane in *The Everlasting Mercy* are also examples of the common man to whom Masefield dedicates himself in "A Consecration," the first poem of his first book.

The Common Man and "The Beaten Man"

In the first poem of *Salt-Water Ballads* (1902), Masefield pledges himself to the common man, the man "with too weighty a burden, too weary a load." When the common man is handicapped, the underdog, the one against many, the defeated, then Masefield loves him the more. He takes for his province "the scorned—the rejected—the men hemmed in with the spears," and promises that "of these shall my songs be fashioned, my tales be told."

Many writers have issued credos and manifestos early in their careers and have lived to abandon their beliefs. Masefield is true throughout his life to the men he promises to serve in "A Consecration." Though he writes about the man with "too weary a load" and "the scorned—the rejected," he does not belong to "the literary school which has sprung up from our awakened social conscience." Like Chaucer, he describes and narrates, but, still like Chaucer, he does not moralize or preach. Henry Seidel Canby points out Masefield's dissimilarity in this regard to the "Church of England moralist," Crabbe, and his similarity to "the greatest of modern dramatists in English, Synge"; like Synge, Masefield views "all this vivid world of ill-timed emotion and errant endeavor, not as a reformer but with the tender sentiment of a lover of life in all its manifestations."[19]

Masefield knew poverty and hardship and the life of the poor from his own experience as sailor, bartender, farm-laborer, factory worker, and struggling writer. He can present the life of the poor in all its ugliness and all its reality. But from it he can also distill much goodness and beauty—in Nan of *The Tragedy of Nan* (1909), for example, and Saul Kane, in the Dauber, Mary and her lovers, and the widow.

Sometimes the Masefield hero is not so much the poor man as the man opposed by insurmountable obstacles or a sequence of setbacks or catastrophes. Sometimes he wins through his own loyalty and the dogged courage that Masefield traditionally associates with the English, aided also at times by spiritual forces or "Helpers." Such winners are Sard Harker and Saul Kane, the circus man aided by King Cole, Charles Cothill and Right Royal, the baker in *Eggs and Baker,* Ned of the two novels that bear his name, the juvenile heroes,[20] and skipper Trewsbury of *The Bird of Dawning.* These books are full of what John O'London calls Masefield's "incorrigible love for the under-dog"[21] and of the optimism that leads the poet to say with King Cole:

> There is a hope that the abandoned know
> Deep in the heart, that conquerors cannot feel.
> Abide in hope the turning of the wheel,
> The luck will alter and the star will rise.

and with Highworth Ridden of *ODTAA* (1926):

> I have seen flowers come in stony places;
> And kindness done by men with ugly faces;
> And the gold cup won by the worst horse at the races;
>   So I trust, too.

Often the Masefield hero is the man who achieves spiritual triumph even in physical defeat; the text is then that "the conqueror's prize is dust and lost endeavour./ And the beaten man becomes a story for ever."[22] The theme of defeat and failure haunts much of Masefield's work from *The Tragedy of Pompey the Great* (1910) through the early narrative poems, *Good Friday* (1916), and *Gallipoli* (1916), and recurs in *ODTAA* (1926) and other later work. The hero is not always an Englishman, but his virtues are the virtues of Masefield's English heroes. Sometimes he is Pompey, or Philip of Spain, or Christ; once the heroine is the ship *Wanderer,*[23] a symbol of great significance throughout the poet's life. The *Wanderer* was an ill-fated ship, doomed to a series of disasters, but queenly and beautiful through them all, "half-divine" to the poet "for having failed." Her story ends with the lines:

> Life's battle is a conquest for the strong;
> The meaning shows in the defeated thing.

In any struggle, it is the loyalty to the ideal that matters, not the actual issue of the conflict. Often the goal is unattainable, but the good fighter reveals its supreme worth to other men. His failure to achieve his goal is a defeat, but in his loyalty, his effort, his self-effacement, and his revelation for others lies the real victory. The great Masefield quest is for Beauty, Understanding, Truth, and it exacts from the artist the ultimate in courage and sacrifice.

> Beauty and Peace have made
> No peace, no still retreat,
> No solace, none.
> Only the unafraid
> Before life's roaring street
> Touch Beauty's feet,
> Know Truth, do as God bade,
> Become God's son.[24]

The Masefield hero is often the artist in life, faithful to an idea or an ideal or a person, who never completely achieves, who is in some way defeated, but who through his very defeat brings others to a consciousness of his goal. "All artists fail," Olivia says to Captain Margaret. "But one sees what they saw. You see that in their failure."[25]

Dauber, though winner of one victory in his final acceptance by his sailor-mates, fails to reach his goal as an artist, and dies. But his dying words are, "It will go on."[26] The mother in *The Widow in the Bye Street* (1912) suffers defeat and loss, but her loyalty is unshaken, and she becomes the "story for ever." *The Sweeps of Ninety-Eight* (1916) and *The Faithful* (1915), like *The Tragedy of Pompey the Great,* are tales of a lost cause, but loyalty unto death gives immortality to those defeated. In *Good Friday,* Masefield's subject is the beaten man, Christ, whose physical defeat is transcended by spiritual triumph and whose story becomes the greatest of all stories "for ever."

One of Masefield's most notable achievements is the book *Gallipoli,* prose epic of the heroic and ill-fated Dardanelles campaign of World War I. It is a detailed picture of the campaign, an explanation of the reasons for its failure, and a supreme tribute to the courage of the English soldier and his Anzac ally. It is a beautifully written and moving account of a great victory cloaked in outward failure, and it is perhaps the poet's finest study of Englishmen who become "a story for ever." In *Gallipoli*, as in "August, 1914," Masefield's love for his countrymen reaches its most eloquent expression.

Notes to Chapter 3

1. *William Shakespeare* (London: Williams and Norgate, 1911), p. 64.

2. *Chaucer* (Cambridge: University Press, 1931), p. 30.

3. *A Letter from Pontus and Other Verse* (London: William Heinemann, 1936), pp. 29–35.

4. (London: William Heinemann, 1942), p. 8.

5. "Fox-Hunting" (introd. to *Reynard the Fox*, New York: The Macmillan Co., 1920), p. vi.

6. *John Masefield: A Critical Study* (London: George Allen and Unwin, 1922), p. 21.

7. *John Masefield* (London: Thornton Butterworth, 1932), p. 188.

8. *Poetry and Poets* (Cambridge: Houghton Mifflin Co., 1930), pp. 191–92.

9. "Reynard the Fox," *Living Age* (Dec. 20, 1919), p. 729.

10. F. N. Robinson, *The Poetical Works of Chaucer*, (Cambridge: Houghton Mifflin Co., 1933), p. 754, quotes J. M. Manly as saying that Chaucer never uses "verray" as an adverb.

11. *Troilus and Criseyde*, 4, l. 288, and *Prologue to Canterbury Tales*, l. 72.

12. *The Legend of Good Women*, Prologue, Text F, 53.

13. See the notes of Manly and Robinson on the *Prologue to Canterbury Tales*.

14. *A Tale of Troy* (London: William Heinemann, 1932), p. 1.

15. *Knight's Tale*, ll. 1035–38.

16. *Physician's Tale*, ll. 32–34.

17. *Knight's Tale*, l. 1055; *Miller's Tale*, l. 3257.

18. See *Squire's Tale*, Introduction to *Man of Law's Tale*, Prologue of *The Legend of Good Women*.

19. Henry S. Canby, "Noyes and Masefield," *Yale Review* (Jan. 1916), pp. 287–302.

20. Martin Hyde, Jim Davis, Charles Harding, and Kay Harker in the juvenile novels, *Martin Hyde, Jim Davis, Lost Endeavour*, and *The Midnight Folk*.

21. From review quoted in advertisement on p. 303 of *The Square Peg* (1937).

22. *The Tragedy of Pompey the Great* (London: Sidgwick and Jackson, 1910), p. 103.

23. *Philip the King and Other Poems* (London: William Heinemann, 1914).

24. "Good Friday," *Good Friday and Other Poems* (New York: The Macmillan Co., 1916), pp. 39–40.

25. *Captain Margaret* (London: Grant Richards, 1908), p. 405.

26. For Dauber's victory and loss, see Fraser Drew, "John Masefield's *Dauber:* Autobiography or Sailor's Tale Retold?" *Modern Language Notes* 72, no. 2 (Feb. 1957).

4

The English Games
and Pastimes

Masefield and English Sport

To John Masefield, no picture of England is complete without
her sports and pastimes, some of them shared, of course, with other
lands, but even these touched with something peculiarly English.

In the introductory poem of *The Country Scene* (1937), a
group of forty-two poems by Masefield and forty pictures by
Edward Seago, the poet asks for a definition of his country:

> What is this England, whom the draughtsmen print
> As such and such, in ever-changing guise,
> Now as a fat boor, whiskered and unwise,
> Now as a shielded, trident-bearing Queen,
> Now as a lion, now as a St. George
> Thrusting a trampled dragon through the gorge?
> From what known image do they take their hint?
> Where is such England met, such England seen?

The next two stanzas synthesize Masefield's England in a rapid
catalogue of the charms of her countryside, the power of her
industry, the courage of her seamen, and "football, though the
grass be blasted bare."

The second poem of *The Country Scene,* its "Prologue," expands the catalogue into "the world of man and his adventure." Here the reader learns that the subject of the poems and pictures to follow will be the country aspects of England and the labors and diversions of her country folk. He is asked to see the horse race and the football match and to "tread the roads with circusmen, with bull-herds, with huntsmen, or with fairs."

In these introductions to *The Country Scene,* Masefield has not listed all the English sports that appear and reappear in his poetry and prose. In forty-four separate pieces in twenty-eight different volumes of his work, English sports and pastimes are mentioned in some detail. One novel, two essays, and four long narrative poems[1] are devoted almost entirely to fox-hunting, the steeplechase, boxing, and the traveling circus, while other sports are the subject of many shorter pieces and constitute central incidents in other novels and long poems. These four activities, and the country fair, are the pastimes described at greater length, while rowing,[2] swimming,[3] running,[4] football,[5] cricket,[6] whippet-racing,[7] and the less attractive diversions of cockfighting and bull-baiting[8] receive less attention. The games and pastimes described in Masefield's work are not exclusively English, although some, like the fox-hunt and the steeplechase, are traditionally English. The English country fair and traveling circus differ in some respects from their American counterparts. Rowing and boxing are as familiar to Americans as to Englishmen, but the sport of boxing is appropriately treated here in the English settings in which Masefield describes it.

Boxing and the Three Boxing Poems

In the absence of a complete biography or autobiography of Masefield, it is not possible to say when he first became interested in boxing. There is no actual evidence that he practiced the sport. In his years aboard the training ship the *Conway,* boxing was not the required activity for cadets that it became after the first decade of the twentieth century. Some boys boxed, and by 1902 instruction was available for those who requested it, but there is no mention of boxing in the biographical sketch, *New Chum* (1944), which records Masefield's first months as a cadet. The book *The Conway*

(1933), a history of the training ship, contains a stirring account, ostensibly from a cadet's diary, of a good fight between a bully and another boy, in a makeshift ring on shipboard.

Several references to boxing in *In the Mill* (1941), the prose study of Masefield's life in Yonkers, New York, from 1895 to 1897, are merely metaphorical usages; four other passages in the book contain more extensive references to boxing.[9] The young Masefield was impressed by the widespread American preoccupation with the sport. One of his first acquaintances in Yonkers was a young fellow named Perce, whose chief interest was boxing and who wanted the young Englishman's opinion on the coming bout between Pete Maher and Bob Fitzsimmons. Masefield apparently was interested in the subject, too, for he records that he and Perce raised similar topics throughout the day, and discussed Sharkey and Joe Choynski as well.

The Maher-Fitzsimmons meeting claimed the interest of most of the workers in the carpet factory where Masefield was employed. Peter Maher lived in Yonkers and some of the workers knew him. Local feeling ran high in his favor, and one American told Masefield that Maher could punch a hole in a brick wall. The English boy, however, had his "own reasons for favouring" his compatriot, who went on to win the fight, and from "that moment the mill talked daily of what would happen if and when Fitzsimmons met Corbett."

Perce and Masefield continue their discussion of pugilism during subsequent days in the mill, and late in the book Masefield devotes three-and-a-half pages to the Corbett-Fitzsimmons championship fight. There had been much friction and tension between the two countries in the months before the battle, and the writer summarizes and explains their grievances. He admits that England's aggressive imperialism of the day had left her "without many friends among the nations," and that Americans were also "appalled by the manners" of the English rich and the squalor of the English poor.

I think that there was a feeling in many minds that England was "old" and that America was "young" and coming to take her place. This fight was looked upon by many as certain to clinch the matter.

Masefield describes the activity of the American press in spreading
excitement and enthusiasm; he doubts that anyone in America
thought very deeply about any other subject in the weeks before the
fight and concludes that no modern fight ever roused comparable
feeling. The writer had seen both fighters in New York and describes them in detail. His pictures of Corbett and Fitzsimmons are
those of the enthusiast, the aficionado, and not of the mere
observer.

The tension of the days before the fight comes alive on the page,
and the reader regrets only that the English boy could not have
seen the fight to record it, blow by blow. There is ample evidence
of Masefield's ability as a fight commentator in one of the poems
to be discussed later, *The Everlasting Mercy* (1911). But Masefield was a working boy, and he heard the results at work in the
mill in late afternoon. The word came, "Fitz in the fourteenth,"
and one of the sweepers, a boy who had saved up ten dollars to
bet on Corbett, burst into tears. The writer ends his account, published forty-five years later, by saying that he thinks Fitz was lucky
to get the decision so early in the fray and that he had expected
a full twenty-five rounds.

During the earlier years of Masefield's writing career, he edited
many books for a variety of publishers, writing prefaces, fore-
words, introductions, memoirs, notes. Two of these editorial essays
contain references to boxing. One, in the introductory essay to
his edition of Defoe, is slight; it speaks of Defoe's lack of interest
in sports, though he "knew enough about boxing not to hit his
man when down."

The other essay, Masefield's introduction to a new edition of
John Hamilton Reynolds's *The Fancy* (1905), is of greater importance. Reynolds, the lawyer-poet and friend of Keats, was
before his marriage a gay young blood who loved and practiced
the sporting life. Masefield finds Reynolds an attractive figure, "a
person delighting in life, who found the statue a cold thing compared to the stripped boxer, with the bright eyes and cheeks."
His introduction includes five delightful pages describing the great
boxers of Reynolds's day and the social life that surrounded them.
There are echoes of this essay in one of Masefield's most recent
poems, "A Tale of Country Things," and the poet writes with
such excitement and color that his familiarity with the sport can-

not seem a purely literary one.[10] The reader is admitted to Jack Randall's in Chancery Lane "to meet the bloods and the sports and to watch some sparring." In an atmosphere of cigar-smoke, he meets the writer Pierce Egan, the trainer Captain Barclay, Tom Cribb the champion, Jack Randall the Nonpareil, and the painter Belcher. He goes the round of sportsmen's bars and takes the road out of London to a fight held in some corner on the border-line of two counties. He observes the costume of the sports, their gigs and their equipment, the battlefield itself with its varied spectators. The principals appear, with music to welcome them, "swathed in rugs, and sucking oranges." Gypsies with whips drive the crowd back from the ropes, the fighters toss their hats into the ring and vault over the ropes, and the fight begins. "It was," Masefield quotes Hazlitt as saying, "the high and heroic state of man."

Boxing plays a part in only one Masefield novel, the adventure story, *Sard Harker* (1924). Here, however, is no English boxing match, but a contest between a Carib and a Mexican in a rowdy Latin American port. Two English sailors, Captain Cary of the English ship *Pathfinder,* and his chief mate, Sard Harker, on a day ashore, have tickets to a fight that is lavishly advertised on handbills as follows:

Feast of Pugilism.
At three o'clock punctually.
Grand display of the Antique Athletic
Contests with the gloves for the decisions.
The Light-Weights, the Middle Weights,
The World Famous Heavy-Weights
At three o'clock punctually.
At three o'clock punctually.
Six contests of the three rounds for the Champions
Of Las Palomas
For the Belt of the Victor.
To be followed by a Contest Supreme.
Twenty Rounds. Twenty Rounds.
Twenty Three-Minute Rounds.
Between
El Chico, Champion Caribe de la Tierra Firme,

And
Ben Hordano, Champion, of Mexico City.
Grand Feat of Pugilism
At three o'clock punctually.

The two Englishmen soon realize that they are about to witness a barbarous and degrading spectacle, a "fixed" fight involving two dangerous ruffians and a disorderly, quarrelsome crowd. It is no sporting English "display of athletics but . . . a very low piece of blackguardism."[11] However, the incident is vividly told with a mysterious undercurrent of suspense that merges with the main current of the novel. Another unattractive boxing match, this one on English soil, is pictured in a short prose article called "Saturday Night's Entertainments." A dull fight ends in shouts of derision from the crowd, and the reporter leaves the brawl "at once to avoid being called as a witness."[12]

Masefield has written three boxing poems: one, "Camp Entertainment," a brief, twenty-line description;[13] one a ballad-like narrative of a famous fight, "A Tale of Country Things," nearly a thousand lines long; the third, *The Everlasting Mercy,* perhaps his most famous long poem, containing a boxing incident some two hundred lines in length.

The first-written of these, *The Everlasting Mercy,* is the long and powerful narrative of Saul Kane's conversion, in which Saul's fight with Billy Myers is an exciting incident early in the poem. Saul Kane and Billy Myers are poachers whose argument over the division of their poaching territory leads to a fight on Wood Top Field, where the "grass is short and sweet/ And springy to a boxer's feet." The local bookie, Silas Jones, makes a "purse five pounds a side," and both men have their backers. The scene, with its makeshift ring and its "warner" (two brandy flasks struck together), is graphically described by the poet.

From the start of the fight, Bill is obviously the better man, but Saul is quick and keeps away from him until the fourth round. Then follows one of those passages in which Masefield demonstrates his remarkable ability to portray speed and violent action. These lines are perhaps not the equal of the sustained flight of the hunted animal in *Reynard the Fox* (1919), or of the midnight race run by the naked Saul later in *The Everlasting Mercy,* but will serve as example of one of the reasons why Masefield narratives succeed.

> I don't know how a boxer goes
> When all his body hums from blows;
> I know I seemed to rock and spin,
> I don't know how I saved my chin;
> I know I thought my only friend
> Was that clinked flask at each round's end
> When my two seconds, Ed and Jimmy,
> Had sixty seconds help to gimme.
> But in the ninth, with pain and knocks
> I stopped: I couldn't fight nor box.
> And round the ring there ran a titter:
> "Saved by the call, the bloody quitter."
>
> They drove, (a dodge that never fails)
> A pin beneath my fingernails.
> They poured what seemed a running beck
> Of cold spring water down my neck;
> Jim with a lancet quick as flies
> Lowered the swellings round my eyes.
> They sluiced my legs and fanned my face
> Through all that blessed minute's grace;
> They gave my calves a thorough kneading,
> They salved my cuts and stopped the bleeding.
> A gulp of liquor dulled the pain,
> And then the two flasks clinked again.

The pace does not slacken from this point until the end of the bout. A lucky accident saves the fight for Saul; he stops Bill's right on his shoulder bone and hears him groan. Bill's thumb, sprained once before, has "crocked again," and Saul gains strength as Bill gives ground. Saul's second, Jimmy, warns him to be careful for a round or two and then the fight will be his. Even in the blackguard Saul, there are signs of good sportsmanship at this point. He feels sick "that luck should play so mean a trick," and give him the chance to beat a man who had so clearly been his better. For five rounds more Bill fights on gamely. Masefield pays tribute to his courage in Saul's words:

Try to imagine if you can
The kind of manhood in the man,
And if you'd like to feel his pain
You sprain your thumb and hit the sprain
And hit it hard, with all your power
On something hard for half an hour,
While someone thumps you black and blue,
And then you'll know what Billy knew.
Bill took that pain without a sound
Till halfway through the eighteenth round,
And then I sent him down and out,
And Silas said, "Kane wins the bout."

After the fight and Bill's unwillingness for a reconciliation with Saul, the winner and his backers go down the hill for an all-night carouse at the Lion, the local pub. There, after some argument as to whether or not the fight had been "cross," the bets are paid and Saul receives his purse from Silas, the pubkeeper, who had "never seen a brisker bout." The purse is quickly spent in gin punch for the crowd and the carouse is under way.

Thirty-two years elapse before Masefield's second boxing poem, a twenty-line description of a fight held under very different circumstances. Eight hundred English and American soldiers are gathered inside a circus tent to watch a bout between two bombardiers on a lighted stage draped with the allied colors. The two fighters shake hands after the verdict and leave the ring talking, while an old comedian, "benign with spirits," sits down at the piano to continue the "Camp Entertainment."

"A Tale of Country Things," the longest poem in *On the Hill* (1949), is a thirty-page ballad, mostly in five-line stanzas, of an old-time fight, in 1829, between Bill Cop of Dym and Jock of Dyne. Once again, the occasion of the fight is a quarrel, but this is a disagreement initiated by the gossip of "knaves with serpent tongues" who lie to each man about the other in order to arrange an exciting and lucrative bout.

Although Bill and Jock are not completely admirable characters, they are very different from the battling poachers in *The Everlasting Mercy*. Bill has the same weakness as Saul for drink, but it is his only vice, and he is trying to conquer it in order to wed his sweetheart, Meg of Stad, "that sterling heart who hopes that, once they are wed," Bill may be dissuaded "from painting half the country red." Jock of Dyne is very different. He "never took to games for fun" but only for the sake of mastery over all. He too had a sweetheart, Anne of Prior's Dall.

The poet describes the good old days when boxers fought, bare-knuckled, out of doors "where grass was flat and firm," and when London sportsmen gave purses worth fighting for. The gossip about Jock and Bill achieves its purpose. The two become enemies and prepare for their fight. Jock takes as trainer Sergeant Wood, a hero of Waterloo; Bill's trainer is Cocker Joe, a former light-weight champion whose knowledge extends to cock-fighting and dog-fighting as well as boxing. The training days are described and we see Jock and Bill abstaining from "barley-brew." The whole countryside becomes intensely partisan, but two hearts are sore, the loving hearts of Meg and Anne. Meg warns the local magistrates that the fight is to be held, and the watchful marshals surprise Bill's trainer at cocking and put him up for the night in the Pound "which sinners shared with horse and hound." Deprived of Joe's guardianship in this unexpected turn, Meg's man falls prey to a stratagem of the wily Anne, who has six magnums of champagne sent to her man's rival. Bill yields to temptation, and Joe returns to find his charge with a bad hangover on the day before the fight. But Meg has not finished. Sure now that Bill is going to lose the fight, she again warns the magistrates, who hurry to the scene of the fray. Meanwhile, the stage is set and the crowd has gathered. The marshals of the law arrive and forbid the fight, but its promoters have already foreseen their objection. They merely move across the brook to a site in the neighboring county, a frequent dodge mentioned by Masefield in his introduction to *The Fancy*. Again Meg has a plan. Borrowing a horse from the gypsies, she rides furiously to the magistrate of the new county, and spurs him to action.

> The mob has crossed the brook with cheers,
> As they had planned to do.
> And now the longed-for minute nears,
> The stakes are driven deep like spears
> The ropes are strained thereto.

> And now a stir, but not a roar,
> As Bill comes to the ring.

More enthusiasm greets the entrance of Jock, but he, after smiling at the crowd and enjoying its adulation, slips as he vaults into the ring, and strains his right hand. As in the earlier poem, an accident occurs to change the fortune of the fight, but this fight never comes off. The Buffshire magistrate, a hearty ex-admiral, Sir Falmouth Road, appears in a storm of "Avasts" and "Belays" and stops the fight. Sir Falmouth, however, has a heart of gold. When he learns the circumstances, he makes Jock and Bill shake hands, and each owns the other the better man. Sir Falmouth orders a tremendous celebration for a double wedding and even pays the bill, and "thus ends the tale of country things/ Four generations since."

This piece of rollicking fun is a far cry from *The Everlasting Mercy*. There the fight was a serious business, part of the dark and sordid backdrop against which the conversion of Saul Kane is later to shine; the background of the fight, its setting, its principals, its audience, are all shady and unattractive, while "A Tale of Country Things" is the brightly colored, light-hearted recreation of a story from a bygone day. It is in the tradition of *The Fancy,* and one may safely conclude that it is by far the most "English" of the three boxing poems.

The Traveling Circus

Masefield's catalogue of the world of the Englishman "and his adventure" in the Prologue of *The Country Scene* advises the onlooker to "tread the roads with circus-men, with bull-herds/ With huntsmen, or with fairs. . . ." These men are among those with whom the painters of England, Masefield and Seago, are most concerned. The circus and the fair are English institutions whose sights must be "set down" before a changing world forgets them.

The collaborators of *The Country Scene* have "set down" the traveling circus and the country fair for readers in other lands and later days. Seago's book, *Circus Company* (1933), illustrated with his drawings, is a very readable story of his own experiences with a traveling circus, and Masefield has written an introduction for the book. Four poems in *The Country Scene* have circus themes, and the long poem *King Cole* (1921) presents the circus at both its gloomiest and its attractive and glamorous best.

The introduction to *Circus Company* reveals Masefield's love for the circus tent and for the men and the animals who perform beneath its top. Going to the circus is a delight that most of us have shared in our childhood, he writes, and a delight that lessens very little, as time goes on, for "those with imagination." Its appeal is well nigh universal.

> The old have been known to leave the circus tent saying that thus, surely, Paradise will first appear to the entering soul, as a world of strangeness and beauty in which all the inhabitants have a loveliness, a skill or a swiftness not before seen, and where even the oldest jokes take on new life. The young can seldom leave the circus-tent without the thought that this is life itself, real life, the heart and glow of life, not the ordered pretense of grown-ups, and that this very night, when the grown-ups are asleep, that way of life shall be trodden by young feet.

Masefield finds that even in recent years, when circuses have changed somewhat, children still delight in them, though it may no longer be necessary, as it was in his day, to circulate anti-circus propaganda booklets among the very young in order to dissuade them from running away to join "the brotherhood."

The circus life is a hard one, both Masefield and Seago point out, demanding great skill and effort and sacrifice, as well as resistance to bad weather, hardship, and discomfort. Yet both men present this life as good and attractive, with freedom, the open air, comradeship, and artistic expression as its compensating values. The politician and the schoolmaster, Masefield writes, may recommend other ways of life, but the wise child knows that it is surely much better to belong to a circus. It is interesting to note that of the little quotations from various authors with which Seago prefaces his twenty chapters, five are from the poetry of Masefield.[14]

As for *King Cole,* Cecil Biggane remarks that the "shy, gentle, humorous" spirit of England pervades the poem like a sweet and wholesome air. She finds it a "gracious fantasy, mellow and kindly and full of pleasant, childish things . . . as though the poet had suddenly recovered his lost childhood with all its vanities and absurdities and simple pleasures."[15]

The hero of the narrative is the legendary British king whose spirit still wanders England, helping the brave and good who are vexed with trouble and sorrow. A combination pied piper, scholar gypsy, and *deux ex machina,* he gives his magic assistance this time to a traveling showman whose circus has had a long run of misfortune and who, in spite of his own troubles, is kind to the disguised spirit.

The story is slight enough, the rehabilitation of a ruined show-man through supernatural aid, but the poem becomes memorable for the poet's picture of circus life and circus people in England, his charming catalogues of the creatures of the field, forest, and air who follow King Cole's piping, and the air of mystery and fairyland with which he (or perhaps King Cole!) invests the lines.

The poem begins with the story of King Cole's happy reign and of his return to earth as a benevolent spirit disguised as "an old, poor wandering man, with glittering eyes." Then the reader meets a circus company, plodding wearily along the muddy roads through the rain, "broken by bitter weather and the luck." The owner is a beaten man who despairs of any good turn to his fortune and who says: "This is the end; I'm ruined; I'm defeated." The men traveling with him are discouraged, too, and disaffected, ready to leave the showman. Each is introduced: the second clown, "a snub-nosed youth,/ Fair-haired, with broken teeth"; his wife, "who leaped the hoops" and who now "nursed sour twins, her son and jealousy"; the cowboy, and his wife, "the rat-eyed bag-gage with red hair," who had joined the show to do tight-rope walking and now attracts the attention of the second clown; the clown, old Circus John, with his complaint that women are killing the circus trade when "horses and us are what men want to see." There are others: the juggler, "red-cheeked, with eyes like boxer's, quick and keen"; Molly, the singer, who watches the juggler, with "big black eyes that love had brimmed with tears," and "the music," bitterly plotting rebellion and demanding "A shilling more, or never play again." In each van are cross fathers, haggard-eyed mothers, crying children. These are the circus people.

A stranger meets the disconsolate circus troupe and begins to talk with the showman, who complains bitterly of his misfortunes. Then, pitying the sorrier lot of the poor old wanderer, the showman invites him inside the van to share a meager supper. They talk long of the plight of show business, and the disguised spirit of Cole comforts the unhappy man and his wife and prophesies success in the city ahead, for ever since "the grass was green, all men have loved a show."

The circus enters Wallingford, but because the Prince is visiting the city, the caravan must pass directly through and out into the countryside. This is another blow to the showman, who sits in his van with bowed head.

Now King Cole slips from the van to march at the head of the leading team. His fluting calls "the spirits that inhabit dream," and the rain ends in a "rush of sun and glittering cloud." The city people stare with amazement at the "bright waggons led by the bright-haired," while the horses crest to the tune and step "like centaurs to a passionate festival."

> And to the crowd, the circus artists seemed
> Splendid, because the while that singing quired
> Each artist was the part that he had dreamed
> And glittered with the Power he desired,
> Women and men, no longer wet or tired
> From long despair, now shone like queens and kings,
> There they were crowned with their imaginings.

Even the creatures of the forest and the meadow come to walk in procession to Cole's fluting. This is no everyday circus, and Wallingford is a new Wallingford, touched with magic.

Once through the city, the circus becomes again the weary, muddy company, grumbling beneath a dripping sky, but King Cole goes to the Prince, who is restless and dissatisfied with his own lot. He invites the Prince to attend the circus performance that night, and in answer to the question, "What can they do?" offers an enticing list of the troupe's abilities. King Cole also persuades the whole Court and the townspeople to attend the performance, in order to behold man's skill and woman's beauty "imaged to the height."

The discouraged show people are getting ready for the night's performance. Sick at heart, the showman's wife, dressed in spangles for her song and dance on the barebacked horse, sits at the ticket window, fearing that no one will come. Inside the tent, the bandsmen in their scarlet cart tune their bugles, flageolets, and strings, while the horses stand waiting, nosing at the grass. Only a few children have appeared. Suddenly King Cole's piping is heard, and a great crowd approaches. The piper tells the showman's wife that the Prince and the Queen are coming and gives her a sack of minted gold, the ticket money for the people of the Court and town. She rushes from the van to tell her husband, who quickly bids the band strike up "God Save the Queen." The piebald horses kneel at the Court's entrance, and the performance begins.

It is an inspired performance, partly because of the happiness of the artists, partly because of King Cole's magic.

> There in the Ring, indeed, the stranger stood,
> King Cole, the shining, with his flute of wood,
> Waiting until the chattering court was stilled.
>
> Then from his wooden flute his piping thrilled,
> Then all was tense, and then the leaping fluting
> Clamoured as flowering clamours for the fruiting.
> And round the ring came Dodo, the brown mare,
> Pied like a tiger-moth; her bright shoes tare
> The scattered petals, while the clown came after
> Like life, a beauty chased by tragic laughter.
> The showman entered in and cracked his whip.
>
> Then followed fun and skill and horsemanship,
> Marvellous all, for all were at their best.
> Never had playing gone with such a zest
> To those good jesters; never had the tent
> So swiftly answered to their merriment
> With cheers, the artist's help, the actor's life.

The delighted monarchs invite the circus to perform at the Court at Christmastide, and they give a feast for all the circus company. Not only are the fortunes of the company rebuilt, but friendship and peace are restored; the wandering son of the showman and his wife miraculously returns, and the juggler declares his love for the patient singer, Molly. At the close of this scene of perfect happiness, King Cole breathes "a piping of this life of ours," until the stroke of twelve on the belfry tower tells him that his hour is come. And then "He dimmed like mist till one could scarcely note/ The robins nestling to his old gray coat."

After this extended picture of the circus in adversity and in felicity, the brief circus poems from *The Country Scene* are only slight snapshots. They are four in number; one of them, "Elephants in the Tent," has an unexpected flash of humor in Masefield's treatment of the elephants:

> "They're not the draw they were," the showman said.
> "I never like them much; they're queer things, very.
> For anything they happen on, they'll eat;
> Your spanners, or galoshes off your feet;
> One day you'll have em well, the next day, dead.
> And take my word, they're hellish jobs to bury."

In "The Tight-rope Walker," Masefield, the ballet lover, treats the circus performer with almost the same respect that he accords to the ballerina. "Their Canvas Home" shows the tent and its occupants in the hours just before and just after the show, and the lamp-lit wagons starting away again down "summer-drowsy lanes." "Nomads" takes these vans on their journey, when the last visitor has left the ground and "declining stars behold them trudge the night." Then with Cole-like optimism the poet prophesies that "Tomorrow they will prosper and be bright,/ Beauty will triumph and the clown will please."

The English Country Fair

It is a logical transition from the English traveling circus in Masefield's work to the English country fair. Frequently the two

offer similar attractions, and apparently the circus sometimes
visits the fairs in its travels. In *King Cole,* for example, the circus
is on its way from Reading to St. Giles' Fair, and later the showman tells the disguised spirit of the king that his troupe has been
at Wycombe Fair. Generally, however, the traveling shows that
appear at country fairs are not circuses, but other attractions of
various sorts. The traditional circus, before its more recent trend
toward "turns which would better suit an aquarium or menag-
erie,"[16] would have scorned the antics of the showmen at fairs
described in *The Widow in the Bye Street* (1912), *The Hawbucks*
(1929), "Young John of Chance's Stretch" (1931),[17] and elsewhere: the circus performers, jugglers, clowns, tight-rope walkers,
singers, trainers of horses, riders, are all artists. Against "counter-
attractions" of less artistic worth, the showman of *King Cole*
inveighs bitterly.

In the Prologue of *The Country Scene* Masefield speaks of the
fair as an important phase of English life; he also cites the October
Fair as among the earliest memories of his childhood in the poem,
Wonderings (1943), and the "fragments of autobiography" entitled *Grace Before Ploughing* (1966). Mention is made in various
places of "May fairs" and "winter fairs," but the October fair is
commonest in Masefield's work.

> But best of all, was the October Fair
> When in the market-place the beasts were cooped,
> And horses whirled to the steam-organ's blare,
> And many coloured swing-boats hove and swooped;
>
> And shiny stalls were there of painted toys,
> Fairyland stalls, all brightly gardened round
> With life of man and beast, exciting noise,
> And paper zinnias stuck into the ground.
>
> Ah, the October fair, the hiring-day,
> The sunny day, when it could never rain,
> When bells were rung for sorrows put away,
> And men rejoiced for life begun again.

The main elements of the fair that the child Masefield remembered in later life reappear in the fair described in *The Hawbucks*. This novel provides a detailed picture of the country fair when the chief character, George Childrey, visits Hilcote fair in the hope of seeing the half-sister of his sweetheart. While he looks for her, the reader follows him from one end of the fair to the other.

George finds Hilcote square crowded with the booths of merchants selling crockery, china, cakes, linen shirts, and caps. Further along are other booths, such "as there had been for 350 years . . . for the sale of country things and country skill." Among the occupants of these booths are: a china-mender, who uses an ancient Egyptian device, the dancing-ball drill, in his work; a woman who mends rush-bottom chairs while the owner waits; a turner selling wooden cups and plates of his own making; two women selling the increasingly rare country lace of that region; another woman who makes "the original old Hilcote pies, being the boat of St. Nicholas in ginger-bread, stuffed with currants and spice"; and sellers of flowers, brushes, and other articles of various sorts. Many of these merchants are honest local folk. Some are gypsies and other people of questionable honesty, like the hawkers of posies made of stolen flowers and the other "Fair-time rogues" against whom the boy's mother warns him in "Young John of Chance's Stretch."

> Four shows are busy at the Hilcote fair, a merry-go-round with a steam organ which played "White Wings"; a smaller merry-go-round, with a steam organ and cymbals, which played "Cheer, boys, cheer"; a smaller merry-go-round, with a trumpeter and drummer, who played what sounded like selections from "Annie Laurie," and a double stand of swing-boats in full swing, with the swingers singing to all three.

These are the swing-boats and steam organs and painted horses described in a number of Masefield poems. *The Country Scene* describes them in two brief pictures of the tumult of October Fair.

George is interested in the rifle saloons, because he is a good shot. He pauses to shoot a few times at the "glittering balls tossing in the air," and wins a china dog and five other trinkets, which he gives to children near the booth. In *The Widow in the Bye Street* there are similar booths, "And if you hit you get a good cigar," and throughout this scene of the poem, the crack of the rifles mingles with the "whanging" of the steam organs, the "thud" of the Sally-shy-sticks, the "clanging" of the brassy cymbals, the "clash" of the cheapjacks' crockery, and "brazen patter of the touts."

The Hawbucks describes more fully the Aunt Sally shies and the cheapjacks mentioned in the poems. The reader hears the Aunt Sally men bawling and the shouting of the cheapjack, who stands on a wagon and auctions off cheap crockery pudding-basins, smashing them on the pavement from time to time to attract attention when the bidding is not brisk. George meets various local characters as he makes the round of the fair, including one old laborer, Punch, who has just won a turkey in a raffle. Many fairs, like this one at Hilcote and the October event at Cholsington described in the novel *Dead Ned* (1938), are Hiring Fairs. At Hilcote George sees a hiring stand near the church where loitered a few men and women known as the "Hilcote Hard Bargains," who had been discharged by their employers after Michaelmas.

The Cholsington fair, being very near London, attracted "much rascality from London," selling cheap jewelry, shoelaces, and buttons while they looked out for whatever they might steal. The Cholsington fair is much like the one described in *The Hawbucks,* with a few additional noises, such as

> the exhilarating bell-ringing, not only from the church ringing for its patron saint, but from the auctioneer's assistant. . . . Besides these there were solitary musicians, of sorts. A one-legged sailor leaning on a crutch, played upon a whistle; a man in an almost worn-out red soldier's coat played "Jockies to the Fair" and similar tunes. Then there were the Irish harper and the Scottish piper, both followed by little gangs of boys imitating the noise they made.

There is also an excellent picture of a "remarkable fair character," called Jane Jollycok, whom the hero, Ned Mansell, has seen before at the Pie Fair beyond Islington.

Masefield has two long poems that include country fair scenes. "Young John of Chance's Stretch" offers little in addition to what is to be found in *The Hawbucks,* but there are several vivid scenes through which Young John wanders, a country boy alone at his first fair.

In *The Widow in the Bye Street,* the October Fair is the place of meeting for the two chief characters of the tragic tale—the light woman, Anna, and the boy Jimmy. The opening stanzas describe the typical scenes to which "the country folk flock from far and near." Anna goes to the fair to meet her lover, Shepherd Ern, who makes his wife stay in the house and promises to bring "fairings" for the children. The reader meets Ern, angry at Anna's lateness, drowning his troubles in a noisy inn and then going away with the strapping gypsy girl, Bessie. The reader also meets Jimmy, at the fair with his widowed mother, an old lady "dressed in her finest with a Monmouth shawl."

This fair presents a ram-wrestling contest and the other attractions missing from *The Hawbucks* and *Dead Ned,* such as "The Oldest Show on Earth," "The Last Hanging," and "The Murder in the Barn," the last named "with real blood." It is Jimmy's victory in the ram-wrestling contest that attracts Anna's attention and leads to his infatuation and the dramatic climax of the poem. Jimmy's battle with the ram is one of several delightful, homely anecdotes in the poem.

At the end of this section of *The Widow in the Bye Street,* Masefield describes the closing of the fair:

> The fair's lights threw aloft a misty glow.
> The organ whangs, the giddy horses reel,
> The rifles cease, the folk begin to go,
> The hands unclamp the swing-boats from the wheel,
> There is a smell of trodden orange peel;
> The organ drones and dies, the horses stop,
> And then the tent collapses from the top.
>
> The fair is over, let the people troop,
> The drunkards stagger homewards down the gutters,
> The showmen heave in an excited group,
> The poles tilt slowly down, the canvas flutters,
> · · · · · · · · · · · · · · · ·
> · · · A concertina plays
> Far off as wandering lovers go their ways.

In the traveling circus and country fair passages, Masefield frequently draws the reader's attention to the animals. The first stanza in the country-fair sequence of *The Widow in the Bye Street* describes "pens of heifers blinking in the sun," and Lemster sheep "which pant and seem to doze," while at the end of the fair, new owners drive home their cattle and "many a young calf from his mother parts." The prize-winning bulls draw comment in *The Country Scene;* of the bull's importance in English civilization, Masefield, describing a picture by the artist Munnings, writes in one of his essays:

> The first (picture) is that of the foundation of civilization, and the rough ground on which we are built. It is that of a man leading a bull. The man leads the bull by a twitch hooked to a ring in the bull's nose. It is a picture of the elements of man's life on earth; his conquering of the beasts by which he lives. Without the bull, man would be little indeed. He could hardly cultivate, he could hardly live.[18]

However, it is the horse that attracts attention in most of the fair and circus descriptions. One poem, "Pony Fair," from the volume, *A Letter from Pontus, and Other Verse* (1936), presents this type of fair as a tradition five centuries old, and shows evidence, corroborated extensively in other poetry and prose, of Masefield's love and sympathy for horses.

> Twice every year for full five centuries
> This grass beside the road has held a fair,
> Where horses have been sold from everywhere,
> Each with some gloss of not-believed-in lies,
> Here they have huddled close with frightened eyes,
> Hearing the trumpets of the showmen blare,
> Here they have cropped the roadside selvage bare,
> And gone with their new masters down the rise.
>
> Within the dream where horses run career,
> (Being set free of men, when death at last
> Slips halter off and knocks the shoes from feet),
> How many must retread this quiet street,
> Hoping to find some mistress of the past,
> Or mother mare, or foal last looked on here.

"Horses and shipping" appear as two of Britain's traditional concerns in one of the poems from *The Country Scene*. Here the horse fair is seven centuries old, and the picture is painted from a historical as well as from a sentimental viewpoint:

> King Cymbeline bought ponies here, they say;
> And haply twenty centuries from today
> Horses will still be priced here, to these cheers,
> Horses and shipping being Britain's Law.

Horses, Horse-Racing and Right Royal

Love for horses is characteristic of many of Masefield's men and women, not only in *Reynard the Fox* and *Right Royal*, where horses are a primary concern of every character in the poems, but elsewhere in his work. Often a common love for the horse will bridge serious difficulties of opinion, and sometimes an otherwise unpleasant person is redeemed by this appealing trait.[19]

"Gallopping horses," says the old man in the dedication poem of *Tribute to Ballet* (1938), are one of the "three lovely things"; and of Edward Seago, his collaborator in *Tribute to Ballet* and other books, Masefield writes that "horses fill his waking dreams." In *The Country Scene,* one of Seago's loveliest pictures is accompanied by lines about white horses of the sea, and for another Seago picture Masefield writes "The Mare and Foal at Grass," in which the two are enjoying the warmth of Spring when, still far away from the foal's young life are the "switches on his thighs and iron on his feet and in his mouth."

In the novel *ODTAA* (1926), the hero, Highworth Ridden, belongs to an English family passionately fond of horses: the mother, "a loud, fresh-coloured, robust mare of a woman"; the daughter, a sweet and gentle girl who loves to ride and to work in the stables; and the father, "an ugly devil, foul-mouthed and rude," whose character is redeemed by his strange gentleness with women and horses. Bill Ridden's language is filled with figures of speech from the world of horse-breeding, racing, and the fox-hunt, and he believes the horse to be the very hub and pivot of English life. Opposing an engineering career for his son, he urges the boy to stay at home at "a needed job; a pleasant job; and a gentleman's job." One of the more interesting minor characters in *Eggs and Baker* (1936) is young Bob Mansell's mysterious grandfather, a gentleman of irregular habits who lived a colorful life in the sporting world and whose character, like Bill Ridden's, is redeemed in the English boy's eyes because he "was said at the time to be the best man on a bad horse in all England."

In the essay written as a foreword to a catalogue of pictures exhibited by Alfred Munnings, Masefield affirms the importance of the horse in English life and speaks of "our fondness for animals, and our deep fondness for the horse" as "one of our characteristics" as a nation. Commenting on Munnings's work, he writes that "no one has so deeply felt the beauty of our horses." He concludes by praising the artist's capture of "the unmatchable beauty of the English horse," and he writes, "Somebody ought to have put all these scenes into poems."

Masefield has done just this. He has given us some exciting and beautiful pictures of the horse in action,[20] in the fox-hunt and the steeplechase, "which were once the needs and are still the delights of our race."

The Country Scene has two racing poems. One of them, "The Road to Epsom," gives a quick view of the crowds hurrying to Epsom Downs for the races, blackening "all the face of all the downs." The other poem, "Point-to-Point," describes the scene at the races and then the racers themselves. "The Racer," a sonnet from the *King Cole* volume, almost personifies the horse but is less successful than *Right Royal* in its attribution of human qualities to the animal.

The Hawbucks, like the poems *Right Royal* and *Reynard the Fox,* is thronged with English countryfolk of all social levels, who are horse lovers. When George Childrey returns to his old home after several years in America, one of his first wishes is to visit the stables. There conversation about the horses ensues between George and his brother Nick. Of the two, George is clearly the true horse lover, and in this difference lies an index to their characters. The reader's almost immediate preference for George is quickly justified. The most attractive people in the novel, Carrie Harridew, Bun Manor, and Charles Cothill, are all deeply fond of horses. All three, like George and Nick, are characters first

presented to the reader in *Reynard the Fox*. Charles Cothill, who
represents in Masefield's work the ideal of English manhood, is
also the central figure in *Right Royal*.

Perhaps the most exciting episode in *The Hawbucks* is a point-
to-point race that occupies twelve pages of the novel. The fact
that four of the competitors are competing also for the favor of
Carrie Harridew lends interest to the race. Masefield describes
the candy and amusement booths, some of which are like those
found at the country fairs. The sellers of score cards and the
bookies, "in loud check suits, often hung about with bright tin
medals," are present, as well as an old huntsman hawking copies
at sixpence each of his poem on Pyeford Bridge Day, thirty years
before. The assemblage of people is almost as varied as that which
Masefield describes at the great hunt in *Reynard the Fox,* for "all
the countryside was there: the middle period folk as actors, the
old and the young as spectators."

The chief excitement of the race is afforded by the villain,
Vaughan, who is barred from the race, but enters it illegally at
the very start, drunk and dangerous. After his fall and elimination
from the race, interest flags a little, although the finish is close.
As they come into the straight, Charles Cothill on a beautiful
black, George Childrey on Kilkenny, Bun Manor on his big Irish
hunter Muckish, and a Tencombe man riding a light chestnut
chaser are all neck and neck.

> The black led, Tencombe led, Kilkenny led, Muckish led
> again. Then Kilkenny's effort seemed to grow greater, as
> though he were suddenly become a greater horse: instantly
> there came a final, swift, fatal sorting out of values. George
> was past the white post a neck ahead, the black second, Muckish
> third; and all four horses went careening on for fifty yards
> before they could come to a canter or pull up.[21]

It is a good race, but it is nothing compared to the steeplechase in
Right Royal. In *Right Royal* the race is the whole poem, and
Masefield's rushing lines give the story a thrilling quality absent
from the prose of *The Hawbucks*.

The poem *Right Royal* opens an hour before the English
"Chasers" Cup on Compton Course, a race to be watched by
seventy thousand men and women from every walk of English

life, and by spectators from all over the world. Of the chief characters, Emmy Crowthorne is a newcomer to Masefield's stories,[22] but Charles Cothill has appeared elsewhere;[23] they represent much that is best in the English character, and their future life together depends upon this race.

The night before, Charles Cothill had dreamed a strange dream, so moving and so real that it led him to stake everything he owned on victory in this race. In the dream, as he stood on the race-course, his horse, Right Royal, had appeared at his side, saying "It is my day, today." This in itself was remarkable enough, but on the following morning, other strange things happened. Right Royal, usually cold-mannered and unfriendly, had greeted his master at the stable, nuzzling him with signs of joy, as his startled trainer said "It is his day today, that's plain to see." Struck by these things, Cothill had gone directly to the bookies and backed himself to win. When the reader first sees Right Royal, he is impressed with the horse's beauty and nobility; his record, however, has not been good. Mistreated by a jockey, he had become sulky, undependable, and crowd-shy and had lost his races. His owner sold him to Charles, who had retrained him with love and patience, but even the devoted trainer Harding is skeptical of Royal's chances in the race, while Dick Cappell and others do not give him a thought.

Masefield's description of the huge crowd arriving at Compton is full of excitement and bright colors, and he sketches several race-goers with a few deft strokes. There is a bookie like the one in *The Hawbucks,* "his clothes a check of three-inch squares." Forty swift lines catalogue the visitors from foreign lands who are at the race, men from the mines of the Cordilleras, Greeks, Russians, Bengalese, even "Oregon men of six feet seven/ With backs from Atlas and hearts from Heaven." The fashionable sports from London are like the gay blades who crowd the pages of *The Fancy*—"bucks from city and flash young bloods/ With vests 'cut saucy' to show their studs."

It is time for the start. Em wishes her lover well and assures him of victory; John Harding has some advice about the pace and the course. Then Masefield calls the vivid roll of starters, thirty-six in all, characterizing some with an adjective, but the favorites, Soyland and Sir Lopez, with several lines each. Right

Royal's reaction to the crowd is surprisingly good, and Charles smiles with relief that the roaring throng is "to his horse's mind." The start is agonizingly delayed, with some riders jockeying for an unfair start, others controlling their nervous mounts with difficulty. There is an accident even before the start, and after the start a steady succession of falls and injuries. But for those who survive the first thorn-bound ditch, there is "a tide of horses in fury flowing,/ Beauty of speed in glory going."

Part Two of the poem records the race, stride by stride, hazard by hazard. The reader is certain that all is lost when Royal jumps too early at one bad ditch and hurdle, but horse and rider are uninjured and, though shaken, resume the race, thirty lengths behind the leaders.

Only a perfect unity of spirit in man and mount could overcome this handicap. Charles waits wisely for the exact moment, and at that moment Right Royal responds. He is neck and neck with the favorite, Sir Lopez, coming down the straight.

> Right Royal went past him, half an inch, half a head,
> Half a neck, he was leading, for an instant he led;
> Then a hooped black and coral flew up like a shot,
> With a lightning-like effort from little Gavotte.
>
> The little bright mare, made of nerves and steel springs,
> Shot level beside him, shot ahead as with wings.
> Charles felt his horse quicken, felt the desperate beat
> Of the blood in his body from his knees to his feet.
>
> Three terrible strides brought him up to the mare,
> Then they rushed to wild shouting through a whirl of blown
>   air;
> Then Gavotte died to nothing; Soyland came once again
> Till his muzzle just reached to the knot of his rein.
>
> Then a whirl of urged horses thundered up, whipped and
>   blown,
> Soyland, Peterkinooks, and Red Ember the roan
> For an instant they challenged, then they drooped and were
>   done;

Then the White Post shot backwards, Right Royal had won.

The pace never flags through the second half of the poem, and the right reader droops with relief at the end. But the poem does not end with the finish of the race. The poet has a four-stanza ending in which the reader learns that

> Charles married his lady, but he rode no more races;
> He lives on the Downland on the blown grassy places,
> Where he and Right Royal can canter for hours
> On the flock-bitten turf full of tiny blue flowers.

Asked to explain the weakness of the poem's ending, Masefield admitted in a letter that the end was "a little flat." After most climaxes, he felt, there came a moment of dismissal "with calm of mind all passion spent," but here his attempts to produce the desired effect had failed and he decided that "the thing ended with the race."[24] Whatever one's reaction to the ending, the importance of *Right Royal* is that it is a thrilling tale and the glorification of the English horse race and the English horse.

Fox-Hunting in the Poems

Reynard the Fox (1919) is probably Masefield's best-known long poem. It is said to have been immensely popular in England and to have been largely responsible for its writer's appointment to the laureateship. Its popularity is not hard to explain, for it is the most eloquent presentation in English literature of the sport traditionally associated with England—the fox-hunt.

In "Fox Hunting," an introduction to the 1919 first illustrated edition of *Reynard the Fox,* Masefield gives his reasons for writing the poem. He writes, "A man wanting to set down a picture of the society of England will find his models at the games," and then shows that at a fox-hunt one finds the best cross-section of English society. The fox-hunt appeals to "both sexes, all ages and all classes" and is a game in which "all who come may take part, whether rich or poor, mounted or on foot." But Masefield's use of the fox-hunt as a setting for a Chaucerian gallery of English portraits is of less concern at this point than his second reason for writing the poem.

> . . . to all Englishmen who live in a hunting country, hunting is in the blood, and the mind is full of it. It is the most beautiful and the most stirring sight to be seen in England. In the ports, as at Falmouth, there are ships under sail, under way, coming or going, beautiful unspeakably. In the country, especially on the great fields on the lower slopes of the downland, the teams of the plowman may be seen bowing forward on a skyline, and this sight can never fail to move one by its majesty of beauty. But in neither of these sights of beauty is there the bright colour and swift excitement of the hunt, nor the thrill of the horn, and the cry of the hounds ringing into the elements of the soul. Something in the hunt wakens memories hidden in the marrow, racial memories, of when one hunted for the tribe, animal memories, of when one hunted with the pack, or was hunted.

This introduction traces the historical development of fox-hunting in England from the days when the hunt was a necessity for man. Masefield speaks of its prevalence in England and Ireland and of its growing popularity in the United States, where "it is rapidly becoming a national sport." In later years he must have come to admit to over-optimism in his predictions for Ireland and the United States. Football, hurling, and horse-racing in Ireland, and football, baseball, and basketball in the United States are not likely to share their top ranking with the English sport. Masefield discusses as reasons for the popularity of fox-hunting in England its social nature, its beauty and excitement, and the fact that "we are a horse-loving people who have loved horses as we have loved the sea."

In this introductory essay Masefield includes imaginary accounts of typical hunts, the first as "the ideal run of 1750 might have been described," the second a hunt of "the present time." The first is a most entertaining account in the form of a letter written to "your Lorp" by his "most obedient Charles Cothill," an ancestor, no doubt, of the hero of *Right Royal.*

The poet also tells us of his own early interest in foxes and the hunt in both "Fox-Hunting" and the 1966 *Grace Before Ploughing.* Born in "a good hunting country, partly woodland, partly pasture," he had seen hounds, "the loveliest animals," on most days of his life and had seen many meets, "each as romantic as a circus."

> Often, as a little child, I saw and heard hounds hunting in and near a covert within sight of my old home. Once, when I was, perhaps, five years old, the fox was hunted into our garden, and those glorious beings in scarlet, as well as the hounds, were all about my lairs, like visitants from paradise.[25]

No one fox was the original of Masefield's Reynard. The fox's "grace, beauty, cleverness, and secrecy" had always thrilled him, and he admired the animal as "one against many, who keeps his end up, and lives, often snugly, in spite of the world." The pirate and the nightrider cannot rival him for romance or danger. The combination of adventure and an underdog is irresistible to Masefield, whose work is filled with men who triumph against great odds or fail gloriously in a "lost endeavour."

The introductory essay closes with a portrait, part verse, part prose, of Baldy Hill, the "earth-stopper," who to Masefield is "Primitive Man survived," the essential and basic English countryman.

Reynard the Fox is a long poem in two parts; the first sets the stage for the hunt, the second records the actual hunting. Masefield describes the "Cock and Pye," an ancient inn where the meet is to start. The inn and its yard and stables are alive with activity from dawn until meeting time, and the reader receives a minutely detailed account of this activity. By ten o'clock the hunters begin to arrive, one by one, or in groups, and the poet describes each. They form a fascinating array, a late-nineteenth-century reincarnation of the Canterbury pilgrims, although Masefield's reader is less intimately a part of the crowd than Chaucer's. Masefield's reader observes the people at a distance, as if he were watching the stage or the cinema screen; Chaucer's reader drinks and jokes at the Tabard and then jogs along the Canterbury road with fellow-pilgrims. Yet the men and women of *Reynard the Fox,* discussed above in chapter 3, are real enough and interesting enough for our instant recognition and delight when we meet them again in later poems and novels. The horses are real, too, and "those feathery things, the hounds." Masefield calls several by name, as they wait uneasily, tongues lolling, noses questing, for the start of the hunt.

The hunt moves slowly to Ghost Heath Wood, where the "chacking" cry of "that blue-winged Judas, a jay" warns of the fox's presence. The hounds pick up their scent, and the run is on.

Part Two of the poem first introduces the fox. This fox is no ordinary creature whose pursuit the reader is to follow objectively. On the contrary, he is to become an object of real solicitude, with whom the reader almost merges in self-identification because he sees much of the hunt from the fox's viewpoint.

The poet describes the fox's haunts and follows him on a hunting and mating expedition of the night before.

> Before the dawn he had loved and fed
> And found a kennel and gone to bed
> On a shelf of grass in a thick of gorse
> That would bleed a hound and blind a horse.
> There he slept in the mild west weather
> With his nose and brush tucked well together,
> He slept like a child, who sleeps yet hears
> With the self who needs neither eyes nor ears.

The fox, awakened from his nap by a passing boy and his dog, scents the approaching hunt. He plans his campaign, while Masefield begins that attribution of human qualities and emotions to the beast which may constitute an artistic flaw for some readers but heightens absorption in the story for others.

The chase is in full cry now, and the reader follows over brook and fence, through pasture and wood. As the fox finally draws near his earth on Wan Dyke Hill, the pace is beginning to tell on him. When he reaches the hill at last, a heart-breaking reverse is in store for him: "The earth was stopped. It was barred with stakes." Here one's sympathy goes at once, if it has not gone before, to the fox, who now has to run as he changes his plan. He knows another earth and heads for that, but here again is frustrated. A boy, hunting rabbits, stands beside the hole, with gun, ferret, and terrier pup. The fox, strength failing, must run on. He has some brief respite when the terrier's scent kills his, but the pack is soon on his trail again. He tries his best tricks, running among sheep and swimming a brook, to throw his pursuers off scent. For all this, they gain on him steadily as Mourne End wood looms ahead. Nearly exhausted, the fox reaches the thorn fence at the wood's edge and fails in his first attempt to leap it. Over the top in a second try, he meets another in the staggering series of reverses. This earth too is stopped, filled with stones. For a moment his courage fails, but fear drives him on into the wood, where the "taint of fox was rank in the air." At long last fortune intervenes for Reynard. The hounds change scent in the wood and crash off after a new fox, in whose fate the reader has no stake.

The poem ends with the hounds and the hunt limping home after the "fastest and longest" run in their memory. The hounds have caught and killed, and everyone is happy and weary. The reader follows the hounds to their supper and their bench, the horses to their straw.

> Then the moon came quiet and flooded full
> Light and beauty on clouds like wool,
> On a feasted fox at rest from hunting,
> In the beech wood grey where the brocks were grunting.
> The beech wood grey rose dim in the night
> With moonlight fallen in pools of light,
> The long dead leaves on the ground were rimed.
> A clock struck twelve and the church-bells chimed.

Masefield appears to be an authority on fox-hunting, and nowhere does any critic, whatever his attitude toward the poem's characters or its setting or its versification, challenge the authenticity of the hunt itself. Douglas Gordon's dissertation on foxes and fox-hunting states that Masefield "knows his fox, and in his luminous, impulsive verse, draws his psychology with a suggestive pen, limning the Reynard of his epic on a heroic scale."[26] Coulson Kernahan recalls Harold Monro's remark about a sportsman who approved the hunt but not its human participants, calling it "a damned good run, but a Bank Holiday Field."[27] Siegfried Sassoon, both fox-hunter and poet, once told Edward Davison that "Masefield's account of the chase . . . throughout its exhaustive particulars, is faultlessly accurate."[28] It is, therefore, a surprise to read in Masefield's Sheffield University remarks in 1946:

In answering to this toast, please let me begin by saying that I know nothing whatever about fox-hunting, but I discovered a few who did, and I discovered that those who are passionate about fox-hunting are poets on that theme. It is to their inspiration that I owe any quality which that poem may contain.[29]

Two years after the appearance of *Reynard the Fox*, Masefield wrote in the foreword to the Munnings exhibition catalogue that there was no sight in the countryside more beautiful than the "moving of hounds and huntsmen on a mild winter day." Commenting on one of the paintings, he writes, "I love the raw February scene of the hounds going out in the snow." Years later, in *The Country Scene*, the poet paints these hounds in a picture of his own called "The Hounds in Snow." The only other hunting poem from *The Country Scene* is a quasi-historical treatment of the sport from its earliest days as a necessity for life to its present status when "all is idle, but the idlest still/ Feels in his marrow the ancestral thrill."

Fox-Hunting in the Novels

In *The Hawbucks* (1929) the many country folk who love horses and horse racing participate even more eagerly in the fox-hunt. The novel is full of references to the hunt and discussions of it. Early in the book, when George Childrey returns to his old home in England after several years abroad, he is looking forward to hunting once more. A meet is scheduled for Godsdown on the following Wednesday, and both he and his brother Nick plan to be present. George hunts for the pleasure and exhilaration of the sport, Nick because of the potential social and business contacts with the important people of the country.

George's first visit after his return is to the Harridew House, where he renews acquaintance with the three daughters and their irascible old father, the Squire, and where Jane Harridew shows him a picture of the Harridew pack, 1799. George misses the Godsdown meet, so that the reader has only brief descriptions of it from other characters, but soon attention is fixed on a larger meet to be run from the "Cock-and-Pye." This is the inn of the hunt in *Reynard the Fox*, and as the hunters gather, the reader recognizes many of the people he met at the earlier hunt at the Cock-and-Pye. Although Masefield did not develop the characters introduced in Part One of *Reynard the Fox* in the second part of that poem, he apparently liked many of them too well to abandon them entirely. Chapter 3 surveys some of these characters and their appearances in Masefield's poetry and fiction.

The Hawbucks is the novel in which the Reynard people reappear en masse. All its chief characters and many minor figures, to the number of thirty-two, as well as several of their relatives, derive directly from *Reynard the Fox*.

The Cock-and-Pye meets in *Reynard the Fox* and *The Hawbucks* are not identical, but they do have similarities other than those of location and participants. In *The Hawbucks*, however, the emphasis is upon George's courtship of Carrie and not upon the drama of the flight and final escape of the fox. The description of the hunt in prose is far less exciting than that in *Reynard*. Here, too, the fox gets away, through a change of scent in Mourne End Wood, but the hunt fails to kill its new quarry. When George and Carrie are riding home, an incident occurs that is another variation from the *Reynard* story. A blue jay is swearing in a tree near a blackthorn fence.

> George had good country eyes, quick to catch subtle changes. He saw nothing as he passed, but just after he had passed he saw something move, ever so slightly, as though with relief at a danger gone. He said nothing for half a minute; then he said: "That was our fox in the hedge, lying down to die. He'll never get up after such a gruelling. They changed in the wood, as I said."[80]

The climax of the novel is another hunt. George, heartsick at his rejection by Carrie, who is to marry his worthless brother, rides recklessly to a hunt at St. Margarets. He is first to see the fox break cover and for four miles leads the hunt; the fifth mile takes him into rough and unfamiliar country. Bill Ridden and Charles Cothill catch up with him and suddenly turn aside, Bill to the right, Charles to the left, both shouting something. George is warned too late and he and his mount go over into Stonepits Old Quarry. The novel ends as George recovers consciousness, with Carrie's beautiful half-sister in attendance upon him. A happy ending does not improve the book, which is weak in plot but strong in English landscape, open air scenes, and pictures of the fair, the point-to-point, and the hunt.

The novel *The Square Peg* (1937) is another *locus classicus* for the English fox-hunt, but its pictures of the sport are far different from those in *The Hawbucks,* the essays, and the poems. Here the reader finds the other side of the fox-hunt, for several of the characters in the novel attack the sport and its followers as cruel, useless, vain, and ridiculous.

When Frampton Mansell and his fiancée buy an estate near Stubbington, they plan to make a bird sanctuary and game preserve of the grounds. On one of their first visits to the property, they find evidence of a recent hunt; the fox has been killed and eaten there, and both had the "feeling of being haunted by a terrible event."

A conversation between Mansell and an old countryman who is making fences for him reveals the new owner's hatred of the hunt. Old Zine tells him of a recent hunt at which the fox had escaped but two horses were "ridden until their hearts burst." When Mansell questions the old man about hunting, Zine is perplexed by the attitude of this stranger from the city, but he attempts to explain:

> It's in man's nature to like sport, sir; they take to it naturally. And it gives a chance to every man to enjoy what he likes best. A lot cares for hunting because the others care for it, and because it puts life into a country-side, to see a lot of life in it. And it is a fine sight, on a moist morning.[31]

The old man then tells Frampton the history of Spirr Wood, now part of his property and traditionally the place where fox-hunting began, and sings him the old ballad which begins: "To Spirr Wood we came on the opening day." Mansell is not touched by this account and writes to the Hunt Secretary, Sir Peter Bynd, a note informing him that Spirr Wood is to be a bird sanctuary and game preserve and that hounds are to avoid it.

After Margaret's death in a motor accident a few days later, Frampton's father, "a frail and sweet old man," comes to see him. He asks if he will hunt, to tide him through a bad time. The old man thinks that his son underestimates fox-hunting, which, along with "puritanic religion," has been one of the "two pleasures" of the English in recent centuries. Frampton's reply is that he loathes the sport because it is based on cruelty and that no man would tolerate the torture of the sport if he would stop seriously to consider it.

The father makes one more attempt to justify the hunt on the grounds of its beauty: "The beauty of the hunt is so great that people forget the cruelty." Frampton, however, is not impressed. In his opinion it is the "swank and display" of the hunt that appeal to most participants, and not the beauty. "They don't give a tuppenny curse," says he, about beauty, but are interested only in "going fast in an expensive suit." The old man's last word is that his "own youth would have been the poorer without that beauty."

Negotiations between Sir Peter Bynd and Frampton Mansell might have been successful in reaching a compromise, for the two men liked each other at first. Lady Bynd, however, is arrogant and spiteful, and her insults, added to the fact that her chief ally, Colonel Annual-Tilter, is a political enemy of Mansell, steel the new owner against any concessions with Spirr Wood.

The remainder of the novel is chiefly concerned with the struggle between the Bynd-Tilter faction and Mansell. Sir Peter's manly frankness and good sportsmanship, and his story of the Tuncester Hunt and Spirr Wood Day, make fox-hunting the glamorous and colorful sport that it appears in the Munnings pictures and the Masefield poems and essays. On the other hand, the reader meets a group of drunken, stupid, irresponsible, decaying young aristocrats whose championship of the hunt make it an unattractive and useless show.

The hunt breaks into Mansell's property and he sues for damages. He wins his case and becomes the most unpopular man in the district. He buys adjoining properties to close them as well, posts his land with insulting signs, and threatens to turn the old beauty spots into cheap housing projects and artillery ranges. Finally he confronts a second invasion of the hunt in person, shoots their exhausted fox and flings the corpse into the lake, and cows the infuriated hunters into retreat.

To an unprejudiced reader, the novel does not offer an immediate verdict on the fox-hunt. Eventually the story ends with

Mansell as a popular benefactor of the district, nature lover, model house builder, and patron of the arts.

What is Masefield's own attitude toward the sport? Does he speak through Frampton Mansell, or Mansell's father, or Sir Peter Bynd? What conclusion can one draw from the evidence in this and other work of Masefield? One wonders if he may not have divided feelings like those of old Bob Mansell, or like those of an unnamed man in *The Hawbucks* who "has a sort of feeling about the place where a fox is killed."[32]

Without the existence of *The Square Peg*, Masefield's attitude would be easily established. Gilbert Thomas approaches the subject without weighing the evidence in the novels or the minor poems. Calling attention to the fact that *Reynard the Fox* "appeals as strongly to the opponents as to the devotees of hunting," he suggests that the first part of the poem and the essay, "Fox-Hunting," were written by Masefield, the "practical man of affairs, the calm and detached spectator" who "deals objectively with the hunt and the huntsmen" and delights in the picturesqueness and the fellowship of the hunt. The second part of *Reynard*, Thomas feels, was written by Masefield, the "poet and humanitarian," who, with his "intense compassion for all life's hunted creatures," must pity the fox even to the extent of crediting him with "exaggerated sensibility."[33]

It is clear, at any rate, that the poet did not intend in *Reynard the Fox* to raise any moral issue. In the essay, written, Masefield says, because "I have been asked why I wrote this poem," he avoids specific statement on the moral issue of fox-hunting. He does, however, say, when asked if hunting will be soon abolished, that he thinks not, since people are not willing to give up their pleasures and hunting is also "an instinct in man." Masefield then discusses the effect that the increase of small holdings is likely to have on hunting. Although small holdings may become prevalent near the towns, he believes that they can never become the "national system of farming."

> Even if the small holdings system were to prevail, it would hardly prevail over the sporting instincts of the race. Beauty and delight are stronger than the will to work. I am pretty sure that a pack of hounds, coming feathery by, at the heels of a whip's horse, while the field takes station and the huntsman,

drawing his horn, prepares to hunt, would shake the resolve of most small holders, digging in their lots with thrift, industry, and self-control. And then, if the huntsman were to blow his horn, and the hounds to feather on it and give tongue, and find, and go away at head, I am pretty sure that most of the small holders of this race would follow them. It is in this race to hunt.[34]

In spite of the fact that *The Square Peg* is a later work, one feels that the poet's most frequent and characteristic concern with the fox-hunt is for its beauty, its Englishness, and the fellowship and happiness that it brings to many people. He is glad because men are

> . . . kindled and cheered by the beauty and the glory of the horses, the colour, life and manhood of the sport, and the sympathy that linked the world to friendship and fellowship. Religion moved thus once, so did poetry.[35]

Only this last sentence, with its suggestion that, for all its glory, the sport is less worthy than those deeper sources of fellowship and joy which it now supplants, may qualify Masefield's praise of fox-hunting. Even *The Square Peg* does not deny the beauty or the Englishness of the hunt, or the happiness that it brings to men. The satire of the novel is directed, not against the institution of the hunt, but against certain practitioners of it. And the satire is directed equally against the prejudiced outsider, Frampton Mansell.

Although the following lines were written in 1920, it is easy to believe them Masefield's final word on the subject.

> Hunting makes more people happy than anything I know. When people are happy together, I am quite certain, that they build up something eternal, something both beautiful and divine, which weakens the power of all evil things upon this life of men and women.

It is equally easy to believe that this is the basic reason for his love of all sport. At the end of the poem "Biography," in which his happiest moments, some of which were passed in sport, are catalogued, the poet writes:

> Best trust the happy moments. What they gave

Makes man less fearful of the certain grave,
And gives his work compassion and new eyes,
The days that make us happy make us wise.[36]

Notes to Chapter 4

1. *The Square Peg* (1937); "Fox-Hunting" (introd. to *Reynard the Fox,* 1920), and introd. to J. H. Reynolds, *The Fancy* (1905); *The Everlasting Mercy* (1911), *Right Royal* (1920), *King Cole* (1921), and "A Tale of Country Things," in *On The Hill* (1949).

2. See *The Conway, New Chum,* "Evening—Regatta Day" in *Salt-Water Ballads,* and "Biography."

3. See *The Conway, New Chum,* and "Biography."

4. See *The Everlasting Mercy* and *Sard Harker.*

5. See "Fox-Hunting," *Reynard the Fox, The Conway, New Chum,* "Young John of Chance's Stretch" in *Minnie Maylow's Story, The Country Scene,* and an extended simile in *Right Royal.*

6. See the characterization in *Reynard the Fox,* (New York: The Macmillan Co., 1919), pp. 36–41, and in *The Hawbucks,* (New York: The Macmillan Co., 1929), pp. 132–36, of Edwin Hyacinthus Armytage Manor, "the famous Tantshire bat." See also *The Conway* (London: William Heinemann, 1933), p. 127, *New Chum* (London: William Heinemann, 1944), pp. 86–87, and "Eighty-Five to Win" in *The Bluebells* (London: William Heinemann, 1961), pp. 73–81.

7. See "Whippet-Racing," *Manchester Guardian* (Aug. 19, 1905).

8. See introductions to *The Fancy* (London: Elkin Mathews, 1905), pp. 10, 12, and to *Defoe* (London: George Bell and Sons, 1909), p. xxvi.

9. Pp. 2 and 30; 13, 49, 60, 108–11.

10. See Fraser Drew, "Poetry and Pugilism: John Masefield's Fights," *Canadian Forum* 38, no. 453 (Oct. 1958): 155–56.

11. Pp. 33, 54.

12. *The Speaker* (Mar. 25, 1905).

13. *A Generation Risen* (London: Collins, 1943).

14. P. 9, from *King Cole* (London: William Heinemann, 1921), p. 36; p. 44, from *King Cole,* p. 28; p. 174, from "Laugh and Be Merry," *Ballads* (London: Elkin Mathews, 1903), p. 44; p. 229, from "Tewksbury Road," *Salt-Water Ballads* (London: Grant Richards, 1902), p. 24; p. 262, from "Laugh and Be Merry, p. 45.

15. *John Masefield: A Study* (Cambridge: W. Heffer and Sons, 1924), p. 41.

16. Introduction to *Circus Company* (London: Putnam, 1933), p. xi.

17. *Minnie Maylow's Story* (London: William Heinemann, 1931), p. 90.

18. Foreword to exhibition catalogue, *Pictures of the Belvoir Hunt and Other Scenes of English Country Life* by A. J. Munnings, A.R.A. (1921), pp. 3–4.

19. In his introduction to a 1909 edition of Defoe, p. xxvi, Masefield records Defoe's lack of interest in sports but cites one exception in the earlier writer's fondness for horses and horse-racing, which "gave joy to his leisure" and "brought beauty to his work."

20. See also the horse-race metaphor in "Naia and Edward," *Tribute to Ballet* (London: Collins, 1938), p. 55.

21. *The Hawbucks*, p. 294.

22. Later she appears in *The Hawbucks* (1929) as a minor character, a friend of the Cothills, pp. 152–60.

23. *Reynard the Fox*, pp. 46–47 and several times in Part Two; *The Hawbucks, passim*.

24. Unpublished letter to W. H. Hamilton (n.d., *c.* 1920).

25. "Fox-Hunting," *Reynard the Fox*, illustrated ed., (New York: The Macmillan Co., 1920), p. xv.

26. "Reynard the Fox," *Quarterly Review* (Oct. 1922), pp. 265–78.

27. *Six Living Poets* (London: Thornton Butterworth, 1922), p. 29.

28. "The Poetry of John Masefield," *English Journal* (Jan. 1926), pp. 5–13.

29. Sheffield University pamphlet (June 25, 1946), p. 2.

30. *The Hawbucks*, pp. 214–15.

31. *The Square Peg* (London: William Heinemann, 1937), pp. 46–47.

32. *The Hawbucks*, p. 218.

33. *John Masefield* (London: Thornton Butterworth, 1932), pp. 190, 193–94.

34. "Fox-Hunting," p. v.

35. *Ibid.*, p. 180 (as revised in *Recent Prose* [London: William Heinemann, 1924]).

36. *The Story of a Round-House* (New York: The Macmillan Co. 1912), p. 209.

5

The English Ship

*Masefield's Sea Experience
and the Nautical Theme in His Work*

It is a commonplace to refer to John Masefield as the sea poet
or the sailor's laureate; yet only the reader familiar with the great
body of Masefield's poetry and prose can realize the extent to
which the sea, the ship, and the sailor have dominated Masefield's
life and his work. His first book, *Salt-Water Ballads* (1902), is
a collection of fifty lyrics and ballads, of which only thirteen are
not sea poems; his last three books of poetry[1] contain two poems
on Sir Francis Drake and such titles as "On Pilots," "A Storm,"
and "Lines on the Shipwreck of Admiral Sir Cloudsley Shovell,"
although the poet had left the sea seventy-two years before the
publication of the last of these volumes.

In the introductory poem of *Salt-Water Ballads,* the credo poem
called "A Consecration," Masefield assigns to himself the cause
of the common man, and specifically the cause of the sailor—
the chantyman, the man at the wheel, the tired lookout. Throughout this first book the sailor is the man sung, not the English
countryman, or the soldier, the artist, the worker. In the sixty-six
years of Masefield books, the sea, the ship, and the sailor have been
the subject of five novels and three volumes of short stories,[2] nine
essays,[3] five miscellaneous books of prose,[4] two plays,[5] more than
one-hundred-fifty prose articles and reviews in newspapers and

magazines, and more than one hundred poems, while they have played minor parts in other books.

Almost equally commonplace is the statement that Masefield's early life offers the key to this lasting preoccupation with the sea. A review of his experience as a sailor is perhaps the best preface to an examination of his nautical writing.

In the poem *Wonderings* (1943) and in the prose sketch, "Bredon Flood," from *Grace Before Ploughing* (1966), Masefield records his first experience on water. One of his earliest memories is of a path through an orchard to a boat "wherein my pilgrim self first went afloat."

> I was then three; two half-remembered men
> Launched with me forth and brought me back agen,
> But half a century later, I was told
> What risks beset us in that bliss of old.
> The boat was crazy, like her merry crew,
> And many drowned men's deaths that mill-race knew.
> Life, looking on her lamb, postponed the slaughter
> And stamped within my soul delight in water.

This delight seems to have persisted through childhood, and in September 1891, when the boy was "thirteen years three months and three weeks old," he went on board the training ship H. M. S. *Conway* in the River Mersey to train for a career as officer in the merchant service.[6]

After two years and some months of training, he went to sea;[7] he must have remained at sea for about one year, for the date of his arrival in New York City has been established as April 1895.[8] Masefield nowhere tells the exact course of his sea voyages. Internal evidence in the poems and the early prose sketches indicate a trip around Cape Horn and experience in Atlantic, Pacific, and Caribbean waters, with some time ashore in Chile and Argentina.

In April 1895, he came ashore in New York City and worked in a Greenwich Village bar and a Yonkers carpet factory and at other odd jobs until July 1897,[9] when he returned to England. He never went to sea again, except on war service and as a traveler.

The impression made upon the young man by his years aboard the *Conway* and at sea can hardly be overestimated. Masefield has been consistently reticent about much of his early life and has voiced his attitude toward biographers in the 1912 poem, "Biography," and as recently as 1936 in the closing poem of *A Letter from Pontus*. "Sweet Friends" from the latter volume may sound like a semi-serious echo of the pleas of many poets: "Print not my life or letters; put them by:/ When I am dead let memory of me die." "Biography," however, is explicit in its reasons why the important events of a life can be only imperfectly chronicled and known, why "work that obscures those moments seems impure." In spite of this reticence Masefield has recorded, in "Biography" and elsewhere, some of the "golden hours" and "bright days of action," and in *Wonderings, New Chum* (1944), *In the Mill* (1941), *So Long to Learn* (1952), and *Grace Before Ploughing* (1966), published in later years, the reader learns much about the poet's childhood, his days on the *Conway* and in New York, and his development as a writer.[10]

"For the most part," Masefield writes in "A White Night" in *A Tarpaulin Muster* (1907), "My significant memories are of the sea." The poem "Biography" is filled with such recollections; a catalogue of significant memories begins:

> By many waters and on many ways
> I have known golden instants and bright days;
> The day on which, beneath an arching sail,
> I saw the Cordilleras and gave hail;
> The summer day on which in heart's delight
> I saw the Swansea Mumbles bursting white,
> The glittering day when all the waves wore flags
> And the ship *Wanderer* came with sails in rags.

The ship *Wanderer* is a memory and a symbol that haunt the poet, inspiring a long poem in 1914 and an entire book in 1930, as well as echoes throughout at least thirty years of his work and as late as 1944.

The list in "Biography" continues with "wild days in a pampero off the Plate," surf-swimming, days of hard work at winch and capstan, and

> The dawn when, with a brace-block's creaking cry,
> Out of the mist a little barque slipped by,
> Spilling the mist with changing gleams of red,
> Then gone, with one raised hand and one turned head;
> The howling evening when the spindrift's mists
> Broke to display the four Evangelists,
> Snow-capped, divinely granite, lashed by breakers,
> Wind-beaten bones of long since buried acres.

In counting the gifts received from "life's hands," he includes

> The gift of being near ships, of seeing each day
> A city of ships with great ships under weigh,
> The great street paved with water, filled with shipping,
> And all the world's flags flying and seagulls dipping.

Masefield fears that after his death his "penman" may not know the ships that were the source of wonder and of inspiration to the poet, or the friends with whom he shared his love of ships. These are the "happy moments" which Masefield believes "make us wise," and, in his own life, the source of the sea fever that has produced much of his wisest and most attractive work.

Rarely has Masefield written more movingly of his love for the sea than, as recently as 1941, in the autobiographical *In the Mill.* At several times in the book he reconstructs a scene in the Yonkers factory or in his room when his longing for the old life was strongest. Often he would go to New York harbor to see the "best display of ships in the world." To pass slow hours of mechanical work in the mill, he would pose for himself, and then answer, problems in navigation and seamanship, or formulate plans for an ideal Maritime Service College. Often he regretted his exchange of the sailor's life for the landsman's.

> Compared with the life at sea the mill life lacked the companionship of the sky and the continual interest of the weather. Memorable beauty companions the sailor. I longed for morning watches in the tropics, or sunsets in the second dog watch. I longed also for the sight of ships and the interest of rigging. . . . I missed very much the link of the ship; no man can fail to feel for a ship as for a living thing, and though the affection can be

very well disguised, it is there, she is a living thing, sometimes almost a divine thing, who demands and receives service.

In later years Masefield the writer found compensation for Masefield the exiled sailor in the making of ship models,[11] the drawing of ships, the talking with old seaman-friends and new, and chiefly in his books, many of which were labors of nautical love.[12]

The Ship in Masefield's Early Books and His Novels

In the dedicatory poem of *Tribute to Ballet* (1938), Masefield has an old man list the three lovely things: "Gallopping horses; and a ship at sea;/ And men and women, dancing from delight." The poet's collaborator, Edward Seago,[13] knew and could draw horses, and in this book the two artists unite their efforts to pay tribute to the beauty of the dance; the ship at sea, "under topsails dark with rain," is Masefield's own province.

The early books, the poems of *Salt-Water Ballads* and *Ballads* (1903), and the prose stories and sketches of *A Mainsail Haul* (1905) and *A Tarpaulin Muster* (1907), are filled with the beauty and romance of the sea and with sailor lore, but there are few references to the beauty of the ship itself or to its significance in the life of the poet and the life of his nation. The only ship poem of the early volumes is the favorite anthology piece, "Cargoes" (1903), with its three ships and their cargoes that symbolize three civilizations. The third ship, the dirty "coaster with a salt-caked smoke stack," is English. Its use in this poem is all the more striking and effective because it is not the type of English ship that moves the poet so much elsewhere; the stately clipper generally symbolizes for Masefield the greatness of his people.

One sketch in *A Tarpaulin Muster* is unlike most of the early prose pieces. "A Memory" is a quiet, fireside story that begins like an essay on the moods and the nature of recollection. The writer then speaks of one memory that is different from his others, a memory persistent and recurring, "charged with meaning, beautiful and solemn, hinting at secrets," a "thing so beautiful that it could not be a chance, a mere event." The memory is of a clipper seen from the narrator's own ship at dawn "in the tropics, not very far from the Doldrums, in the last of the Trades." The scene is described, and then the ship appears, to windward.

> There was no man aboard of us but was filled with the beauty of that ship. I think they would have cheered her had she been a little nearer to us; . . . The old mate limped up to me, and spat and swore. "That's one of the beautiful sights of the world," he said. "That, and a cornfield, and a woman with her child. It's beauty and strength."

Two early prose articles, never reprinted in book form, reveal Masefield's consciousness of the beauty of the ship and of the ship's importance to England. "Liverpool, City of Ships" (1907) is a short essay illustrated by nine photographs by Alvin Langdon Coburn. It describes the city that "of all the great English ports, . . . alone gives the visitor a sense of the glory and wonder of the sea" and the shipping in the River Mersey where "in the beauty of the ships . . . the business and the romance of the world break in full tide upon the heart." "The Passing of the Glory of the World" (1907), a longer essay, recalls many of England's finest ships and concludes nostalgically that the great days of shipbuilding and seamanship have passed, that "their glories are over."

During the first decade of his literary career, before he won widespread attention in 1911 with *The Everlasting Mercy*, Masefield published two books that might be called long historical essays, *Sea Life in Nelson's Time* (1905) and *On the Spanish Main* (1906). He also wrote introductory essays for new editions of Anson's *Voyage*, Hakluyt's *Navigations, The Travels of Marco Polo*, Dampier's *Voyages*, the *Chronicles of the Pilgrim Fathers* and Southey's *Life of Nelson*. In these essays are frequent and sometimes detailed references to the ships of those times and often to such famous ships as the *Mayflower* and the *Centurion* However, these essays are concerned primarily with great seamen and their exploits rather than with their ships. *The Conway* (1933) and *New Chum* (1944), later books concerning the training ship on which Masefield spent two and a half years, are devoted chiefly to the routine of life aboard the ship, although *The Conway* doe include an exhaustive history of the three training ships that served under the Conway name.[14]

In 1909 Elkin Mathews published one of Jack B. Yeats's books for children, illustrated by Yeats and called *A Little Fleet*. It is a mini-saga of toy boats with which Yeats and Masefield amused themselves in the Gara River near the painter's home in Devon. The illustrations are of five ships called the *Monte,* the *Moby Dick,* the *Theodore,* the *Pasear,* and the *New Corinthian.* The construction of each is described in detail (e.g., the *Pasear* is made of "a bright green cardboard tie box, with a lid, and stones inside to ballast her"), and her fate on the stream or the pond is told in a prose sketch. Four pieces of verse, ranging from four lines to twenty in length, appear with no author listed; however, a note at the beginning of the book reads, "The owners and myself are indebted to the Fleet Poet for the verses throughout the book." The verses are attributed to Masefield by the Simmons bibliography and by Sean O'Faolain and Elizabeth Corbet Yeats in letters. A more cautious letter from Jack Yeats includes this statement: "The text of the *Little Fleet* was written by me, but all I can say about the verses is that they were handed to me by Masefield. All these things were long ago."[15] The verses are slight indeed, but they are perhaps as revealing a commentary upon Masefield and Jack Yeats as are some of the nonsense verses of A. E. Housman upon that poet. One verse commemorates the *Moby Dick,* whose anchor caught in a weed:

> She came to flying anchor
> At the twilight time of day,
> But the strain on the cable sank her,
> And her crew, oh, where were they?[16]

The Masefield sea novels, although packed with motion and incident, invariably pause for a few beautifully written descriptions of the ships involved. A survey of the seven novels in which the sea plays a major or supporting role yields a memorable gallery of old-time sailing vessels. In *Captain Margaret* (1908), the ship aboard which almost all the action takes place is the *Broken Heart.* The reader meets her at the very start of the novel and knows her before he knows the men and women who are to people the book. She appears first at dawn, in Salcombe harbor, when the dim light gives her "the beauty of all half-seen things."

> An artist's heart, hungry for beauty, had seen the idea of her in dream; she had her counterpart in the kingdom of vision . . . She had the impress of her builder in her, a mournful state, a kind of battered grandeur, a likeness to a type of manhood. There was in her a beauty not quite achieved, as though, in the husk of the man, the butterfly's wings were not quite free. There was in her a strength that was clumsy; almost the strength of one vehement from fear. She came from a man's soul, stamped with his defects. Standing on her deck, one could see the man laid bare—melancholy, noble, and wanting—till one felt pity for the ship which carried his image about the world. Seamen had lived in her, seamen had died in her; she had housed many wandering spirits. She was, in herself, the house of her maker's spirit, as all made things are, and wherever her sad beauty voyaged, his image, his living memory voyaged, infinitely mournful, because imperfect, unapprehended.

Throughout the novel there are pictures of the *Broken Heart* in various kinds of weather, and, as often occurs in Masefield writing, there is a brief picture of another ship, passed at sea. This one is a "sixth-rate, under plain sail," a lovely thing, and the *Broken Heart* salutes her.

Sard Harker (1924) is more a land novel than otherwise, but its hero is a sailor from the ship *Pathfinder,* which is described in three sonnets as well as in the prose of the novel. In the sonnets she is not especially memorable, but she plays an unusual part in the land adventures of her Mate. When Sard is lost in the desert mountains between Tlotoatin and San Agostino, one of those dreams, or visions, that characteristically guide Masefield heroes, brings him the spirit of the *Pathfinder,* "fierce, hard, and of great beauty." She leads him and he awakens later to find himself safely over the crest of the mountains.

The Bird of Dawning (1933) and *Victorious Troy* (1935) abound in pictures of clipper ships in the Tea Race from China and the Grain Race from Melbourne. The tea race in the former novel is run by seven clippers, the *Blackgauntlet,* the *Natuna,* the *Fu-Kien,* the *Min and Win,* the *Streaming Star,* the *Caer Ocvran,* and the *Bird of Dawning.* The novel is a stirring tale of the sinking of the *Blackgauntlet* and the abandoning of the *Bird of Dawning* by her superstitious skipper. The *Blackgauntlet* castaways board the *Bird of Dawning* and in an exciting finish just manage to win the race. The best picture in the book may be that of the *Caer Ocvran* as she races the *Fu-Kien* and the *Bird of Dawning* in the Channel.

> Presently they were abreast of her, and forging ahead upon her, so that they could see her in her glory. In a light air no ship of her time could touch her, and she could run with the swiftest. She had a name through the seven seas for being wet: her decks now were running bright: for she was a caution in a head sea. They were watching and tending her now, getting some of her after-sail off her to keep her from burying her bow.

Victorious Troy has one of the most extended and dramatic tales of shipwreck to be found in fiction. The clipper in this novel is called the *Hurrying Angel*.

A Latin-American revolution and war add interest and suspense to the seamanship of *The Taking of the Gry* (1934). The central action of the novel is the feat of an English sailor and his friends in stealing an arms vessel, the *Gry,* from Santa Barbara harbor and guiding her through an almost impassable channel to join the Santa Ana fleet. There is a vivid picture of the fleet under way in the early stages of the war, but nowhere in the novel is to be observed the love of the ship for her own actual and symbolic beauty that is to be found in much of the Masefield poetry and prose.

Dead Ned (1938) and *Live and Kicking Ned* (1939) are not primarily sea novels. However, the first presents the interesting figure of Admiral Sir Topsle Cringle and his ship, the *Hannibal,* while the first part of *Live and Kicking Ned* records the voyage of the *Albicore* and her macabre captain and crew from England to the African coast, where she is wrecked and abandoned.

The Ship in the Narrative Poems

One could make a good case for the argument that practically all Masefield's best work was done in the nine years from 1911 to

1919, and this would be a well-deserved rebuke for those anthologists who represent Masefield by a handful of pleasing lyrics and ballads from his first two books. Some readers (but not this writer), sacrificing *Lollingdon Downs* (1917) and *Reynard the Fox* (1919), would be willing to list 1911–1916 as the golden years. During this period the four long narrative poems that brought their writer to quick fame were written, and to these years belong some fine shorter poems and sonnets, the prose *Gallipoli* and *William Shakespeare,* and the dramas, *The Faithful, Good Friday,* and *Philip the King.* Much of Masefield's best sea-writing was published at this time, most significantly in *The Story of a Round-House and Other Poems* (1912), which contains "Dauber," "Biography," and "Ships," and in *Philip the King and Other Poems* (1914), with its title piece and "The Wanderer."

"Ships" begins with a reiteration, like that in "Biography," of the poet's inability to capture for others the magical beauty of the ships he has known.

> I cannot tell their wonder nor make known
> Magic that once thrilled through me to the bone,
> But all men praise some beauty, tell some tale,
> Vent a high mood which makes the rest seem pale,
> Pour their heart's blood to flourish one green leaf,
> Follow some Helen for her gift of grief,
> And fail in what they mean, whate'er they do:
> You should have seen, men cannot tell to you
> The beauty of the ships of that my city.
> That beauty now is spoiled by the sea's pity;
> For one may haunt the pier a score of times,
> Hearing St. Nicholas' bells ring out the chimes,
> Yet never see those proud ones swaying home
> With mainyards backed and bows a cream of foam,
> Those bows so lovely-curving, cut so fine,
> Those coulters of the many-bubbled brine,
> As once, long since, when all the docks were filled
> With that sea-beauty man has ceased to build.

These are the graceful ships of a bygone day, the ships whose passing is lamented by bitter Captain Duntisbourne in *The Bird*

of Dawning, and which Sard Harker and Captain Cary discuss in
a later story. Masefield is grateful to these ships for their contribution to his own life, and he begins a long catalogue of remembered
names, too long to quote.

> Yet, though their splendor may have ceased to be,
> Each played her sovereign part in making me;
> Now I return my thanks with heart and lips,
> For the great queenliness of all those ships.

After his list of the old ships (one of them the *Wanderer,* whose
story will be told later in this chapter), the poet cites a dozen
steamers and liners as well, including the *Magdelena, Puno, Potosi,*
and "Lost *Cotopaxi.*"

In the closing lines of the poem, Masefield links his country's
destiny and glory to her ships and her seamen, as he does in *Sea
Life in Nelson's Time.* There is more than a suggestion that
England's greatest days were those when her seamanship and
shipbuilding were at their peak, a suggestion to be forgotten later
in his Englishman's pride in the magnificent achievements of
English courage by land and sea at Gallipoli and Dunquerque.[17]

The major poem of the *Round-House* volume, and one of
Masefield's greatest achievements, is the narrative *Dauber.* It is
the story of a boy who goes to sea to learn to paint the sea, the
ship, and the sailor as they really are; the story is one that Masefield had sketched six years earlier in a prose tale published in the
Manchester Guardian.[18] Derisively nicknamed "Dauber" by his
unsympathetic fellow-seamen, the boy finally proves his manhood and wins their respect by his courageous behavior in a Cape
Horn storm, but in his hour of triumph as a man he falls to his
death, never to taste triumph as an artist. *Dauber* is primarily a
tale of the sea and of a boy's struggle at sea, but there are some
stirring scenes of the ship as well. When the reader first meets
Dauber, he and the apprentice Si are watching the sunset, standing
by the rail. Dauber tells Si how he hopes to "paint great ships at
sea" before he dies, and

> Even as he spoke his busy pencil moved,
> Drawing the leap of water off the side

> Where the great clipper trampled iron-hooved,
> Making the blue hills of the sea divide,
> Shearing a glittering scatter in her stride,
> And leaping on full tilt with all sails drawing,
> Proud as a war-horse, snuffing battle, pawing.

> "I cannot get it yet—not yet," he said;
> "That leap and light, and sudden change to green,
> And all the glittering from the sunset's red,
> And the milky colours where the bursts have been,
> And then the clipper striding like a queen
> Over it all, all beauty to the crown.
> I see it all, I cannot put it down."

Later in the poem are many scenes of the ship in various seas and weathers, painted in words as Dauber wished to paint them in oils. At one time she loiters "south, slowly, with no white bone across her mouth." Again, in the ominous hours before a great storm:

> All through the windless night the clipper rolled
> In a great swell with oily gradual heaves
> Which rolled her down until her time-bells tolled,
> Clang, and the weltering water moaned like beeves.
> The thundering rattle of slatting shook the sheaves,
> Startles of water made the swing ports gush,
> The sea was moaning and sighing and saying "Hush!"

The final lines of the poem bring the ship into Valparaiso harbor[19] and depict a scene that Dauber did not live to see or draw.

> Cheerly they rang her in, those beating bells,
> The new-come beauty stately from the sea,
> Whitening the blue heave of the drowsy swells,
> Treading the bubbles down. With three times three
> They cheered her moving beauty in, and she
> Came to her berth so noble, so superb;
> Swayed like a queen, and answered to the curb.

The title piece of Masefield's next volume, *Philip the King and Other Poems* (1914), is a verse play. Although the action takes place on land, the poem is, in its account of the sailing of the fleet and in the messenger's long report of its defeat, the epic of the Spanish Armada. But these ships are Spanish, not English. Their description is colorful and dramatic, but it does not have the deep feeling that characterizes Masefield's treatment of English ships, particularly his portrayal of the ship *Wanderer*.

The Saga of the Wanderer

The ship *Wanderer* has been mentioned earlier in connection with "Biography" and "Ships." In *New Chum* (1944) Masefield writes a prose account of his first sight of the *Wanderer* fifty-three years before. On the day of his arrival, a boy of thirteen, at Liverpool to go aboard the *Conway,* he caught a glimpse of "the masts of a splendid ship, known by me to be splendid, although I knew nothing of ships or splendour." A few days after his arrival, he went aloft alone for the first time. Again he saw the great ship that had caught his eye on his first day in Liverpool; this was his first long look at the *Wanderer*.[20] On a trip to the Liverpool Baths, the new chums again see the *Wanderer;* the seniors tell the younger boys that she is "by much the finest ship now in dock" and that they plan to visit her if she does not sail before the day of their Liverpool leave. Even her name fascinates Masefield with its suggestion of "skies of desolation" and "seas of loneliness with that ship in sail." But the *Wanderer* sails before the boys have their holiday. On the following Sunday morning a great cry of "The *Wanderer*" brings all hands on deck to the fo'c's'le head.

At that instant, the fog in the lower Sloyne went, and the river there brightened. The Wanderer came out of the greyness into sunlight as a thing of such beauty as the world can seldom show. She was in the act of preparing to dock with tugs, sidling, so that I saw her slowly come forward and turn away. She had been lopped at all her cross-trees, and the wreck of her upper spars was lashed in her lower rigging. As she turned, her tattered sails (nearly all were tattered), suddenly shone all over

her; her beautiful sheer, with its painted ports, shone. I had
seen nothing like her in all my life, and knew, then, that something had happened in a world not quite ours.

This story of Masefield's first sight of the ship whose beauty is to
haunt him for the rest of his life has at least a partial parallel in an
experience related in Dauber's tale to Si, a moving passage from
that poem about another English country boy who went to sea.

Two years after the references to the *Wanderer* in "Biography"
and "Ships," "The 'Wanderer'" appeared in the *Philip the King*
volume. This is a longer story of the ship, beginning with her
appearance in the harbor at Liverpool. Here, as in the *New Chum*
account, the ship goes to sea and returns one morning after a
terrible gale. Called to watch her coming up the river, the poet
sees "a full-rigged ship unutterably fair."

> Beauty in desolation was her pride,
> Her crowned array a glory that had been;
> She faltered tow'rds us like a swan that died,
> But although ruined she was still a queen.
>
> . . . .
>
> So, as though stepping to a funeral march,
> She passed defeated homewards whence she came
> Ragged with tattered canvas white as starch,
> A wild bird that misfortune had made tame.

Now the story goes beyond the limits of the prose account. The
Wanderer is repaired and refitted and goes seaward, only to return again, "A wounded sea-bird with a broken wing." Once
more the unlucky ship sails and then comes back to port. This
time a "stay had parted like a snapping reed," and the superstitious crew, sensing an omen, refuses to proceed. Time elapses
before another crew will sign, but finally the *Wanderer* sails and
this time sails far. The teller of the story often looks for her when
he is in foreign ports. Years later, one Christmas Eve, near a
Southern port, he watches a gale and its passing and is strangely
prompted to climb a hill from which he can look at the sea.

> And on the instant from beyond away

That long familiar sound, a ship's bell, broke
The hush below me in the unseen bay.
Old memories came: that inner prompting spoke.

And bright above the hedge a seagull's wings
Flashed and were steady upon empty air.
"A Power unseen," I cried, "prepares these things;
"Those are her bells, the Wanderer is there."

He hurries to the crest of the upland and looks down upon the
shipping in the bay.

I did but glance upon those anchored ships.
Even as my thought had told, I saw her plain;
Tense, like a supple athlete with lean hips,
Swiftness at pause, the Wanderer come again—

Come as of old a queen, untouched by Time,
Resting the beauty that no seas could tire,
Sparkling, as though the midnight's rain were rime,
Like a man's thought transfigured into fire.

And as I looked, one of her men began
To sing some simple tune of Christmas day;
Among her crew the song spread, man to man,
Until the singing ran across the bay;

And soon in other anchored ships the men
Joined in the singing with clear throats, until
The farm-boy heard it up the windy glen,
Above the noise of sheep-bells on the hill.

The last of these closing stanzas, which are so reminiscent of the
last lines of *Dauber* and *The Daffodil Fields* and, to a lesser degree,
of *The Widow in the Bye Street,* is another chorus-like pronounce-
ment of the "beaten man" theme:

Over the water came the lifted song—
Blind pieces in a mighty game we swing;

Life's battle is a conquest for the strong;
The meaning shows in the defeated thing.

In this stanza is one key to an understanding of the significance
of the *Wanderer* in Masefield's life. Gilbert Thomas comments
that this poem has all the elements of "The essential Masefield"—
his love for the sea, the ship, and the sailor, for the countryside
and the common man, for "the defeated thing," even his "simple
joy in the spirit of Christmas. And implied throughout is his phi-
losophy that beauty, glimpsed in moments of intense vision, is
the revelation of something beyond itself."[21]

It was not until 1930 that the whole story of the *Wanderer* was
told. In that year, the year of his appointment to the laureateship,
Masefield published *The Wanderer of Liverpool.* The larger por-
tion of the book is a carefully documented history of the *Wanderer*
from her construction at Liverpool in 1890 to her fatal accident
in the mouth of the Elbe in 1907.

The book begins with these lines from the *Odyssey,* which tell
the reader again that the *Wanderer* is the most beautiful ship in
the poet's long experience and the perfect ship of that day: "There
are many ships, both new and old, in sea-girt Ithaca, I'll choose
you out the best."[22] The description of the ship is complete and
detailed, with many photographs and tables, an account of her
ten voyages, with dates, cargoes, itineraries, and names of crew,
even the analyses of two astrologers who were given "the time of
high water as the approximate moment of her launch." For the
average reader, the verse sections of the book have more interest
than the prose. Two episodes in the *Wanderer's* life, "The Setting
Forth" and "The Ending," are told in long anapestic lines, which
are unusual in Masefield.

In "The Ending" the *Wanderer* on her last voyage is addressed
by the spirits of wrecked English ships of the past, as she passes
over their graves—the *Khyber,* the *Peregrine,* the *Cromdale,* the
Queen Margaret, the *Panama Bay,* and the *Siren.* The latter, a
ship that once docked beside the *Wanderer* in Queenstown, recalls
the days when she had raced down the Channel "with skysail
poles bending, the lee scuppers flashing with spray." Included in

"The Ending" is a song of the spirits or "watchers" of the ships, a lyric containing the central statement that all beauty "lives in the attempt to make it ours."

After the account of the *Wanderer*'s sinking, when she had been rammed at night by a German steamer, the poet writes of her physical death, "sunken, unminded." But the ship's real self, "being Beauty Eternal," wanders the seas "with white wing on wing/ Star-lighted, star-guided, the sea-gleaming beautiful thing."

The Wanderer of Liverpool contains, in addition to the prose and verse accounts of the ill-starred ship, a brief poetic drama called "A Masque of Liverpool," and twelve shorter sea pieces, some of which concern the *Wanderer* and her home port. Of all these the finest is the concluding poem, "Wanderer and Wonderer," the poet's final summation of his relationship with the heroine of his book—the ship which, "unutterably fair," shines "on my mind's sea everywhere." The poet's praise of the ship ends with his farewell to the "sea-wandering bird," which in another life he will surely see again.

> However changed upon the chain
> Your shape and mine will meet again.
> When ship meets ship,
> Sea-wanderer, the colours dip.
> The hidden then may be made plain.

If "Ships," "The 'Wanderer,'" *Dauber,* and *The Wanderer of Liverpool* offer Masefield's finest poetic treatment of the English ship, probably the finest prose description is to be found in *Gallipoli,* in that long passage which will be quoted in part in chapter 7. This is Masefield's picture of the Aegean harbor of Mudros in the spring of 1915 when in the bay were "more ships, perhaps, than any port of modern times has known." There follows the description of the French and English warships, the transports, the picket-boats, the tugs from the Thames and Mersey, and, mingled with them, "strange beautiful Greek vessels . . . under rigs of old time."

The Ship and the Sea in Figures of Speech

Throughout Masefield's poetry the sea, the ship, and the sailor appear and reappear. In the most landlocked of poems, a simile or metaphor of the sea will suddenly light up and make vivid an inland scene or an inland thought, for the poet always turns, whenever in search of a clarifying or life-giving image, to the world which he knows and loves best. So, suddenly, in the closing lines of *The Daffodil Fields,* "all the ocean opens," the mates cry, and the crew sings. In *Right Royal* are several sea similes, particularly one in which the horses, exulting in the swiftness of the race, quicken with final energy and the excitement of the Straight and are compared to a porpoise which

> . . . grown weary of his rush through the dim
> Of the unlitten silence where the swiftnesses swim,
> Learns at sudden the tumult of a clipper bound home
> And exults with this playmate and leaps in her foam.

In the same race, the feeling of the hero, as he passes a respected rival, is described in the following extended simile:

> Charles felt like a captain whose ship has long chased
> Some ship better handled, better manned, better placed,
> And has all day beheld her, that ship of his dream,
> Bowing swanlike beyond him up a blue hill of gleam,
> Yet, at dark, the wind rising makes his rival strike sail
> While his own ship crowds canvas and comes within hail;
> Till he see her, his rival, snouting into the grey,
> Like a sea-rock in winter that stands and breaks spray,
> And by lamplight goes past her in a roar of song
> Shouting, "Let fall your royals: stretch the halliards along!"

Even at the hunt in *Reynard the Fox,* the sea is not forgotten. Charles Cothill, Masefield's ideal young English countryman, "loved the downland like a sea," and among the hunters there is, in keeping with the Chaucerian atmosphere of the poem, a modern shipman who "looked ahead as though his craft/ Were with him still in dangerous channels."

In the beautiful lines of the double sonnet, "On Growing Old," the youth is he "whose young passion sets the spindrift flying," and the first regret of the aging man is "I cannot sail your seas . . . ever again." Another use of the sea and the ship in metaphor is in the poem "Truth" from *Enslaved and Other Poems* (1920). The figure of speech is a familiar one that Masefield turns in this poem to the service of his characteristic optimism.

> Man with his burning soul
> Has but an hour of breath
> To build a ship of Truth
> In which his soul may sail,
> Sail on the sea of death.
> For death takes toll
> Of beauty, courage, youth,
> Of all but Truth.
>
> Life's city ways are dark,
> Men mutter by; the wells
> Of the great waters moan.
> O death, O sea, O tide,
> The waters moan like bells.
> No light, no mark,
> The soul goes out alone
> On seas unknown.
>
> Stripped of all purple robes,
> Stripped of all golden lies,
> I will not be afraid.
> Truth will preserve through death;
> Perhaps the stars will rise,
> The stars like globes.
> The ship my striving made
> May see night fade.

The ships of this chapter are English ships, built in English shipyards, captained and manned by the English seamen to be described in the following chapter, sailing in English commerce or to fight English wars. Masefield best identifies them as English in the closing lines of his poem "Ships," partially quoted above. Speaking of his fellow countrymen, he writes:

"They built great ships and sailed them" sounds most brave
Whatever arts we have or fail to have;
I touch my country's mind, I come to grips
With half her purpose, thinking of these ships.

These are the ships "born of a manly life and bitter duty," which

. . . are my country's line, her great art done
By strong brains labouring on the thought unwon,
They mark our passage as a race of men,
Earth will not see such ships as those again.[23]

Notes to Chapter 5

1. *On the Hill* (1949); *The Bluebells and Other Verse* (1961); *Old Raiger and Other Verse* (1965).

2. *Captain Margaret* (1908), *Sard Harker* (1924), *The Bird of Dawning* (1933), *The Taking of the Gry* (1934), and *Victorious Troy* (1935); *A Mainsail Haul* (1905 and, revised and enlarged, 1913), and *A Tarpaulin Muster* (1907).

3. His introductions and prefaces to editions of the voyages of Anson, Dampier, Hakluyt, and the *Chronicles of the Pilgrim Fathers,* to Visiak's *Buccaneer Ballads,* the 1911 edition of Southey's *Life of Nelson,* Lubbock's *Adventure by Sea from Art of Old Time,* Cameron's *Goodbye Russia,* and his own compilation, *A Sailor's Garland.*

4. *Sea Life in Nelson's Time* (1905); *On the Spanish Main* (1906); *The Wanderer* (1930); *The Conway* (1933); and *New Chum* (1944).

5. *Philip the King* (1914), and "A Masque of Liverpool," *The Wanderer.*

6. *New Chum* (London: William Heinemann, 1944), p. 1.

7. George Schreiber, *Portraits and Self-Portraits* (Boston: Houghton Mifflin Co., 1936), p. 89.

8. Louise T. Nicholl, "John Masefield in Yonkers," *Bookman* (Jan. 1919), p. 544.

9. *Ibid.,* p. 547.

10. For information about Masefield's life in and near New York City from 1895 to 1897, see Nicholl, and internal evidence in: "A Measure of Shifting Sand," *The Speaker* (Apr. 26, June 21, June 26,

July 26, Aug. 23, 1902); "Johnny Good" (*Manchester Guardian*, Nov. 21, 1905); "In a New York Saloon," *A Mainsail Haul* (1905), pp. 97–103; "A Steerage Steward," *Manchester Guardian* (June 21, 1906); "On the Palisades" and "A Raines Law Arrest," *A Tarpaulin Muster* (London: Grant Richards, 1907), pp. 127–29 and 205–11.

11. See his review of E. Keble Chatterton's *Ship Models, Manchester Guardian* (Oct. 16, 1923); he also made a fine ship model as a gift for Thomas Hardy.

12. See W. R. Titterton in *Living Age* (Jan. 1931), pp. 537–38.

13. Artist collaborator with Masefield in *The Country Scene, Tribute to Ballet,* and *A Generation Risen;* Masefield also wrote introduction for Seago's *Circus Company* (1933).

14. Among the book reviews that Masefield wrote for the *Manchester Guardian* are the following primarily concerned with ships: "Ancient and Modern Ships" (Dec. 28, 1906); "Encyclopedia of Ships" (Oct. 23, 1907); "Sailing Ships and Their Story" (Aug. 20, 1909); "The King's Ships" (Aug. 28, 1913; Jan. 23, 1914; Apr. 13, 1915); "The China Clippers" by Basil Lubbock (May 12, 1914); "The Lookout Man" (Sept. 19, 1923).

15. Letters from Sean O'Faolain to Fraser Drew, Mar. 23, 1951; Jack B. Yeats to Fraser Drew, July 13, 1950 and May 31, 1951; Elizabeth C. Yeats to L. G. Thornber, July 14, 1922; see also *The Dial* 86 (July 7, 1929): 586–88.

16. For more detailed accounts of the friendship and collaboration of Masefield and Jack B. Yeats, see Hilary Pyle, *Jack B. Yeats: A Biography* (London: Routledge and Kegan Paul, 1970), chaps. 7 and 8; and Fraser Drew, "The Irish Allegiances of an English Laureate," *Eire-Ireland* 3, no. 4 (Winter 1968): 24–34.

17. See *Gallipoli* (1916), and *The Nine Days Wonder* (1941).

18. "In the Roost," *Manchester Guardian* (Mar. 16, 1906); in this story a boy named Ash ships as "dauber" aboard the *Joppa* and is killed in a fall from aloft; see Fraser Drew, "Masefield's *Dauber*," *Modern Language Notes* 62, no. 2 (Feb. 1957): 99–101.

19. For Valparaiso, see "Vallipo," *Manchester Guardian* (Nov. 14, 1904), and "Valparaiso," *Ibid.* (Aug. 25, 1906).

20. On back of photograph of the *Conway,* by Robinson and Thompson of Liverpool, given to Fraser Drew, Masefield has written, "I first saw the *Wanderer* from this ship."

21. *John Masefield* (London: Thornton Butterworth, 1932), pp. 81–82.

22. *Odyssey* 2: 292, quoted in *The Wanderer of Liverpool* (London: William Heinemann, 1930), p. 1.

23. *The Story of a Round-House* (New York: The Macmillan Co., 1912), pp. 216–18.

6

The English Sailor

Masefield's Sea Fever and the Sailor's Life

When the reader of Masefield leaves the English ship and turns to the sea itself, he will find treatments of the subject varying from the very romantic to the very realistic. It will not surprise him to learn that one of the three earliest extant Masefield poems is called "Sonnet—To the Ocean."[1] The poem is ponderous and grandiose, with none of the grace of the first published poems like "Sea-Fever," but it is Masefield's first recorded tribute to "the thunder of the never-silent sea."

Masefield's best-known poem, "Sea-Fever," stamped him early as a romanticist. In "Sea-Fever," as in "A Wanderer's Song," "Roadways," and other poems from the 1902 and 1903 collections,[2] the picture is clean, clear, bracing, and glorious, with white clouds flying and the wild Atlantic shouting on the sand. The same fever, which has affected Masefield all his life,[3] is also to be found in such less-attractive pictures of sea life as the 1902 "A Pier-Head Chorus" and "Hell's Pavement." In the latter, a sailor leaves the sea "for ever" when his ship comes into Liverpool; a week later, however, he ships again, "in the clothes upon his back."

There is a wide range in these early ballads, from the pure beauty of "Sea-Fever" to the rough-and-tumble "Bill," "Fever-Chills," and "Burial Party," with their dialect, occasional

160

"bloody's," and admissions like the following from one of the sketches in *A Tarpaulin Muster* (1907):

> You see some queer goes at sea. . . . But if you ask me about the sea, I say it ain't a life; not properly it ain't. It's an existence, that's what the sea is. And it's a yaller dawg's existence even at that.

This range of presentation and interpretation of the life at sea indicates Masefield's willingness to tell the whole truth when he tells his stories of "the sailor . . . the chantyman . . . the tired lookout." The same range is to be found in the early collections of short stories and sketches. "Being Ashore," from *A Tarpaulin Muster,* is a eulogy of the beauty and joy of life at sea, as remembered by an English sailor now ashore. Here is a typical passage:

> We were at sea off the River Plate, running south like a stag. The wind had been slowly freshening for twenty-four hours, and for one whole day we had whitened the sea like a battleship. . . . In this old sailing ship, the joy of the hurry was such that we laughed and cried aloud. The noise of the wind booming, and the clack, clack, clack of the sheet-blocks, and the ridged seas roaring past us, and the groaning and whining of every block and plank, were like tunes for a dance. We seemed to be tearing through it at ninety miles an hour. Our wake whitened and broadened, and rushed away aft in a creamy fury. We were running here, and hurrying there, taking a small pull of this, and getting another inch of that, till we were weary. But as we hauled we sang and shouted. We were tearing along across a splendour of sea that made you sing. Far as one could see there was the water shining and shaking. Blue it was, and green it was, and of a dazzling brilliance in the sun. It rose up in hills and in ridges. It smashed into a foam and roared. It towered up again and toppled. It mounted and shook in a rhythm, in a tune, in a music. One could have flung one's body into it as a sacrifice.

This ecstatic paean is less convincing than the calm restraint of the poet's later praise of the sea. It may be contrasted with the equally unconvincing ugliness of a scene in "A Deal of Cards," from *A Mainsail Haul* (1905), in which a company of English seamen, "a rough lot of gallows-birds" later to be hanged for piracy, are drinking and dicing around a cabin table. One of them

> had been hurt with a knife by a mate that morning, since when he had been at the rum. His head was singing like a kettle, what with the cut, the drink, and the heat of the between decks. . . . Perhaps he was a little touched with fever, for of a sudden he refilled his pannikin and drank it dry. He rose unsteadily, clutching at the bowl, at the table, and at the shirts of his companions. He leaned his head through the window, flinging his empty can far astern into the still, blue sea where the sharks swam. "A rot on all salt water," he shouted. Then he collapsed over a Newgate man.

In two prose articles of 1904–1905,[4] not collected in book form, Masefield records his own first impressions of actual life at sea, "a life brutal as that of the convict, a life foul, frowsy, whose one refinement was that of the low tavern by the dock."

The negative side of Masefield's ambivalence toward the sea is startlingly revealed in comments that he wrote in the margins of the galley proofs of Ashley Gibson's article, "Mr. John Masefield," written for the April 1909 issue of *The Bookman*. Reacting sharply to the critic's comment on the importance of his sea experience and the inevitability of his having become a sailor, Masefield explicitly denies ever having wished to go to sea at any time and dismisses sea life as something he had loathed unspeakably.[5] His ambivalence is reflected in the attitudes and experiences of his sea characters and may explain his later success, as in *The Everlasting Mercy, The Widow in the Bye Street,* and *Dauber,* in using extremes of beauty and brutality, of joy and suffering, effectively in a close juxtaposition that becomes a favorite Masefield device.

Among the sea poems, this contrast between hardship and happiness is to be found in *Dauber*. Man's cruelty to man becomes most painful to the reader when Dauber's shipmates smear and cut his pictures and then jeer at his grief. The sailor's life nowhere seems harder than in the storm stanzas when Dauber, after being buffeted about in the icy rigging, goes below shivering and freezing, only to climb into a bunk that has been soaked by the inrushing seas. Yet here, as in the earlier poems and stories,

Masefield tips the balance in favor of the sea life. The poem is filled with passages of great beauty when the sea and the sky are Dauber's friends and life aboard ship becomes a good life for Dauber the seaman as well as for Dauber the artist.

> "This is the art I've come for, and am learning,
> The sea and ships and men and travelling things.
> It is most proud, whatever pain it brings."
>
> He leaned upon his arm and watched the light
> Sliding and fading to the steady roll;
> This he would some day paint, the ship at night,
> And sleeping seamen tired to the soul;
> The space below the bunks as black as coal,
> Gleams upon chests, upon the unlit lamp,
> The ranging door hook, and the locker clamp.
>
> This he would paint, and that, and all these scenes,
> And proud ships carrying on, and men their minds,
> And blues of rollers toppling into greens,
> And shattering into white that bursts and blinds,
> And scattering ships running erect like hinds,
> And men in oilskins beating down a sail
> High on the yellow yard, in snow, in hail.

Dauber tells the reefer Si that he wants to learn and to paint not only ships and the sea but the men and their life.

> "It's not been done, the sea, not yet been done,
> From the inside, by one who really knows."

This is the life that Masefield portrays in his own medium, and "from the inside," in many of his novels, short stories, and poems, and in several of the "sea books" and essays. Although these early essays, *On the Spanish Main, Sea Life in Nelson's Time,* and the prefaces and notes for *A Sailor's Garland, Southey's Life of Nelson,* and the editions of Hakluyt, Anson, and Dampier, cannot be considered in the same light as Masefield's sea poems and sea novels, they do offer further evidence of his preoccupation with nautical subjects.

Sea Life in Nelson's Time (1905) is a careful study of the construction and armament of the late eighteenth-century English ship, the duties of her officers and crew, and various phases of their life on ship and ashore. The sailor's life in the earlier time of Lord Anson's voyage around the world is more graphically, if more briefly, described in Masefield's introduction to the Everyman's Library 1911 edition of that famous voyage of 1740–1744. Here there is little attempt to make the eighteenth-century sailor's existence an attractive one.

> Life at sea has always been, and may always be, a harder life than the hardest of shore lives. . . . Much in it was brutal, dirty, and debased; but it had always behind it an order and a ceremony grand, impressive, and unfaltering. That life in that society was often barbarous and disgusting cannot be doubted. The best men in the ships were taken by force from the merchant service. The others were gathered by press-gangs and gaol deliveries. They were knocked into shape by brutal methods and kept in hand by brutal punishments. The officers were not always gentlemen; and when they were, they were frequently incompetent. The administration was scandalously corrupt. The ships were unhealthy, the food foul, the pay small, and the treatment cruel.

In his introduction to the Everyman edition of Hakluyt's *Principal Navigations* (1907), Masefield presents a similar picture of Elizabethan sea life, which was "harder than it is today; though perhaps not very much harder than it was to those who sailed with Anson, in the middle of the eighteenth century."

The sea life pictured in the Masefield fiction is generally that of the nineteenth century and has, in spite of its brutal captains and hardships of weather, shipwreck, and mutiny, its pleasant aspects. There are the "joys of life at sea" which "it does not become a sailor to sing,"[6] and which one rarely finds, perhaps for that reason, in such accounts as those of Lord Anson. Masefield fiction is full of both sides of the sailor's life; *Captain Margaret* (1908) and *A Tarpaulin Muster* are two storehouses for detailed pictures of the English sailor's working and playing hours. The authenticity of Masefield's sea life has rarely, if ever, been questioned.[7] May Lamberton Becker reports that a sailor gave her a copy of *A Mainsail Haul,* saying "It's the real thing."[8]

Of the Masefield poems, *Dauber* and several pieces from *The Wanderer of Liverpool* (1930) offer the best pictures of life aboard ship. *Dauber* presents the sailor in both fair weather and foul. The *Wanderer* poems are more limited, but two that show seamen going ashore after "long months of water and sky" and a scene at "Eight Bells" aboard ship are excellent photographs.

Sailors' Yarns and Sailors' Singing

Sailors are traditionally addicted to telling yarns and to singing songs, and these pastimes are common in Masefield sea literature. There are some yarns in *Salt-Water Ballads,* but the best are in the prose of *A Mainsail Haul* and *A Tarpaulin Muster,* where half the stories and sketches are old sailor tales, many of them told to the author by the famous Wally Blair. Masefield dedicates *A Mainsail Haul* to the memory of Wallace Blair and acknowledges in a note his indebtedness to the old sailor who taught seamanship aboard H.M.S. *Conway* when Masefield was a "new chum." Among the best of these yarns, which generally show the sailor getting the better of a landsman, or the mate, or "the old man," or the Devil, is "The Devil and the Old Man" from *A Mainsail Haul,* a delightful variant on the themes of Dr. Faustus and *The Devil and Daniel Webster.* Often the yarns are prefaced by a descriptive scene in which the writer is working or talking with an old salt; one such story is "Port of Many Ships."

Singing sailors are familiar figures in nautical literature. Seamen sing as they work and sing for entertainment in the fo'c's'le aboard ship and in the tavern ashore. Sea poems in the form of songs or ballads contain their meaning in an especially appropriate form, and many Masefield sea ballads are easily set to nautical tunes. In his first book, *Salt-Water Ballads,* the title links the poems to the singing of sailors, and seven of the poems are called "songs," or "lyrics," or "ballads." In *On the Hill* (1949) the three sea poems are all ballads. One is the tale of a seaman, Count Arnoldos, who sings a compelling song, while the other two, "Sailorman Bold" and "The Wind of the Sea," have ballad refrains, one of them a chanty-like refrain. Not only do many Masefield poems have the swing and savor of a sailor's song, but many poems and prose pieces discuss or record the seaman's love of singing.[9] In a long note in *A Sailor's Garland* (1906), Masefield defines the chanty and classifies its various types.[10] He then gives the text of two dozen of the best chanties.

Masefield's definition of the chanty is "a song sung by sailors when engaged in the severest of their many labours." The sheet, tack, and bowline chanties are the most ancient, but the capstan and halliard types are much more commonly heard in Masefield's time. "The most beautiful of all the chanties" is the capstan "In Amsterdam there dwelt a maid," which is like a song in the fifth act of Heywood's *Lucrece,* and which "is sung to an old Elizabethan tune which stirs one's blood like a drum-tap."

Among the favorite halliard chanties are "Lowlands," "Whiskey! Johnny!," "Blow the Man Down," and "Hanging Johnny." Of the last-named Masefield writes:

> It has a melancholy tune that is one of the saddest things I have ever heard. I heard it for the first time off the Horn, in a snowstorm, when we were hoisting topsails after heavy weather. There was a heavy, grey sea running and the decks were awash. The skies were sodden and oily, shutting in the sea about a quarter of a mile away. Some birds were flying about us screaming. . . . I thought at the time that it was the whole scene set to music. I cannot repeat the words to their melancholy wavering music without seeing the line of yellow oilskins, the wet deck, the frozen ropes, and the great grey seas running up into the sky.

Masefield, the former merchant seaman, writes that the chanty is the invention of the merchant service, on whose invariably undermanned ships "one sings whenever a rope is cast off the pin." Without the chanties, efficient work could not be done, especially in foul weather off Cape Horn, where "a song is ten men on a rope" and "as comforting as a pot of hot drink. A wash and a song are the sailor's two luxuries."

There are several references to chanties in such poems from *Salt-Water Ballads* as "A Wanderer's Song" and "Nicias Moriturus" ("The Turn of the Tide" in later editions) and in "A Valediction," with its "salt Atlantic chanty" refrain of "A long pull, a strong pull, and we're outward bound!" In the final scene of *The Tragedy of Pompey the Great* (1910), at the sign of Pompey's death, the sailors hoist sail, and a chantyman leads them in song. Four of his solo lines are:

And the conqueror's prize is dust and lost endeavour.
And the beaten man becomes a story for ever.
For the gods employ strange means to bring their will to be.
We are in the wise gods' hands and more we cannot see.

After each of these lines is the halliard chorus of "Away, i-oh" or "So away, i-oh." Although the setting of the play is, of course, far from England, the sailors haul and sing like English seamen aboard an English sailing vessel, and their chanty tune is "Hanging Johnny." The reader must judge for himself if the English chanty is appropriate for a play of two thousand years ago, if the solo lines are appropriate for a chanty, and if inappropriateness in either event does any violence to the play.

Sailors sing in several of the narrative poems. In the last stanza of *The Daffodil Fields* (1913), the crews of ships going out to sea are handling the halliards and singing while "the topsail fills/ To this old tale of woe among the daffodils." In *Dauber* the initial stanza shows a watch free from work, some singing, others playing at check, still others mending clothes. After the worst of the Cape Horn storm, later in the poem, the Mate, drunk on the remnants of an issue of hot whiskey and lime juice, strips and dances in the cabin, "singing in tenor clear that he was pipped." Twice there is mention of chanty singing, once only the brief mention of singers "clapped to the halliards, hauling to a tune/ Old as the sea." The ending of the poem shows the crew bringing their ship into Valparaiso after Dauber's burial at sea. The men are singing the halliard chanty called "Lowlands," with its haunting music and its Ceyx-and-Alcyone theme of death in the sea.

The climax stanzas of "The 'Wanderer,' " with their bells and their singing of "some simple tune of Christmas day," have already been quoted; they recall two early poems, "Christmas, 1903" and "Christmas Eve at Sea."[11]

The stories of *A Tarpaulin Muster* are filled with singing English seamen.[12] "In a Fo'c's'le" laments the passing of the old stories and the old songs and the substitution of "music-hall lyrics." The good singer or musician is still a popular man aboard ship, however, and one old sailor refuses to criticize a mate's faulty seamanship because "he sings pretty good." "El Dorado" begins with an evening aboard an English ship ready to leave a South American port, and a sing-song is in progress under the stars. The singing, Masefield writes, is filled with "a haunting beauty which thrilled and satisfied me."

There are several references in *A Tarpaulin Muster* to chanties. In "Anty Bligh" a sailor in a night watch is singing a new chanty of his own, beating out the tune with his pipe stem and repeating the words over and over as though he could never tire of their beauty. The nostalgic essay, "On Growing Old," recalls two famous chanties, one of them the old "furling chorus" of Paddy Doyle. The writer and his sailor friend of bygone days are thinking about the lighthouse to which they had once planned to retire together in their old age. Life will be simple there, and good; it will also be full of song, especially:

> I dreamed a dream the other night,
> > Lowlands, Lowlands, hurrah, my John;
> I dreamed a dream the other night,
> > My lowlands a-ray,

Masefield does not speak of "Rolling Home" in *A Sailor's Garland*, but in "The Cape Horn Calm" he calls it "the most popular of sailor songs" and quotes one stanza.

> I think I would rather have written "Rolling Home" than "Hydriotaphia." If I had written "Rolling Home" I would pass my days at sea or in West Coast nitrate ports hearkening to the roll and the roar of it as the yards go jolting up the mast or the anchor comes to the bows.

> > Pipe all hands to man the capstan,
> > > see your ca—bles run down clear,
> > Heave away, and with a will, boys,
> > > 'tis to old England's shores we steer;

And we'll sing in joyous chorus in the
     watches of the night,
For we'll sight the shores of England when
     the grey dawn brings the light.

I used to think that stanza, as the old sailor sang it in the
dark watches, the most beautiful thing the tongue of man ever
spoke.

Perhaps the best singing incident in *A Tarpaulin Muster* is in
the story, "One Sunday." A piano-playing sailor in a Welsh tavern
s telling the story of his experience. Sick at sea, he lies in his
bunk and listens to the noises overhead and on the shore. The
ship is anchored in the harbor of Junin and he longs to sail.

"And then I heard them at the capstan, heaving in. They
were singing 'Amsterdam.' It's the only chanty worth a two-
penny. It broke me up not to be heaving round too.

"And when they come to get under sail, setting the fore-
topsail, and I heard them beginning 'There's a dandy clipper
coming down the river,' I lit out a scritch, and I out of my
bunk to bear a hand on the rope. I was as weak as water,
and I lay where I fell. I was near hand being a goner.
The first words I said was 'Blow, bullies, blow.' It was that
chanty cured me. I got well after that."

He turned again to the piano and thumped out a thundering
sea chorus. The assembled reefers paid their shot and sallied out
singing into the windy streets, where the lamps were being lit.
As we went we shouted the song of the sea:—

                    A-roving,
                    A-roving,
          Since roving's been my ru-i-n,
               I'll go no more a ro-o-ving
               With you, fair maid.

There are a number of poems and prose pieces of sailors
ashore on liberty, drinking, dicing, and singing in the seaport
taverns. "The Emigrant," from *Ballads* (1903), is nostalgic, while

"A Night at Dago Tom's," from *Salt-Water Ballads* (1902), is merry and raucous.

Several of the novels, including *The Bird of Dawning* (1933), *The Taking of the Gry* (1934), and *Victorious Troy* (1935), have good singing scenes, but the best of them is in *Captain Margaret* (1908). The *Broken Heart* is ready to sail for America. The scene is one of intense activity aboard ship and intense interest on shore. The fo'c's'le is thronged with hurrying sailors; the trumpeter sounds his 'Loath to depart'; and the bars are shipped.

> Someone at one of the bars, down in the half-darkness, began to sing. The crowd made chorus together, lifting the tune. Voice after voice joined in. Bar after bar sounded and shouted. The ship rang with song. The music of the tune floated out over the harbour. In the sixth-rate, the men joined in, till the whole crew were singing. Ashore they heard it. On the schooners at anchor, in the inns ashore, in the dance-house up the town, the music made echo, stirring the heart. As the light wind moved or failed, so died the tune or lifted. With a great sweep it rose up, towering on many voices, then dropped to the solo, to soar again when the men sang. They were singing that they would go no more a-roving. To Margaret and Perrin, standing there at the poop-rail, hearkening to them, much moved by the splendour of the song, the coarse old words seemed touching, infinitely sad, the whole of sea-life set to music.

Masefield's Seamen

In an introductory essay to *A Sailor's Garland,* Masefield remarks that "nearly all the English poets, from Chaucer to Keats, have a dislike for, or a dread of, the sea, and a hatred of sea-life and no high opinion of sailors." In a discussion of English nautical literature before his own generation of writers, Masefield deplores the lack of great sea poetry and of a great epic of English sea-heroes, but he does find some "unmatchable sea characters in our poetry and our prose fiction." He then discusses the treatment which the sailor has received in English literature, admitting that the sailor has been presented "with perfect art and perfect truth," although he is nearly always an unattractive character.

So far as I know there are not half a dozen attractive naval characters, created and celebrated in poetry or in prose fiction, prior to the early nineteenth century. If a poet or a novelist desired a common seaman or a sea captain in his art, he followed the type of Chaucer's shipman or of Shakespeare's boatswain for the one, and that of Congreve's "young Ben" or Smollett's Commodore, or Edmund Thompson's Captain Mizen for the other. Heywood's sea captains, at the inn, are perhaps the best we have prior to Miss Austen and Captain Marryat, though our fiction makers have always done well with pirates, as with Captain Ward and Captain Roberts.

Masefield has no quarrel with the earlier writer for his portrayal of the ordinary English seaman. This type he finds little changed from Chaucer's day to his own. The sailor is hard-drinking, noisy, and rough-mouthed and can be found "on blue water ships at the present time." Chaucer's shipman is then analyzed as the prototype of English sailor such as one can still find by the dozen "in any dock in Liverpool or New York or Sydney or San Francisco."

He no longer wears "faldyng," or rough Irish frieze, but he is never without a knife (as he will tell you himself in a coarse proverb), and he is tanned by the wind and the sun, and he is a "good felawe," a good comrade, a stand-by in any sudden trouble.

Masefield emphasizes the fact that Chaucer, after his description of the shipman's appearance, admits that "certainly he was a good felawe." Chaucer's sailor is a ruffian, willing to steal and to fight and to dispose of his captured enemies without compunction. Yet Chaucer respects the shipman for his knowledge of his craft and because he is "hardy . . . and wys to undertake." Masefield concludes that the shipman is, on the whole, "the most perfect sailor in creative writing."

Shakespeare's boatswain in *The Tempest* is in the direct line of sailors extending from the Shipman to some of Masefield's own seamen. Like his Chaucerian forebear, he is intent on his work and he is ruthless to all who stand in his way. The reader will encounter many like him in Masefield poetry and fiction, although his characteristics are often isolated and typed into such Masefield figures as the old salt, the cruel captain, the worthless and dangerous seaman, and the hero.

Among Masefield's English sailors who are reminiscent of Chaucer's Shipman and Shakespeare's Boatswain are Bill Harker of "Davy Jones' Gift" from *A Tarpaulin Muster,* old Bill Purple of *Victorious Troy,* and the Mate and Bosun of *Dauber.* Bill Harker is undoubtedly English. His name is common in Masefield fiction, as the hero of *Sard Harker,* little Kay of *The Midnight Folk,* and Sir Theopompus Harker and Mr. Aston Tirrell Harker of *Victorious Troy* will testify. When the reader first meets Bill in the story "Davy Jones' Gift," he is walking down Mary Street in Cardiff, "on both sidewalks and all the road." He is a reefer or apprentice, and he is "brass-bound fit to play music." In his dress he is most unlike the Shipman, for he cuts a brave figure with the gold badge on his cap, bright brass buttons, and trousers "cut like windsails round the ankles." Davy Jones and the Devil, on an inspection tour in Cardiff, are playing cards for souls. Davy has just won a bishop from the Devil, and now he awards the reefer to his crony. The Devil is pleased, for the reefer is "a beauty," and he follows Bill to sea in order to catch his soul at the proper time. Bill is as good at his craft as the Shipman, and shows such courage that one of the sailors remarks, "Ah, come off . . . them reefers, they haven't got souls to be saved," and this sets the devil to thinking. Bill is a hard drinker, and blasphemous, too; he exceeds all his mates at the invention of new blasphemies. After a shipwreck, survived only by the Devil and the reefer, the Devil finally gives up his quest for Bill's soul. For when they have reached land safely, Bill does not give thanks, as the Devil expects. He only looks around for some smooth, round shells to use in a game of knucklebones. The Devil cries, "You've no more soul than the inner part of an empty barrel," and vanishes in a flame of sulphur.[13]

Old William Purple of *Victorious Troy* is a less glamorous figure than Bill Harker, but even more like the traditional English sailor. No reefer, he is a veteran of many years at sea. He is a "truculent-looking ruffian, . . . rough as a bear, surly, sour, and apt to bully," vain of his own seamanship and intolerant of new methods. He has the traditional taste for spirits. His fellow-sailor Jim Alfrick, a shepherd's son from the Cotswolds, is "the very pick of the prime seamen of his time." He has no ambition to rise in his profession, or to command, but he has no peer as a helmsman and practical seaman. In *Victorious Troy* Masefield calls the roll of each watch aboard the *Hurrying Angel,* and the resulting gallery of sea portraits is an interesting one. Each sailor is described briefly, and as the novel proceeds, each character is further developed in the action. Here are apprentices, young lads like Bill Guller, Kit Pillows, and Ed Newbarn; old salts like Bill Purple, Nab Wallers, and Bert Kempley; and the villains Kruger Evesbatch and Morritz. The latter is a stowaway, "a bad specimen from some unknown part of Central Europe." The captain had been furious at his discovery aboard, "for it had been his boast that the ship carried an all-British crew."

The Bird of Dawning affords a similar series of characterizations, and here each sailor is tested by hard days and slim rations in an open boat after the sinking of the *Blackgauntlet.* Villains and heroes emerge under these conditions, and once more, as in *Victorious Troy,* the bad sailors are those with un-English names, Llewellyn Efans, Karl Bauer, Johan Jacobson, and Ewyas Stratton.

The seamen in the poem *Dauber* are characterized with less detail than those of the novels. As a group they are rough, hard-drinking, and foul-mouthed, but able and devoted practitioners of their craft. Unsympathetic toward landsmen and weaklings, they are respectful of courage and skill. The Bosun and the Mate, completely lacking in "nyce conscience" toward Dauber in the early stages of the narrative, are friendly "good felawes" once the boy has proved his manhood in the Cape Horn storm. The Bosun teaches Dauber "square sennit," while the Mate says: "Why, holy sailor, Dauber, you're a man!/ I took you for a soldier."

Heroes and Sea-Captains in Masefield's Fiction

Two special classes of seamen in Masefield fiction are worth some consideration: the heroes and the captains, both good and bad. The heroes of five Masefield novels are sailors: Charles Margaret and Chisholm Harker in *Captain Margaret* and *Sard Harker,* Cruiser Trewsbury in *The Bird of Dawning,* Charles Tarlton in *The Taking of the Gry,* and Dick Pomfret in *Victorious Troy.*

Trewsbury, Tarlton, and Pomfret are all very young, their ages ranging from 18 to 22, and they have been at sea for seven years or less. No one of them is a captain, but each in the events of his story assumes a captain's responsibility and acquits himself with great credit. Since Charles Tarlton is the teller of the story in *The Taking of the Gry,* there is less objective description of him. He shares the position of hero with his cousin, Tom Browne, a lieutenant in the Santa Ana Navy but of English descent and still closely tied to England, her language, and her traditions. Tarlton is much like Trewsbury and Pomfret, of whom we have extended description.

In *The Bird of Dawning,* Cyril ("Cruiser") Trewsbury is presented thus:

> He was an excellent sailor and shipmate; he had a fairly good tenor voice; he made it a rule to learn a new language on each round voyage; and had written but had not published a little manual on Compass Deviation.

Cruiser is a second Dauber, too, for his greatest delight is in painting sailing ships and his ambition is to "pass for Master" on his return to England from this voyage, to give up the sea and to go to Paris to study art.

The picture of Dick Pomfret in *Victorious Troy* is less detailed, but it is interesting to note that he is similar in appearance to Cruiser. Both Dick and Cruiser are old Conway boys. With less experience at sea than Trewsbury, Pomfret met with equal courage and success a situation requiring bravery, intelligence, and skill. These young men are Masefield's ideal young English sailors, as Charles Cothill is his ideal young English countryman. Their identities and their deeds in these stories, at least in *Victorious Troy,* are imaginary, Masefield states in a note at the beginning of the novel. They are, however, real in the sense that similar English seamen, often mere boys, have performed similar exploits, which are "among the glories of their profession." The novelist tries only to "make an image" of what English sailors actually "have done, when there was 'Hell to pay and no pitch hot.' "

Sard Harker and Charles Margaret are older men. Margaret, nearly forty, is the most complex character of the five. Tall and handsome, with the pale face, burned by wind and sun, characteristic of the Masefield sailor-hero, he has intelligence and a noble, idealistic nature. He fails as a man of action because an unrequited love of many years' standing has sapped his energy and decisiveness and left him withdrawn from the outside world. His chivalry and patience become more annoying as the novel progresses. While he obviously has his creator's sympathy and even voices Masefield's own thoughts and feelings at times, he is hardly in the tradition of the English seaman.

Sard Harker has Margaret's idealism, his reticence, and his long-time devotion to the dream of a loved woman, but he is much more the English seaman and man of action. A Berkshire lad who had come to sea at fifteen, when the reader first encounters him in the novel he has been a sailor for ten years. He is described in one of the sonnets that appear at the beginning and the end of the novel, "silent behind triple bars/ Of pride, fastidiousness and secret life." Like Charles Margaret, the Dauber, and Cyril Trewsbury, Sard Harker has a bookish and an artistic side that sets him apart from other seamen. A natural reserve also sets him apart from his mates, who gave him his rarely-used nickname because of his sardonic nature.

The heroes of the Masefield sea fiction are not the beaten men, the failures, of many of his other narratives. All but Captain Margaret are conspicuously successful, and even the oft-beaten Margaret finally wins the love of his sweetheart in the closing pages of the novel.

Generally of more interest than the heroes of these novels are the several sea captains who appear. They range from the admirable John Craig Cary of the *Pathfinder* in *Sard Harker* to the mad and cruel Paul Ashplant of the *Albicore* in *Live and Kicking Ned;* from the bitter and brilliant young Captain Duntisbourne of the *Blackgauntlet* in *The Bird of Dawning* to queer old Admiral Topsle Cringle of the *Hannibal* in *Dead Ned,* retired after several failures and living in the memory of early successes.

Captain Cary had commanded the ship *Venturer,* in which Sard Harker first went to sea. Later Sard followed him into the *Pathfinder,* where he served as third, second, and finally chief mate. The events of the novel explain why Sard is not with Captain Cary aboard the *Pathfinder* on her final voyage. The two men respect and trust each other completely, and the captain is generally described as he appears to his chief mate, the man who probably knows him best.

Captain Cary is a famous sailor, eminent in his profession and even the subject of a ditty written thirty years before. He had won the gratitude of Don Manuel, dictator of Santa Barbara, by allowing him to come aboard the *Venturer* as a refugee of an earlier war. Later a model of the ship is erected in bronze in Santa Barbara; it bears a medallion portrait of Captain Cary with the inscription:

In eternal gratitude
To Captain John Craig Cary
And the officers and company
of the English Barque Venturer,
For their nobleness to the ruined in the Noche Triste.

Below are engraved the English names of the *Venturer's* seamen, including Sard, with lines of praise for their bravery. At the time of the novel, *Sard Harker,* Captain Cary is growing old. He is given to periodic attacks upon modern trends in shipbuilding and the merchant service and to "an old-maidish inquisitiveness about his officers' doings ashore." Captain Cary takes Sard to a boxing match ashore in Santa Barbara, but in spite of the referee's declaration that he is "for the sport, the sport English, the sport antique," the bout is a disgraceful, brutish exhibition. Captain Cary and Sard, with the Englishman's regard for good sportsmanship, leave the arena with a characteristic comment from the captain.

Captain Cary's opposite in many respects is the villainous commander of the *Albicore* in the last pages of *Dead Ned* and the first part of its sequel novel. Paul Ashplant, when sober, has a "lowering, pale, evil eye and downward scowl," and "the real Newgate look." Like many captains in the "African trade," he is reputed to be a "Devil from Hell," and he lives up to his reputation. Instead of the geraniums and canaries that Captain Cary keeps in his cabin, Ashplant has a savage mistress, the Black Mantacaw, who practises voodoo magic and is an accomplished murderess.

The night before the *Albicore* is to sail, Captain Ashplant, who has been drinking heavily, threatens a gang of drunken seamen who have been dragged aboard to serve as unwilling crew for the slaving expedition. Although Ned, the hero and narrator of the two novels which bear his name, calls Captain Ashplant "quite the murkiest savage I have ever met," still he has some word of praise for the captain, who is "at all times diligent in his business, if ever man was."

Between the extremes of Paul Ashplant and John Craig Cary are seven other sea captains of the Masefield novels. *The Taking of the Gry* has two, the captain of Charles Tarlton's first ship, the *Malinche,* who is a "testy old bear, about to be retired at the age of sixty-five, and angry about it," and old Commodore Roarer Bosbury of the *Oquendo,* to which Charles is promoted as fourth officer. The Roarer is "a great big lion of a man" whom Tarlton likes at once.

In *The Bird of Dawning* the original captain of the ship by that name is a strange character. He is called "a fine seaman" by his very critical rival, Captain Duntisbourne of the *Blackgauntlet,* and Cruiser Trewsbury remembers him as "a big, black-haired man with a white face and a kindly manner" of whom he has heard "no ill spoken . . . except that he was 'a religious man, fond of his glass.' " The novelist then comments that "all the captains of the China fleet were religious men, and fond of a glass on occasion." Captain Miserden's failure in the tea race and his retirement from the sea result from his reliance upon his religious belief in the Prophet Habakkuk. In a vision the prophet bids him to cut through a pipe, wreck the pumps, and abandon the ship. He follows instructions, with the result that Cruiser and the survivors of the *Blackgauntlet* find the abandoned *Bird of Dawning,* repair the damage, and go on with her to win the tea race.

Captain Duntisbourne in the same novel is truer to the tradition of the English sea captain, although his stubbornness and his disappointment at the *Blackgauntlet's* fatal accident carry him down with his ship. At the start of the novel he seems to have all the attributes of a brilliant English seaman. Young, ambitious, and able, he captains the *Blackgauntlet* at twenty-seven, "a spare, slim man . . . active beyond the ordinary, and ever restless." A consuming desire to win the tea race reduces Captain Duntisbourne to an irritable, completely unreasonable man, "all frayed nerves and anger." His insulting and contemptuous treatment of Cruiser Trewsbury and the men strips away from him the sympathy of the reader, who admires Trewsbury's later statement in defense of the captain as a seaman.

Like Captain Duntisbourne, Robin Battler Cobb of the *Hurrying Angel* is a ruthless driver of men and ships, a man of "rude courage, with much ignorance and intolerance." Captain Cobb, after a "good many nips," tries to pick a quarrel with his mates Duckswich and MacLerrinan as well as with Dick Pomfret, but he lacks the cold, controlled sarcasm of Duntisbourne. A serious injury and respect for Dick's seamanship, after the deaths of the two mates leave the boy in command of the ship, change the Battler, however, and at the end of the voyage he "swallows the anchor" and accepts a shore billet.

Since Captain Cammock of Charles Margaret's ship, the *Broken Heart,* is a reformed pirate, he belongs to another section of this chapter, and only Admiral Topsle Cringle remains to be called in the roll of Masefield sea captains. His name might lead the reader to expect the caricature of a seaman, but Captain Cringle is a well developed and convincing figure. Retired at the time of the events in *Dead Ned,* he is living in Hannibal House, named for the ship in which he won fame. Hannibal House is crowded with relics and memories of the old ship and is in the charge of a servant named, too appropriately, Will Coxswain. Captain Cringle's career had been an interesting one. Ned Mansell, narrator-hero of the novel, sums up the story, after recounting the Admiral's early successes and later failures, by describing him as a brave boy who never grew up and who was forced into early retirement with the memories of his successes in the *Hannibal.*

Masefield and the Great English Sea-Heroes

In Masefield's introduction to *A Sailor's Garland* (1906), he comments on the scanty recognition accorded England's great sea heroes by English poets. Before the nineteenth century there were few poetic tributes to English seamen except in ballads, and often the singers of these were "greater in their zeal than in their poetry." Only a handful of poems by Peele, Drayton, Marvell, and a few others may be cited as exceptions. Masefield finds the true sea epics of England's great sailors not in verse but in prose;

he cites "the three folios of Hakluyt, . . . the four quartos of Purchas," Mandeville, Raleigh's story of the *Revenge,* "Sir Francis Drake Reviv'd," and the books of Exquemeling, Shelvocke, Dampier, Walter, Cook, and Burney.

England's neglect of her sea heroes is a fault "rather racial than personal."

Until the nineteenth century the English had little sense of the majesty and grandeur of certain aspects of nature; and though they could fear and turn to use, they could not glory in the splendour and beauty, of breaking water. As a nation they have regarded their great men in somewhat the same way. They have broken their hearts or obeyed them or accepted them blindly, but they have never gloried in them, so that we need not look, in books of early English poetry, for any rapture of perception of the sea's beauty, nor rapture of praise of a hero's noble effort.

Much of the work of Masefield's first decade of writing is dedicated to those little-sung heroes, and they appear and reappear in his later work, as recently even as in his last decade. Although much of Masefield's early writing about the sea is the work of student and editor rather than of poet and story-teller, it offers further evidence of his lifelong interest in the sea and the life of the sailor.

The historical essay *Sea Life in Nelson's Time* (1905) is little concerned with Nelson, but later Masefield wrote an introduction for a new edition of Robert Southey's *Life of Nelson* (1911) in which the *Life* is called "pleasant and just" but unsatisfactory for the reader who is a naval officer. Southey states Nelson's achievements but fails to make clear the admiral's "peculiar intellectual power exercised before, during and after" these achievements; this failure Masefield finds at times in the work of the literary man writing about great action. Several pages of the introduction are devoted to the praise of Nelson. He is presented as typically English ("When necessary he could fight in the blunt and brainless way of 'hob, nob, give't or take't' with the most English of his men), but as the possessor also of an unusual faculty for tactics and generalship. Masefield recalls that "to 'go for the enemy' was the maxim of most British naval commanders of that time," but that Nelson added to that enthusiasm "an instrument and a direction." He supports this contention with examples and goes on to cite some of Nelson's least publicized exploits and excellences. The introduction's final tribute to this man so much beloved by his men presents the qualities usually attributed to Nelson and then adds:

> There was also something wistful, magnetic and compelling, which cannot be explained or ignored. It does not get into the books, it cannot be put into words, it is simply mysterious and very beautiful. It was this quality in him which made his rough sea captains shed tears when he explained his plans to them. It was by this quality that he bound men's hearts together, and gave to their virtue purpose and to their strength an aim.

This is Masefield's major tribute to Nelson, although he appears also in a sea-dialect poem in *Salt Water Ballads* (1902), a sailor's acknowledgment of the English naval great called "A Ballad of Cape St. Vincent," and in two newspaper articles and six book reviews written between 1903 and 1913.[14]

Another early historical essay is *On the Spanish Main* (1906). The book discusses life at sea in Drake's time and the exploits of Oxenham, Morgan, Dampier, and other famous sailors. The first third of the book is devoted to the Caribbean exploits of Sir Francis Drake between 1571 and 1573. The book is true to its subtitle ("Some English Forays on the Isthmus of Darien. With a Description of the Buccaneers and a Short Account of Old-Time Ships and Sailors"); it does not attempt a detailed analysis of Drake or of his significance in English naval history.

Drake makes more appearances in the course of the poetry and fiction of Masefield than any other English naval hero. In two of the novels he is mentioned, once briefly in a discussion of the Spanish treasure-trains in *Captain Margaret* (1908), several times in *The Taking of the Gry* (1934).

In *The Taking of the Gry*, Charles Tarlton, on his first visit to Santa Ana and Santa Barbara, recalls a favorite book of his childhood, Nathaniel Clutterbucke's *Golden Voiage of Sir Francis Drake*. In the book one incident was Drake's amazing feat of taking Santa Barbara through the use of a channel deemed impassable for "anie living, above the qualitie of an herring." In the course of the novel, Tarlton and a few friends attempt to steal the *Gry,* which is locked in Santa Barbara harbor with a consignment of military stores intended for the Santa Ana fleet. Since the harbor entrance is blocked by a boom, Tarlton secretly explores Drake's old channel and under cover of night steals the *Gry* and takes her out by that route. One of his helpers, Harry, encourages Tarlton in the bold escapade by his very resemblance to Sir Francis, as if he were "Drake come back to take us out by this channel." Maps and an excerpt in the appendix from the *Golden Voiage* lend reality to the novelist's account of the exploit.

Drake appears also in several volumes of Masefield poetry. In *Philip the King* (1914) he is mentioned three times in accounts of the naval war between England and Spain and of the destruction of the Spanish armada.

A Letter from Pontus and Other Verse (1936) includes a group of eight poems on subjects dealing with the Spanish Main; four of these are about Sir Francis Drake. "Canal Zone" is a sonnet and a contemporary portrait of the isthmus where the "skirt-of-fortune-plucker," Francis Drake, first saw the "bright Pacific basking like a snake." "Nombre de Dios" is a longer poem, a contemporary description of the port that was once of great political importance. The poem echoes the story of the taking of the town by Drake in 1572 and his wounding and withdrawal. In 1595 he visited Nombre de Dios again and burned it. On his second visit to the port, Drake contracted the flux of which he died; Nombre de Dios, then, "witnessed his first triumph and final discomfiture."

"Puerto Bello" begins with a modern description of the port that fell to English seamen five times between Drake's attack in 1595 and Vernon's in 1740. Then the poet writes of a nearby island:

> It is Escudo, where Sir Francis Drake
> "Yielded his valiant spirit like a Christian."
> Some say "His heart is buried there": perhaps.
> His body lies beneath us somewhere here.
> The surf breaks on the island as we pass.

The fourth Drake poem in the volume is called "A Ballad of Sir Francis Drake." It is an account, in traditional ballad form and language, of the seaman's return from sea in time to thwart the wedding of his sweetheart to another man. The story is one, Masefield remarks in "The Joy of Story-Telling" (1951), that particularly pleased him in his childhood.[15]

In the poem "An Art Worker," from *Gautama the Enlightened* (1941), in a catalogue of "the ten tales that still/ Have living power to thrill," the poet refers to "four old tales of ours,/ English as Berkshire flowers." These are the Shropshire tale of Sabrina, the fight between Arthur and Modred on Camlan Sands and Arthur's passing from this world, the Tristan and Isolt story, and the "English quest for gold" by Drake and his ships. Masefield's interest in Drake continues into his last collections of poetry, with the dramatic "A Word with Sir Francis Drake during his Last Night in London" in *The Bluebells and Other Verse* (1961) and the narrative "Two Cousins" of *In Glad Thanksgiving* (1967).

Drake and Nelson are Masefield's chief heroes of the great men in England's naval past, but the others, like Raleigh, Captain John Smith, and Captain James Cook,[16] are not neglected. Masefield is also interested in those English seamen who, like his fictional Captain Cammock and some of the characters in his juvenile tales, have distinguished themselves as pirates and buccaneers as well as in the more lawful activities of Englishmen at sea. Such names as Coxe, Ward, Jennings, Swan, Knox, Coxon, and Morgan, come alive in his pages, in *A Sailor's Garland,* in *A Tarpaulin Muster,* in his introduction to Visiak's *Buccaneer Ballads* (1910), in *On the Spanish Main,* and in a series of sketches in the second, enlarged edition of *A Mainsail Haul* (1913). In a book review of *The Real Captain Kidd* in 1911, Masefield defends two British seamen who "have for many years been vilified by their countrymen," Admiral Byng and Captain Kidd. He praises the book for its fair treatment of a man, no "worse than any other merchant seaman of his time," who did not deserve his reputation of "a monster of iniquity, fabulously rich, rolling home with bloody scuppers, under a Jolly Roger, with a bucket of rum and gunpowder at his blood-stained elbow."[17]

Masefield's edition of *Dampier's Voyages* (1906)[18] is prefaced by an introductory essay that evaluates Dampier as a traveler[19] and explorer and writer. This extraordinary character, of whom Masefield writes that it is pathetic to think of him "writing up his journal, describing a bunch of flowers, or a rare fish, in the intervals between looting a wine-ship and sacking a village," has been praised by many later naval worthies. It is evident from the following statement by Admiral Burney why Dampier had such appeal for the artist and scholar as well as the seaman in Masefield.

It is not easy to name another voyager or traveller who has given more useful information to the world; to whom the merchant and mariner are so much indebted; or who has communicated his information in a more unembarrassed and intelligible manner. And this he has done in a style perfectly unassuming, equally free from affectation, and from the most distant appearance of invention.

It is interesting that Masefield, the self-appointed laureate of the common man, the beaten man, the ordinary soldier and sailor, and not the "be-medalled Commander," should concern himself with captains and admirals as well as with "the drowsy man at the wheel and the tired lookout." Even when he praises Lord Anson's spirit and his "equable and unvaried character," it is the courage and endurance of the common man that moves him most.[20] In somewhat the same vein in his introduction to *Chronicles of the Pilgrim Fathers* (1910), Masefield praises the *Mayflower* pilgrims for their perseverance through a terrible sea passage, a severe winter, and later trials, and calls their story that "of the slow but noble triumph of all that is finest in the English temper."

The English Sailor at War

Chapter 8 will be concerned with Masefield's treatment of the English soldier at war. The English sailor at war also appears in his pages. In the World War I masterpieces, "August, 1914," and *Gallipoli* (1916), the sailor plays a minor part. Yet even in the epic of the British soldier's gallant effort at Gallipoli, the navy's contribution is vital and is fully acknowledged by the historian. He reminds the reader that it was the English navy[21] that brought men to Gallipoli and that evacuated the wounded, brought supplies, bombarded enemy coastal positions, and finally brought the troops away from the peninsula.

The English sailor shares the spotlight with the airman and the soldier in the World War II books. *A Generation Risen* (1942), the collaboration of Masefield and the artist Seago that will be discussed in chapter 7, includes seven short poems on various phases of the sailor's duty in war time. "A Lame Duck," "Here is the Convoy," "The Danlayers," and "Mine Sweepers," are brief sketches in tribute to the seamen "whose simple manhood lets our Nation be." A little humor creeps into "The Ship's Cook" and into the last lines of the grim "Patrol Ships," in which

> The mate on watch behind his screen
> Expecting Death to come to glean,
> Freezing, and ever growing colder,
> Thanks God that he is not a soldier.

The danger traditionally encountered by the sailor of all times is given additional poignancy and horror in "Crews Coming Down Gangways."

> There is no danger seamen have not run:—
> Tempests have drowned them since the world began,
> They have dared shipwreck, frostbite and the sun,
> But these have dared a greater horror: Man.

In the Dunquerque evacuation described in *The Nine Days Wonder* (1941), English seamen, both civilian and naval personnel, are the central figures in that "greatest thing this nation has ever done." The closing pages of the book list the various types of ships and crews that took part in Operation Dynamo, and their casualties; particular tribute is paid to "hundreds of little vessels from half the coast of England," which "deserve to have their names in the Navy henceforward."

Most impressive of all to Masefield is the roused spirit of his nation, which "rose to the lifting of the Armies as to no other event in recent times."

It was an inspiration to all, to feel that will to save running through the land. The event was as swift as Life; no possible preparation could be made; the thing fell suddenly, and had to be met on the instant. Instantly, in reply to the threat, came the will to help from the whole marine population of these islands.

Two of the poems at the end of *The Nine Days Wonder* concern the English sailor. One calls upon postwar England to remember that the peace was bought by men who are "lying blind/ Under the sea in ruined wreckage caught." In the other, a sonnet, "To the Seamen," Masefield addresses the sailors whose hard bread he has eaten and whose ways he has known. He prophesies immortal fame for the heroes of 1940.

> Through the long time the story will be told;
> Long centuries of praise on English lips,
> Of courage godlike and of hearts of gold
> Off Dunquerque beaches in the little ships.
>
> And ships will dip their colours in salute
> To you, henceforth, when passing Zuydecoote.

Masefield's pride in the sailor as the representative of England's finest and most characteristic qualities probably exceeds his pride in the countryman, the sportsman, the soldier, or any other English type. It shows in the foreword to Captain Cameron's *Goodbye Russia* (Adventures of H.M. Transport *Rio Negro*) (1934), which he calls an account of events in which the English character has always shown to advantage, "a chronicle of emergencies that had to be dealt with on the instant by improvised means, with the help of the two great virtues of courage and kindness." It shows in the tale of "Evan Roberts, A.B., of H.M.S. Andromache," the only sea-piece in *Minnie Maylow's Story and Other Tales and Scenes* (1931). This is an account in verse, with two long prose notes, of a deed at sea that "not one man in a million could have been strong, quick and ready enough to do," but that was done by "able-bodied" English seaman Evan Roberts of Liverpool.

Perhaps Masefield's finest acknowledgment of the service and the significance of the English seaman is to be found in one of his early essays, the epilogue of *Sea Life in Nelson's Time*. In this essay he surveys the English scene in 1905 and finds a rich and powerful nation, but a nation that owes its prosperity largely to its sailors. Characteristically, Masefield believes that these seamen of other days are now "spirits moving about us, touching us, rejoicing that evil days should have purchased happy days, and well content that misery should have brought such treasure. He concludes his expression of gratitude with the thought that in the lives of these men is to be found the true patriotism, the love of England—patriotism that "is not a song in the street" or "a flag flying from a window," but "a thing very holy, and very terrible, like life itself."

In three sonnets, "Lines on Sea Adventure," written as preface to Basil Lubbock's *Adventures by Sea from Art of Old Time,* the poet repeats, in 1925, in the more memorable language of poetry, what the historical essayist had written in 1905 in prose. Seeing an "old, rust-spotted ship/ Pass through the dock gates on another quest," he thinks of the seven hundred years during which English ships have gone around the world to bring to "some lone farm in Kent or Devon,/ 'Some crownes, some spoiles, a little dew of Heaven.' " He reviews the hardships and the acts of sacrifice and heroism done by the seamen in these ships and then sums up, in the third of the sonnets, their achievement and their legacy to a later England of "a charted sea,/ A world made little wherein conquering brains/ Can pass from land to new land, setting free."

In the closing lines of this last sonnet, Masefield moves ahead, as he does in the wartime addresses of 1918 and the verse of later years,[22] from a national interest in England alone to an international concern for all mankind. It is one of the glories of England's laureate that, for all the intensity of his regard for the Englishman, his final allegiance is to "this soul of man."

Notes to Chapter 6

1. These three poems Louise Townsend Nicholl found in the possession of two Yonkers men, William Palmer East and Billy Booth, who had known Masefield during his years in the carpet factory; she published them in "John Masefield in Yonkers," *Bookman* (Jan. 1916), pp. 544–49.

2. And in some poems not published in book form, such as "Gara Brook," *Manchester Guardian* (Nov. 18, 1904).

3. The same feeling is evident in "The Wind of the Sea," *On the Hill* (London: William Heinemann, 1949), p. 113, and in poems from his last volumes in the 1960s.

4. "In Dock," *The Speaker* (Nov. 5, 1904, and May 6, 1905).

5. See Fraser Drew, "John Masefield in New Haven," *Yale University Library Gazette* 32, no. 4 (April 1958): 151–56.

6. *A Sailor's Garland* (London: Methuen and Co., 1906), p. xix.

7. In his reviews, however, Masefield sometimes finds other writing about the sea unrealistic, *e.g.*, "Studies in Bed-Rock," review of Bart Kennedy's *A Sailor Tramp*, *The Speaker* (Apr. 5, 1902). In other reviews he praises the realism and authenticity of the writing; see "Old Starm Along," review of Walter Runciman's *Windjammers and Sea Tramps*, *The Speaker* (Feb. 14, 1903), and his review of Joseph Conrad's *The Mirror of the Sea*, *Manchester Guardian* (Oct. 16, 1906). Elsewhere, in reviewing Conrad's *Youth* and the Conrad–Hueffer *Romance*, Masefield's praise is qualified; see *The Speaker* (Jan. 31, 1903 and Nov. 14, 1903). For other reviews of sea books, see "The Banner of Romance" (*The Speaker*, Dec. 12, 1903); "A Wanderer's Oddments," *The Speaker* (Aug. 23, 1902); "A New Marine Magazine," *Manchester Guardian* (Mar. 27, 1911); "Press-gang Days," *Ibid.* (Nov. 17, 1911); "Our Heritage of the Sea," *Ibid* (Nov. 27, 1906); "The British Tar," *Ibid.* (Feb. 22, 1909); "Letters of English Seamen," *Ibid.* (Nov. 8, 1910); "Famous Sea Fights," *Ibid.* (May 1, 1911).

8. "John Masefield," *The Independent* (May 30, 1912), pp. 1158–61.

9. See Fraser Drew, "Those Singing Sailors," *Christian Science Monitor* (May 14, 1957).

10. For other discussions of chanties by Masefield, see prose articles: "Sea Song," *Temple Bar*, n.s. 1 (Jan. 1906), pp. 56–80, and "Chanties," *Manchester Guardian* (Aug. 16, 1905), also a letter by Masefield in *Manchester Guardian* (Aug. 19, 1905), concerning the latter article. See also "On Folk Songs," *The Speaker* (Dec. 23, 1905), a review of *Folk Songs from Somerset* by C. J. Sharp and C. L. Marson concerning sailor's ballads; and reviews: "Old Sea Chanties," *Manchester Guardian* (Mar. 27, 1906); "Sea Songs," *Ibid.* Dec. 3, 1906); "Naval Ballads," *Ibid.* (Apr. 28, 1908).

11. *Ballads and Poems* (London: Elkin Mathews, 1910), pp. 98–99, and *Salt-Water Ballads*, p. 65.

12. See also uncollected stories, "A Trip to Nombre de Dios,"

Manchester Guardian (Apr. 19, 1905), and "Brown," *Ibid.* (Jan. 16, 1906).

13. For another Bill Harker story, uncollected, see "A Duel with Davy Jones," *Manchester Guardian* (Feb. 28, 1907).

14. "Some Sea Dogs," review of W. H. Fitchett's *Nelson and His Captains, The Speaker* (Mar. 21, 1903); "Trafalgar Day: Ship Life under Nelson," *Manchester Guardian* (Oct. 22, 1904); "Nelson's Guns," *Ibid.* (Oct. 25, 1905); "Nelsonian Reminiscences," *Ibid.* (Dec. 15, 1905); "Nelson and Other Naval Studies," *Ibid.* (July 2, 1909); "The Nelson Whom Britons Love," *Ibid.* (Aug. 13, 1909); "Nelson in England," *Ibid.* (Mar. 14, 1913); "The Sailors Nelson Led," *Ibid.* (Nov. 28, 1913).

15. See also review, "The Drake Family," *Manchester Guardian* (May 12, 1911).

16. See Masefield's review of Sir Rennell Rodd's *Sir Walter Raleigh, Manchester Guardian* (Dec. 20, 1904), and "Great Raleigh," *Ibid.* (Sept. 8, 1908); "Great Adventure," review of reprint of *General Historie and True Travels of Captain John Smith, Ibid.* (Mar. 25, 1907); article, "Captain Cook," *Ibid.* (Mar. 10, 1911), and review, "Capt. J. Cook," *Ibid.* (May 28, 1907).

17. "Captain Kidd," review of Sir C. N. Dalton's *The Real Captain Kidd, Manchester Guardian* (June 26, 1911); for buccaneers, see also the reviews, "Buccaneer in the West Indies" (Oct. 27, 1910), and "A South Sea Buccaneer," *Ibid.* (Nov. 15, 1911).

18. Masefield's article in *The Speaker* (Apr. 28, 1906), "William Dampier," is incorporated with some alterations into this introductory essay.

19. For Masefield essays on other travelers, see: "Lithgow's Travels," review of reprint of William Lithgow's *Rare Adventures and Painefull Peregrinations, Manchester Guardian* (Oct. 26, 1906); "Voyages and Travels," review of *An English Garner, The Speaker* (Apr. 18, 1903); reviews of various volumes of *Purchas His Pilgrimes, Manchester Guardian* (June 22, 1905, Aug. 21, 1905, Sept. 19, 1905, Oct. 25, 1905, Jan. 22, 1906, June 1, 1906, July 19, 1906, Sept. 18, 1906, and June 17, 1907); and "Voyages of Elizabethan Seamen," *Ibid.* (June 21, 1907).

20. See also the review, "Life of Lord Anson," *Manchester Guardian* (Mar. 11, 1912).

21. For the English Navy elsewhere in Masefield's writings, see the following reviews in the *Manchester Guardian:* "The Royal Navy" (Jan. 10, 1908); "Inner Life of the Navy" (Jan. 5, 1909); "Naval

Miscellany" (Aug. 13, 1912); "British Battle Fleet" (Nov. 19, 1912); "From Naval Cadet to Admiral" (Oct. 24, 1913).

22. "St. George and the Dragon" and "The War and the Future," *The War and the Future* (1918); *Some Verses to Some Germans* (1939).

7

The English Soldier

Masefield's Interest in the Soldier

The English soldier, fighting in every part of the world to maintain or to extend British dominion "over palm and pine,"[1] found his laureate in the exuberant and vociferous Rudyard Kipling, to whose *Barrack-Room Ballads* (1892) Masefield's own early poems owe some debt. Although Masefield's inclination and his own experience led him to celebrate the seaman more often than the soldier, he neglected no type of English fighting man.

In "A Consecration," that early expression of the credo which he never abandoned, Masefield promises to sing of the common man and names the soldier first. Indeed, his language in this poem is more often military than nautical as he writes of the "men hemmed in with the spears" and "dazed with the dust of the battle." The Masefield novels have nearly as much fighting as they have sailing, but the soldiers are not always English and even when English they are generally fighting as individuals and not as official representatives of England.

In *Sard Harker* (1924) the fighting is limited to individuals, a gang of cutthroats, and the Santa Barbara police, although there is reference to the revolution of the 1880s and the war between the factions of Don Lopez de Meruel and Don Manuel of Encinitas. This war also occupies much of the novel *ODTAA* (1926). However, in these novels, the heroes, Chisholm Harker and Highworth Ridden, both Englishmen, do not appear primarily as soldiers.

One is a sailor who misses his ship and becomes involved in adventures on shore; the other is a boy, seeking his fortune, caught in the toils of the revolution.

The fighting in *Live and Kicking Ned* (1939) is in Africa between native hordes and the white inhabitants of the mysterious inland city of the Kranois. Ned Mansell, the English hero of the story, takes part in the battles, but he is not a soldier by profession or inclination. *Conquer* (1941) and *Basilissa* (1940) are stories of revolution and political intrigue, but the soldiers here are Byzantine, not English. *Badon Parchments* (1947), already discussed in chapter 1, is a novel of King Arthur and the struggle of Britons against the Red and the Black Heathen.

Captain Margaret (1908) is the only Masefield novel in which Englishmen of "modern" times are seen at war. The captain, leading a trading and colonizing expedition along the northern coast of South America, attempts to rescue an English traitor from an Indian city and is betrayed by a mutinous crew and pirate allies. After he has made a gallant and successful assault on the city, only to find the captive dead, he returns from the burial rites to find that his drunken crew and their allies have sacked and looted the city. A Spanish army makes a surprise attack, and Captain Margaret, wounded, barely escapes with his life. Thwarted in his mission and heartsick over his implication in so bloody and disgraceful an episode, he is not only the gallant English soldier but also that favorite Masefield type, the "beaten man." His sweetheart comforts him:

> "There is no dishonour, Charles. You failed. The only glory is failure. All artists fail. But one sees what they saw. You see that in their failure."

The English Soldier in World War I

Masefield's interest in the English soldier is most evident, of course, in his books dealing with World War I and World War II. When war came in 1914, he once told an American audience, he was in an old house in Berkshire.

I had never seen England so beautiful as then, and a little company of lovely friends was there. Rupert Brooke was one of them, and we read poems in that old haunt of beauty, and wandered on the Downs. I remember saying that the Austro-Serbian business might cause a European war, in which we might be involved, but the others did not think this likely; they laughed.

Then came more anxious days, and then a week of terror, and then good-bye to that old life, and my old home in Berkshire was a billet for cavalry, and their chargers drank at the moat. I saw them there. And the next time I saw them they were in Gallipoli, lying in rank in the sand under Chocolate Hill, and Rupert was in his grave in Skyros.[2]

Aside from "August, 1914," Masefield wrote very little poetry about the first World War, because there was "no time for verse" and because he could not write poetry that was "joyless."[3] He took an active part in the British war effort, serving in several different capacities. Five years before, he had written in *Multitude and Solitude* (1909) of the many English poets, like Byron and Chaucer, who had been "much tempted to action," and in the 1914–1918 war he was an active participant.

One of Rupert Brooke's letters to an American friend reported that Masefield was a corporal in Hampstead, drilling hard and expecting to be "promoted soon to a Sergeant."[4] Louise Townsend Nicholl says that Masefield was "refused for actual military service" and "very shortly after the war began" went to France to work in "war hospitals for five or six months."[5] In August, 1915, he went to the Dardanelles to "take charge of a picket-boat and barge for taking the wounded home, money for both of which he had raised in behalf of the British Red Cross." Into this war service, then, went the poet's own training and experience as a seaman and a medical student.

Masefield contracted fever in Gallipoli and came to the United States in January, 1916, to speak of the war to American audiences and to seek more money for the Red Cross work. In sixty days he visited fifty cities, sometimes lecturing more than once in a city. In March he returned to Lollingdon in England and wrote what some critics have called the greatest book of the First World War, *Gallipoli* (1916).[6] Completing the book in June, he spent the remainder of the year and the following year in writing *The*

Old Front Line (1917) and in doing hospital work and "government work" in France. He was made a Lieutenant in the British Army and refused a knighthood offered for his services.[7]

In January, 1918, Masefield came again to the United States, as a representative of the British government. His purpose was to acquaint Americans with England's war effort and to ask for America's cooperation in the war and in the peace to follow. He stayed three months longer than he had expected, in order to fulfill the Young Men's Christian Association's request that he visit camps in many states and speak to the young Americans in training; he remained in the United States until August, receiving honorary degrees at the Harvard and Yale commencements in June. It was after this trip that Masefield wrote *The Battle of the Somme* (1919). Other war prose written during the war years includes an introduction to E. D. G. Liveing's *Attack* (1918) and the newspaper articles, "The Harvest of the Night" and "The Irony of Battle."[8] His address at Yale and two of the 1918 American lectures, all concerned with the war, have also been printed.[9]

Throughout Masefield's books about the First World War, his strongest feeling is not his hatred for war, his love for his country, or his belief that the peoples of the world, after the war, must abandon nationalism for internationalism. It is rather his regard for the soldier—the Englishman (and often the American, the Frenchman, even at times the German and the Turk)—who goes to die, as in "August, 1914," for a half-understood idea of an "English city never built by hands/ Which love of England prompted and made good."

Two of the addresses delivered in America during the early months of 1918 have been published under the titles "St. George and the Dragon" and "The War and the Future." Both, like his address at the Yale Commencement and his article "The Harvest of the Night," are simple, direct, friendly, sincere attempts to give American audiences his own impressions of the war, to thank America for her aid to England and France, and to plead for Anglo-American cooperation during the war and in the future.

Frequently Masefield introduced humor into his speeches, usually in an attempt to illustrate the fine spirit of the men in the trenches. At other times his regard for the common soldier is shown in more serious words. Admitting at one point that no nation is without faults, but calling England's faults those of head rather than of heart, he said:

> When I think of those faults I think of a long graveyard in France, a hundred miles long, where simple, good, kind, ignorant Englishmen by the thousand and the hundred thousand lie in every attitude of rest and agony, for ever and for ever and for ever. They did not know where Belgium is, nor what Germany is, nor even what England is. They were told that a great country had taken a little country by the throat, and that it was up to them to help, and they went out by the hundred and the hundred thousand, and by the million, on that word alone, and they stayed there, in the mud, to help that little country, till they were killed.

Elsewhere in the same speech, asking for the ending of war through internationalism, Masefield spoke for the common people of every nation who have no quarrel with each other.

The Old Front Line and *The Battle of the Somme* are historical essays. Masefield's foreword to the latter explains the circumstances of their composition and the fact that he was "formally requested to write the History" of the Battle of the Somme. He relates that he "walked over every part of the battlefield in which British troops had been engaged . . . at least twice."[10] However, access to certain "Brigade and Battalion diaries," such as he had used in the writing of *Gallipoli* in 1916, was denied, and *The Battle of the Somme* and its prefatory study, *The Old Front Line,* lacked the completeness and the detail that the writer desired. They are careful descriptions and analyses of the campaign and its ground, but even here the humanitarian often pushes aside the objective historian. Masefield introduces actual comments and anecdotes by individual soldiers into *The Battle of the Somme,* and the book closes with a moving tribute to the Englishmen, the Scots, the Irish, the Welsh, the Newfoundland men, the South Africans, and the Australians who fell in the long battle.

The poem "August, 1914," Masefield's noble tribute to the English countryman who "left the well-loved Downs" and the "dear outline of the English shore" for the "misery of the soaking trench," is one of the great poems of World War I and has already been discussed in chapter 2. There are echoes of the war in some of the sonnets that appeared in the 1916 volume, *Sonnets,* and in the 1917 *Lollingdon Downs.* Two of these recall the poet's friendship with Rupert Brooke[11] and his sight of Scyros where his friend was buried. Here Masefield's sympathy for the common soldier of any land and for his fellow Englishman is intensified in his recollection of a loved comrade, "beautiful and wise." The fourth poem of *Lollingdon Downs* is universal rather than personal but records a personal experience in its closing lines.

> Even in the blinding war I have known this,
> That flesh is but the carrier of a ghost
> Who, through his longing, touches that which is
> Even as the sailor knows the foreign coast.
>
> So, by the bedside of the dying black
> I felt our uncouth souls subtly made one,
> Forgiven, the meanness of each other's lack,
> Forgiven, the petty tale of ill things done.
>
> We were but Man, who for a tale of days
> Seeks the one city by a million ways.

Gallipoli

Masefield's great achievement in the war years is his book *Gallipoli.* The gallant but unsuccessful attempt of British troops to secure a foothold on the Gallipoli Peninsula had aroused much comment in America. On his visit to the United States early in 1916, Masefield was repeatedly questioned about the campaign and he met with much criticism of the manner in which it had been conducted. In the first two paragraphs of *Gallipoli* he explains that this criticism and questioning have led him to write the book. His next words show why he was the right man to immortalize the Gallipoli venture.

when there was leisure, I began to consider the Dardanelles Campaign, not as a tragedy, nor as a mistake, but as a great human effort, which came, more than once, very near to triumph, and failed, in the end, as many great deeds of arms have failed, from something which had nothing to do with arms nor with the men who bore them. That the effort failed is not against it; much that is most splendid in military history failed, many great things and noble men have failed.

In 1918, reviewing H. W. Nevinson's *The Dardanelles Campaign,* Masefield describes the undertaking as "the strangest, most difficult, and most heroic effort ever made by the men of our race" and ". . . a failure (redeemed, like all other British failures, by courage and endurance)."[12]

In an earlier chapter Masefield's preoccupation with the glory of failure and with the beaten man who "becomes a story for ever" has been discussed. *Gallipoli,* then, is Masefield's kind of story, as *The Old Front Line* and *The Battle of the Somme* are not. In these later war books, there was no compelling need to vindicate defeat; victory lay ahead, and the soldier-historian wrote his chronicles of the Western Front gladly and conscientiously. But *Gallipoli* is the work of the poet of *Philip the King* and *Pompey the Great* and "The Wanderer," the poet of the loyal and the courageous and *The Faithful* in the face of disaster, who writes that "The meaning shows in the defeated thing."

Gallipoli is all the more remarkable, too, in that it is the work of a man who passionately hates war and who had spoken in *Multitude and Solitude* (1909) and *The Street of Today* (1911) as a pacifist. Roger Naldrett, who is frequently the writer's own voice in *Multitude and Solitude,* tells an army Major who has been recommending conscription and preparedness that war is a "wasteful curse" and the preparation for war "an even greater curse and . . . more wasteful." The transition from *Multitude and Solitude* to *Gallipoli* could not have been an easy one, but it was achieved with dignity and conviction. The Briton celebrated in *Gallipoli* is not the boastful John Bull in his pride of empire, but a Saint George, temporarily, at least, in deadly peril and defeat; the hero of *Gallipoli* is the common soldier—Englishman, Australian, New Zealander—dying on Chocolate Hill, or sailing away in defeat from Anzac Cove.

Gallipoli comprises a careful description of the Peninsula and its terrain, an exposition of the purpose and plan of the campaign, a detailed account of each phase of the campaign, and an explanation of the causes that made failure inevitable. At times the prose attains an epic beauty and dignity, and epic atmosphere is supplied by peculiarly appropriate chapter headings from *The Song of Roland*. One high point of the book is Masefield's description of the harbor of Mudros in the beauty of an Aegean spring and his picture of the British and French ships at anchor there, "more ships, perhaps, than any port of modern times has known." The poet writes of the sacrifices made by these men in leaving their homes to brave death or disfigurement in a far land, and of their courage and spirit as they "went like kings in a pageant to the imminent death."

As each ship crammed with soldiers drew near the battleships, the men swung their caps and cheered again, and the sailors answered, and the noise of cheering swelled, and the men in the ships not yet moving joined in, and the men ashore, till all the life in the harbour was giving thanks that it could go to death rejoicing. All was beautiful in that gladness of men about to die, but the moving thing was the greatness of their generous hearts. As they passed the French ships, the memory of old quarrels healed, and the sense of what sacred France had done and endured in this great war, and the pride of having such men as the French for comrades, rose up in their warm souls, and they cheered the French ships more, even, than their own. They left the harbour very, very slowly; this tumult of cheering lasted a long time; no one who heard it will ever forget it, or think of it unshaken. It broke the hearts of all there with pity and pride: it went beyond the guard of the English heart.

Masefield's glorification of the soldier at Gallipoli is a major theme throughout the book. It is particularly evident and moving in the analysis of the struggle against so many opposing forces— the difficulty of the terrain, the terrible climate of the peninsula, the fanatical courage of the Turk, the inability of the Russians to send promised military aid, and the failure of the home government to provide supplies, equipment, and reinforcements. Writing of the withdrawal from the Peninsula, Masefield says of these soldiers, "the very flower of the world's men," that they lost no honour in failing to take Gallipoli and "fought a battle such as has never been seen upon this earth."

Even so was wisdom proven blind,
So courage failed, so strength was chained;
Even so the gods, whose seeing mind
Is not as ours, ordained.

Between World Wars and the English Soldier in World War II

After the First World War Masefield did not brood on its horrors or concern himself in his writing with the problems of the postwar years. Much of his work in the 1920s and 1930s might indicate an attempt at "escape" from these problems. The decade and a half following the end of the war produced, for instance, a number of novels of adventure and the sea, such as *Sard Harker* (1924), *ODTAA* (1926), and *The Bird of Dawning* (1933); several poems and novels completely English in character, like *Reynard the Fox* (1919), *Right Royal* (1920), and *The Hawbucks* (1929); poetic retellings of the Arthurian and Trojan stories, such as *Tristan and Isolt* (1927), *Midsummer Night* (1929), and *A Tale of Troy* (1932); and a series of dramas on events in the life of Christ, including *The Trial of Jesus* (1925), and *The Coming of Christ* (1928).

Masefield was severely criticized by a number of critics and reviewers during the first years after World War I for turning away from the war instead of continuing to chronicle its great events. *Reynard the Fox* received much praise but was a disappointment to those who expected another *Gallipoli.* One reviewer, Geddes Smith, in the *New Republic,* even attempted to prove that *Reynard* had been written before 1914 and was not a reaction against the war. Among his reasons for so dating the poem were the facts that Masefield's huntsmen knew nothing of Flanders and Picardy and that the only representatives of English arms were veterans of South Africa and the Afghan border.[13] The reviewer seems to ignore the possibility that a poet could write a poem in 1919 and give it a 1913 setting. Another reason cited was a passage in Part One of *Reynard,* of which the critic writes:

Could an English poet today speak coolly of

Songs made before the German King
Made England German in her mind?[14]

That casual deprecation of the Hanoverians would have been natural enough nine or ten years ago; it is out of character today.

Other critics of those years find *Reynard the Fox* "passionately English," something finer born out of the war. Gertrude Campbell, defending Masefield's postwar work in 1921, asks why one should expect him to concern himself exclusively with his own times. She cites Shakespeare's neglect of the momentous events of his day and the fact that England's Napoleonic Wars waited a century for their immortalization by an English poet in *The Dynasts*. *Gallipoli,* then, is not the prelude to an even greater war work; it is "an unprecedented record in itself, such as we have of no other great movement since the March of the Ten Thousand."[15]

Not until the outbreak of the Second World War did the poet, now the Poet Laureate, again show his concern for the soldier and for the nation in peril. The Masefield war books of the 1939–1945 conflict are fewer in number than those of 1914–1918, and slighter than *Gallipoli* and "August, 1914." They include a slim volume called *Some Verses to Some Germans* (1939); *The Nine Days Wonder* (1941), a prose account, with several poems, of the evacuation at Dunquerque; and *A Generation Risen* (1942), a book comprising twenty-four poems by Masefield and forty-three pictures by his collaborator in *The Country Scene* (1937) and *Tribute to Ballet* (1938), Edward Seago. After 1942 Masefield's work does not concern the war.

In 1942 his only son, Lewis, was killed in action. One may conjecture on the influence this tragedy may have had on the father's writing. By 1947, however, Masefield had written a long and tender introduction for the posthumous publication of his son's second novel, *The Passion Left Behind*.[16]

Some Verses to Some Germans recalls the English love for Beethoven, who said, "God bless the English," with his dying breath. It recalls the German love for Shakespeare, whom the poet has heard Germans call "Unser Shakespeare." In 1939 Germany and England are at war; the end of the poem, recalling the words of the dying Goethe a century before, calls upon the two nations to make a fresh start after the horror of this second war.

The Nine Days Wonder is a lesser *Gallipoli*. As careful and detailed as its World War I predecessors, this book comprises a presentation of the events leading up to the Dunquerque evacuation, a description of the port, and a day-by-day account of the Operation Dynamo itself. Unlike the Dardanelles campaign, the Dunquerque operation was a success, although it was a withdrawal made necessary by a great defeat.

Once again Masefield is thrilled with admiration for the exploits of British seamen and landsmen, and for his nation's response in a critical situation. In summary of this action, in which 316,663 British and French troops were evacuated from the Dunquerque trap by an armada consisting of every sort of military and private craft, from tiny boats to mighty warships, Masefield describes the operation as "the greatest thing this nation has ever done." This is high praise from the student of British naval chronicles and the historian of Gallipoli and the Somme.

In *The Nine Days Wonder* the reader will find the same concern for the common soldier that is evident in *Gallipoli* and other Masefield war books. The actual word of the ordinary soldier is again quoted; instances of the nobility and patience of the men are given, as told by participants. Masefield is as proud of the cooperation of "seamen" and "landsmen" as he was in *Gallipoli* in quoting the remark of General Sir Ian Hamilton, "The navy was our father and our mother." For the first time, in this book, the poet praises in verse a relatively new kind of English soldier, the airman, a "smiling, sunburned youth who rode the sky," addressed movingly in an appendix to *The Nine Days Wonder*.

Other poems in the Dunquerque chronicle celebrate the seamen and the footsoldiers who "slogged the Flanders plain to Belgium's aid/ Or stood at Cassel with the grand Brigade." Perhaps the best poem in *The Nine Days Wonder* is an untitled six-stanza poem at the beginning of the book. It records the retreat of the British troops, overland to Dunquerque, "Forever facing front to the attack/ Across the English bones."

> Westward they went, past Wipers, past the old
> Fields bought and paid for by their brother's blood,
> Their feet were in the snapping of the flood
> That sped to gulf them down.

They were as bridegrooms plighted to the mould
Those marching men with neither hope nor star,
The foeman in the gateways as a bar,
The sea beyond to drown.

And at the very sea, a cloud of night,
A hail of death and allies in collapse,
A foe in the perfection of his traps,
A certainty of doom.

When, lo, out of the darkness, there was light,
There in the sea were England and her ships,
They sailed with the free salt upon their lips
To sunlight from the tomb.

In the last paragraph of the book, its similarity to *Gallipoli* in inspiration and dedication becomes most evident. The desperate situation is again summarized, and the British response is praised.

Our Army did not save Belgium; that is a little matter compared with the great matter, that it tried to. In the effort, it lost thirty thousand men, all its transport, all its guns, all its illusions; it never lost its heart.

The Nation said to those men, in effect: "Hold on; we will get you away." They held on, and we got them away.

It is hard to think of those dark formations on the sand, waiting in the rain of death, without the knowledge, that Hope and Help are stronger things than death. Hope and Help came together in their power into the minds of thousands of simple men, who went out in the Operation Dynamo and plucked them from ruin.

In the introduction to *A Generation Risen,* Masefield discusses the importance of records of the scenes and events of wars. His interest in recording them for later generations is obvious from the list of his war books; in *A Generation Risen* he contributes to a record of a different sort from *Gallipoli, The Battle of the Somme,* and *The Nine Days Wonder.*

The book does not attempt a presentation of major figures and events from the 1939–1945 conflict. Instead, as a "tribute to

some of the young people who have come forward to save the
nation in her danger," and "to do dull, dangerous and responsible
work in the midst of mess and dismay," it presents typical English
servicemen in their ordinary wartime activities. Once again, as in
Tribute to Ballet, and *The Country Scene,* the pictures of Edward
Seago and the poems of John Masefield are a happy combination.

The first five poems and their drawings are portraits of men
waiting in railway stations for transportation to the training ground
or the front. The poet recalls past crowds in the same stations,
including one mustered there twenty-five years before, "Full many
a thousand taking train to death." Lovers part, and in one page
are the poem and the drawing of "A Woman and Her Son,"
spending together the last moments before parting. Subsequent
pages are devoted to tank crews and to the sentries who watch
and wonder, "as in other years in other wars." There are several
portraits of airmen, pilots, and ground crews and their love for
their ships; it is this devotion to the care of their charges that
particularly pleases the poet.

The tributes to ships and sailors have already been discussed
in chapter 6. In all these poems it is the common man who is
Masefield's subject. Several poems praise the civilian workers of
England, and several others describe servicemen in their hours
of recreation. Seago's studies of Dame Myra Hess are accompanied by two brief poems addressed to the pianist in whose
concerts Masefield's own soldier-son, during his free hours in
wartime, used to find "one sweet and civilized thing in a world
collapsing and smashing into devilry and anarchy."[17]

Throughout much of Masefield's war work runs a current of
optimism and faith in the future. This is particularly evident in
the 1918 American speeches, *Some Verses to Some Germans,* the
introduction to *A Generation Risen,* and the closing poems of
The Nine Days Wonder. In this peace time to come, the poet's
hope for the future rests on the young English soldier of the
present.

> In our history, our young have done remarkable things.
> When we sent a squadron round the Horn, in the winter,
> manned mainly by pensioners, the one surviving ship with two
> hundred young but sorely-tried men did what was hoped. On

the rising ground of Waterloo, a lot of very young men stood a severe strain, and debated at the end of it (some of them), whether they had been beaten or not. Our young in this war have stood strains as grim or grimmer. Later it will fall to them to remake the England they have saved. If they will keep themselves still like the dauntless inspired chicks they are, our sign will again become the Rose.[18]

Notes to Chapter 7

1. Rudyard Kipling, "Recessional" (1897).

2. "St. George and the Dragon," *The War and the Future* (New York: The Macmillan Co., 1918), p. 10.

3. Louise T. Nicholl, *John Masefield: English Poet,* 6: 19.

4. Arthur Stringer, *Red Wine of Youth* (New York: The Bobbs Merrill Co., 1948), p. 228.

5. If Masefield's 72 letters written to his wife from France in 1917 are published, they should provide a graphic account of his time on this front; the letters are in the collection established by Dr. Corliss Lamont at Columbia University (see *Columbia Library Columns* [Nov. 1970], p. 38).

6. For this opinion, see Newman I. White, "John Masefield, An Estimate," *South Atlantic Quarterly* (April 1927), p. 190; and Gerald Gould, "The Great Book of the War," *Bookman* (June 1925).

7. Louise T. Nicholl, *John Masefield: English Poet,* 6: 2, 3.

8. *Harper's Monthly Magazine* (May 1917), pp. 801–10; *The Nation* (June 16, 1917).

9. "The Common Task," *Yale Alumni Weekly* 27 (July 5, 1918); *The War and the Future.*

10. See Robert Bridges' poem from *October and Other Poems* of the mother who looks into Masefield's *The Old Front Line.*

11. For this friendship, see Arthur Stringer, *Red Wine of Youth,* pp. 18, 21, 118, 120, 126–128, 130, 146, 154, 157, 170, 186, 212, 227–28, 247, 267.

12. "The Most Heroic Effort," *Manchester Guardian* (Nov. 14, 1918).

13. "Reynard the Fox," *New Republic* (Jan. 7, 1920), pp. 174–75.

14. *Reynard the Fox* (New York: The Macmillan Co., 1919), pp. 26–27.

15. "John Masefield of the Present Day," *Bookman* (Jan. 1921), p. 445.

16. Lewis Crommelin Masefield's first novel was *Cross Double Cross*, London, 1936.

17. John Masefield in introduction to Lewis Masefield's *The Passion Left Behind* (London: Faber and Faber, 1947), p. 18.

18. Introduction to *A Generation Risen* (London: Collins, 1943), p. 7.

8
The Laureateship

The English Poet Laureateship and the 1930 Appointment

The English Poet Laureateship has had a varied history and reputation.[1] Its first officially announced incumbent was John Dryden, who was appointed Poet Laureate in 1670 and became an officer of the Royal Household. Many of the succeeding laureates were men of little literary distinction who have been largely forgotten, or are remembered only with ridicule: Shadwell, Tate, Rowe, Eusden, Cibber, Whitehead, Warton, and Pye. With Robert Southey's appointment in 1813, the laureateship assumed more dignity. In Southey's time the obligatory composition of odes in celebration of royal occasions was abandoned, and recent laureates have been free from any compulsion to write. Sir Robert Peel, for example, assured Wordsworth in 1843, "I will undertake that you shall have nothing required from you."[2] Since the time of Southey, the appointment has been regarded as a recognition of poetic distinction, and Wordsworth, Tennyson, Bridges, Masefield, and more recently, Cecil Day Lewis, have brought honor to the post. Among nineteenth- and twentieth-century laureates, only Alfred Austin has failed to win general critical approval, and Wordsworth, Tennyson, and Masefield have had large popular followings.

When Bridges died in 1930, there was no poet whose selection

205

could have won unanimous approval. Binyon, Chesterton, Davies, Gibson, Housman, Kipling, de la Mare, Masefield, Newbolt, Noyes, Watson, Yeats, and others all had their supporters. The Prime Minister, Ramsay Macdonald, would have recommended the appointment of a Scot, W. H. Hamilton believes, "had there been one of adequate fame and power available."[3] The Prime Minister was also the leader of the Labour Party.

On May 9, 1930, John Masefield accepted the appointment to the Poet Laureateship. His remarks in an interview soon after the announcement are characteristic of his modesty:

> I am very happy. It is delightful to receive any honour, particularly a splendid honour of this sort. My only regret is that Dr. Bridges had not lived for another ten or fifteen years. I knew him very well, and I was fond of him and his work. Dr. Bridges was so splendid a man that we thought he might well have lived to be a centenarian.

The new laureate at once asserted that he had no intention of grinding out poems to suit any occasion and revealed his attitude toward "occasional" verse. "I do not think," he said, "that any man can really write unless he is deeply stirred."[4] However, Masefield has been very generous in his celebration of state occasions and important national events and anniversaries. The London *Times* records[5] the publication in its pages, between 1934 and 1950 only, of twenty-two such poems, but none before 1934. There have been later laureate verses and, in addition to these, such poems published in various Masefield books since 1930 as *Some Verses to Some Germans* (1939), *The Land Workers* (1942), "Westminster Hall" (1936),[6] and the poems of *A Generation Risen* (1943) and *The Nine Days Wonder* (1941), fitting expressions of a national poet, if not written purely in virtue and exercise of his office. It is likely that of the Poets Laureate Masefield has been, after Tennyson, the happiest combination of a good poet and a good laureate.

Reaction to Masefield's appointment in England was divided, but in America it was almost uniformly favorable. Masefield's lecture tours of the United States during the First World War and his earlier years of working in New York City and Yonkers, combined with the vigorous narrative style of much of his work, had won him many American friends.

The Canadian Forum, after some frivolous comment on Macdonald's failure to appoint a Scot, called Masefield "a wonderfully fitting choice" politically because he "touches the great British electorate at so many points."[7] *The Forum* also called attention to Masefield's popularity in the United States, suggesting that "an intelligent American public" will "genuinely appreciate" his appointment. *The Outlook, The Nation,*[8] and *The Publisher's Weekly* spoke their approval, and the last named added:

> The English laureate is not required to write poems of occasion as was once the case, but there are scores of Mr. Masefield's poems that so truly interpret the fine spirit of England and English life and the England on the sea that they may take their place as an appropriate part of any public function or anniversary.[9]

Katherine Bregy in *The Catholic World* praised Masefield as equipped for a laureateship not only of England but of "our struggling modern age," and as having a universal appeal in his "compassion."[10]

Winfred Ernest Garrison in *The Christian Century* saw in the appointment of Masefield the coming of a laureate who "will be the poet of the English people as he sees them and knows them, not the poet of the royal family and the army and navy." He further interpreted the appointment as indicative of an important change in England.

> . . . the fact that such a poet has been made . . . the official lyric spokesman for the nation, is a more important fact about England and its government than about Mr. Masefield. . . . In bestowing the laurel upon Masefield, England may be understood to say that she is prepared to listen to medicinal truths about herself and to grant a hearing to the inarticulate masses who, having for the most part no adequate voice, have found in him a messenger to the ears of the world.[11]

In *Arts and Decoration* Burton Rascoe wondered at the surprise in some quarters over Masefield's selection. Dismissing Noyes as a Tory unacceptable to a Labour Government and Kipling as an out-of-style imperialist, Rascoe found Masefield the "one choice . . . who is popular enough, who has fame enough, and who has genius enough to hold the honor. . . ."[12]

One apparently dissenting American voice was that of Odell Shepard, who wrote of Wordsworth, Tennyson, and Bridges, three poets who had "dignified the laureateship" and who had not been democratic in their sympathies. He then proceeded to censure the new laureate for many failings: a journalistic knack of pleasing the public; unoriginal early work; the false realism of his narrative poems; the childishness of his creed, "best trust the happy moments"; his lack of self-criticism; his tendency to over-idealize women; and his failure to reach more often the height of his best work in *William Shakespeare,* "August 1914," *The Faithful,* and "The Hounds of Hell."[13]

The *Saturday Review of Literature* was not over-enthusiastic. Its leading article began:

> It was not who was to be made Poet Laureate of England that was the real problem. Since John Masefield is the man, we shall remember his "Everlasting Mercy" and his "August 1914," surely the best poem in England inspired by the war, and we shall forget his rather dull variations on the Arthurian theme, and hope that, like Robert Bridges, he will stretch his eagle wings again, and soar out of middle age into another flight.[14]

The New York *Times*'s attitude was more typical of the American reaction. Its news report stated that the appointment "was acclaimed everywhere in England" and that Masefield was "hailed as the most intensely English poet who could have been chosen." In the same issue an editorial began with the statement that "The Lancashire (*sic*) lad, the sailor, the New York bar-boy, has become the official successor to Dryden and Tennyson." Here, continued the *Times,* was a life story "of the kind supposed to be peculiar to American soil." The editorial commended the Labor Government of England for choosing "the most gifted and sympathetic poet of daily toil" and for making a selection certain to be greeted "throughout Great Britain and the Empire . . . as worthy and in tune with the mood of the times." "When he writes as Laureate," the editorial concluded, "the world will listen gratefully."[15]

In England Masefield's frequent parodist J. C. Squire censured the appointment in *The London Mercury* as one made "in a very great hurry." He attacked the "penny press for its exploitation of Masefield's past as "good, democratic copy" and attacked Masefield's recent work. His statement concluded that the new Poet Laureate was "on trial."[16] Most of Masefield's English contemporaries, however, received the news with approval. A. E. Housman wrote to his brother Laurence:

> No, I was not given the chance of being Laureate. I thought Masefield the right choice, as all the other good poets are too obviously unsuited for the official duties.[17]

Housman's congratulatory letter to Masefield was a characteristic blend of brevity, common sense, and wit. George Bernard Shaw remarked, "The King could not have appointed a better man," while John Galsworthy said, "It is the greatest delight to me to hear that he has been appointed." John Drinkwater commented: "I don't think a better appointment could have been made. I think he is just the man for the post." G. K. Chesterton's comment was characteristic:

> He is an extremely fine poet and I am very glad to hear that he has been appointed. I hope that he will go on writing poems about the drunkenness of pirates.[18]

The New York *Times* reported that Edith Sitwell "said she was convinced that Mr. Masefield would make an admirable poet laureate."[19] J. B. Priestly commented that Masefield's selection was "not a bad appointment," although he considered Kipling more "popular" and Yeats and Housman more "distinguished." Priestly did, however, praise *Reynard the Fox* as a "genuine slice of this island."[20]

Although the appointment surprised many, it had long been anticipated in some quarters. As early as 1912 a *Literary Digest* article had quoted a *New York Sun* writer as commenting on Masefield's acceptability to both English political parties.

His gift of sympathy for the lowly, his perfect understanding of the toiler, make him persona grata with the friends of labor. Conservatives can not suspect him as they do Shaw, Wells, and Galsworthy of encouraging dark schemes for the reshaping of present society. Masefield goes along taking snapshots, but drawing no conclusions.[21]

Shortly before the appointment the *London Daily Mail* had suggested that the Prime Minister was "not likely to find a more suitable candidate than Mr. John Masefield"[22] and had gone on to cite his qualifications.

In conferring honorary degrees upon Masefield in 1922, Oxford and Aberdeen Universities anticipated the poet's official recognition as a national bard. His citation at the Oxford exercises lauded his portrayal of English country life and sports.[23] At the University of Aberdeen, Professor Mackenzie Stuart praised Masefield as "a writer who has expressed for us all that love of the English earth which is part of the national consciousness" and stated that on that "side alone, without reference to his lyrical or meditative achievements, he has already amply earned the title of a national poet."[24]

During the year of his appointment to the laureateship, Masefield produced *The Wanderer of Liverpool,* the culmination of his long interest in the beautiful but ill-fated ship that he had first seen in his early days aboard the *Conway.* Copies of this book, illustrated by Masefield himself, were presented to the King and members of the Royal family shortly after the appointment and before the appearance of the regular editions. Masefield continued to write of sea, ship, and sailor in the novels *The Bird of Dawning* (1933), *The Taking of the Gry* (1934), and *Victorious Troy* (1935), in a foreword to the exhibit catalogue of Claude Muncaster's marine drawings,[25] and in a few of the poems in the *Minnie Maylow's Story* (1931), *A Letter from Pontus* (1936), *On the Hill* (1949), *The Bluebells* (1961), and *Old Raiger* (1965) collections.

Masefield's first complete volume of verse after 1930 was *Minnie Maylow's Story and Other Tales and Scenes.* Ten of its thirteen poems are on English subjects, as the laureate turned again to Chaucer, to Arthurian legend, to the bravery of the English seaman and the English countryman, for his subject matter. Others of the poems reveal the writer's continuing interest in various periods of English history.

When, in *A Tale of Troy* in 1932, Masefield left the English scene, Louise Bogan expressed concern in *Poetry*[26] lest the laureateship turn him away, paradoxically, from those things closest to him. She advised him to return from Troy to England. The work of the following years includes little that is not English in subject. Only the two Byzantine novels, *Basilissa* (1940) and *Conquer* (1941), the African scenes in *Live and Kicking Ned* (1939), the Harvard University Tercentenary *Lines* (1936), and *In the Mill* (1941) are exceptions to the rule, and Englishmen and English influences appear in all these except *Conquer* and *Basilissa*. The laureateship seems to have caused little or no change in Masefield's preoccupation with England. It is likely that he would have written *Chaucer* (1931), *End and Beginning* (1934), *The Square Peg* (1937), *The Country Scene* (1937), *The Nine Days' Wonder* (1941), and their companion volumes even if he had not been named official bard of England.

After 1934 Masefield began to celebrate significant occasions in laureate verse. Some of these productions, such as "Westminster Hall,"[27] the Second World War poems,[28] and *A Play of St. George* (1948), were published in book form, as were the *Lines on the Tercentenary of Harvard University* which, as England's Poet Laureate and a 1918 honorary graduate of Harvard, he read at the American university's 1936 Commencement. *A Play of St. George* was written to celebrate the 600th anniversary of the founding of the Order of the Garter in April 1948, and is a new version of the old story of England's patron saint and the dragon.

Critical reaction to Masefield's work since 1930 has been varied. The chief trend seems to have been toward neither increased appreciation of his work nor increased censure of it, but rather toward a neglect of it. [29] In general, a survey of reviews in the 1930s reveals that the most favorably received books of that decade were the novels *Bird of Dawning, Victorious Troy,* and *Dead Ned;* least favorably received were the novel *The Square Peg* and the verse collection *A Tale of Troy*. A 1953 *Collected Poems* elicited favorable comment, especially from poet I. L. Salomon, who anticipated the thesis of this book in his statement that "what has absorbed John Masefield in his lifetime has been

England's heritage in song, legend, myth."[30] Later tributes include a *Times Literary Supplement* reference in 1966 to *Grace Before Ploughing* as a "rare and enchanting achievement," comments in prose and poetry by G. Wilson Knight and William Vincent Sieller in the Handley-Taylor bibliography-tribute of 1960, and the address of Robert Graves at Masefield's memorial service in Westminster Abbey in 1967.[31]

The Laureate Verse

Most of the poems written by Masefield in exercise of his official position have not been reprinted in subsequent volumes of his verse. It may be that he did not consider them worthy of inclusion among the poems that he wished preserved. Perhaps he even agreed with *Time* magazine's statement that

> From *On the Hill* . . . the laureate's publishers have mercifully excluded the author's dutiful little odes to George VI, Franklin Roosevelt, Princess Elizabeth and young Prince Charles of Edinburgh.[32]

Indeed, *Time* reported him as having once admitted that "the office of Poet Laureate is responsible for much of the world's worst literature."

With the exception, perhaps, of "Land Workers," Masefield's laureate verse offers little that will enhance his reputation. That poem, with its pictures of the English countryside and the wartime workers on the land and its final affirmation of faith in an England far different from that of his childhood, was separately published, although in paper wrappers, not in book form.[33]

A characteristic but not complete list of laureate poems not reprinted in book form falls into several categories. A number of them celebrate royal anniversaries, births, deaths, or visits, such as an untitled "prayer" of twelve lines in commemoration of the King's Silver Jubilee (1935);[34] an untitled poem of sixteen lines on the unveiling of a memorial to Queen Alexandra in London;[35] an untitled sonnet on the death of King George V (1936);[36] "On the Passing of King George V," twelve lines (1936);[37] "A Prayer for the King's Reign," twenty lines (1937);[38] an untitled

sonnet for Liverpool's Coronation ceremonies (1937);[39] six lines
"To His Most Excellent Majesty the King Upon the Sailing of
the Royal Family for South Africa" (1947);[40] eight lines "To
His Most Excellent Majesty the King Upon His Return from
South Africa" (1947);[41] twenty "Lines on the Occasion of the
Wedding of Her Royal Highness the Princess Elizabeth" (1947);[42]
twenty "Lines on the Occasion of the Silver Wedding of Our King
and Queen" (1948);[43] "A Hope for the Newly Born," four lines
on the birth of Prince Charles (1948);[44] "The Poet Laureate to
His Cathedral Church, Liverpool Cathedral," eight lines at the
time of the visit of Princess Elizabeth to Liverpool (1949);[45]
twenty-three lines "On the Coronation of Our Gracious Sovereign"
(1953);[46] "The Virginian Adventure," a sonnet on the visit of
Queen Elizabeth II to Jamestown (1957);[47] and "On the Prayers
for Our Princess' Happiness," eleven lines on the wedding of
Princess Margaret (1960).[48]

Several other poems comment on events of public significance,
for example, "534," twenty-eight lines on the launching of the
"534" or "Queen Mary" (1934);[49] "The New Figurehead,"
eighteen lines on the unveiling of the Nelson figurehead on the
Cadet School Ship *Conway* (1938);[50] "Neville Chamberlain," four
lines on the occasion of Chamberlain's mission to Hitler (1938);[51]
"Men of the Royal Navy," eight lines for the Trafalgar Day
celebration (1943);[52] "A Moment Comes," a sonnet on the end of
World War II in Europe (1945);[53] twenty-four untitled lines for
the St. Cecilia's Festival of the Benevolent Musicians' Fund
(1946);[54] a twelve-line "prologue" for a rally of the London
Savings Drive (1946);[55] "A Word of Hope," twelve lines com-
memorating the meeting at Oxford of Girl Guides and Girl Scouts
from all over the world (1950);[56] and a sonnet, "Lines for the
Fourth Centenary of William Shakespeare," (1964).[57]

Some of the poems pay tribute to figures of significance in the
modern world of arts and letters, like the two lines, "To Rudyard
Kipling" (1936);[58] a twelve-line commemorative ode for the
birthday of Sir Henry Wood (1944);[59] twenty lines "On the
Ninetieth Birthday of Bernard Shaw" (1946);[60] seventy-four
"Lines for a One Hundredth Birthday: George Bernard Shaw"
(1956);[61] twenty-eight "Lines written in the Memory of Margaret
Babington, A Friend of Canterbury Cathedral who died on

August the 22nd, 1958";[62] thirty-six "Lines for the 25th January, 1959, being the 200th Anniversary of the Birth of Robert Burns";[63] eight Housman-like lines, "In Memory of Alfred Edward Housman, Born March 26, 1859," published on March 26, 1959;[64] and eight lines entitled "East Coker," for T. S. Eliot's burial (1965).[65]

At other times tribute has been paid to men and states outside the British Isles, as in "Melbourne," a sonnet on the centenary of the first settlement in Victoria (1934);[66] fourteen lines "To the Australians Coming to Help Us" (1940);[67] an untitled twelve-line tribute to the Red Army on its twenty-sixth anniversary (1944);[68] twelve untitled lines for United Nations Day (1944);[69] and "Franklin Delano Roosevelt," eight lines on the unveiling of his memorial in Grosvenor Square (1948).[70]

These occasional verses are often nobly conceived and gracefully executed, but like most occasional verse they generally bear the unmistakable stamp of the duty done and the deadline met.

Masefield's Extra-ordinary Activity as Poet Laureate

Most of the published comment on Masefield's appointment to the Poet Laureateship in 1930 comprised estimates of his fitness for the post, evaluations of his achievements as poet and prose writer, and reviews of the history of the laureateship. *The Canadian Forum,* however, looked ahead and prophesied for Masefield an incumbency different from that of Austin and of Bridges.

> it would seem that Masefield can do more for poetry at large than any other man in our time. The Laureateship since Tennyson has been a nominal office only; it has done nothing for national poetry in the better sense of the word. Neither Alfred Austin nor Robert Bridges quickened the nation to poetry and the nation needs quickening; poetry could not mean much less to the great majority of men than it does at this moment. The tide is at the ebb. It is for Masefield to turn it and start it flowing back again. And he can do it.[71]

The *Forum* then proceeded to cite Masefield's qualifications for active service as Poet Laureate, his comparative youth, his vigor and enthusiasm, his understanding of "the great British electorate."

Masefield amply justified the confidence of the *Forum* writer. Not only did he fulfill the ordinary functions of the Poet Laureate, but he was active in many related fields of endeavor. As president of the National Book Council, later the National Book League, "a non-profit-making body founded for the promotion of book reading and the wider distribution of books," he took a leading part in the League's work. The American publisher Frederic G. Melcher, after visits to the Laureate and to the League, reported at some length Masefield's activity:

> That John Masefield should have a deep hold on the people of his own country would be inevitable but that he would use his great influence as poet and as poet laureate to stir up all over the country a deeper interest in books and reading was not inevitable. It is the spirit of the man that does this. . . . All good movements to stir and deepen reading interests of all the people John Masefield supports: the school reading programs, children's book weeks, oral reading in chorus. . . . We doubt if England ever had a poet laureate who has found a way to serve his country, especially its younger generation, by being a living symbol of the power and authority of great books.[72]

Melcher mentions Robert Frost, through his lecture tours and his teaching in American colleges and universities, as a comparable force in the United States.

Beginning in 1938 Masefield served for many years as a devoted and active president of the Society of Authors, a position held, since the Society's founding, only by Lord Tennyson, Meredith, Hardy, and Sir James Barrie. The Secretary-General of the Society in a 1951 statement praised Masefield's service to the organization and his devotion "to the cause of authorship."[73]

Two favorite interests of Masefield were the encouragement of the speaking of verse and the development of amateur theaters[74] and theatrical companies for the production of verse plays. He tells us in the Preface to the 1935 *Complete Poems* that he became "absorbingly and burningly interested in the speaking of verse" when a judge of verse-speaking at the Edinburgh Musical Festival in 1922. The following year he and Mrs. Masefield started the Oxford Recitations, contests in verse-speaking,[75] and for several years the festival was repeated. In 1924 Masefield returned

to Edinburgh as President of the Scottish Association for the
Speaking of Verse and delivered the address later published under
the title, *With the Living Voice* (1925). He records the history of
the Oxford Recitations in a preface to a collection of plays and
poems written for the 1928 festival by Laurence Binyon, Gordon
Bottomley, and himself.[76]

In the 1935 Preface Masefield writes entertainingly of the
amateur theater at Boar's Hill, which he established in the first
years after World War I and which became for several years
a major interest in his life. The theater[77] erected in the garden of
Masefield's Boar's Hill house had "a small stage on two levels
with a balcony above it at the back." Gilbert Thomas calls the
building a visible token of Masefield's failure as "a dramatist for
the commercial theatre" as well as of his indifference to commercial success and his "undaunted passion for his own dramatic
ideals."[78]

Dedications and notes in many of Masefield's books published
between 1922 and 1934 reveal that much of his writing was done
with the amateur theatrical companies and the speakers of verse
in mind.[79] Of *Berenice* he writes that the play was "translated for
the use of the Hill Players" and produced by them on Nov. 24,
1921. The cast included the playwright's daughter Judith, then
sixteen years old, who designed and made costumes and scenery
for the plays and acted in them, as well as illustrating her father's
books, *The Dream* (1922) and *The Box of Delights* (1935).

A King's Daughter (1923) was produced, before publication,
at the "Oxford Playhouse by the Hill Players," while *The Trial
of Jesus* (1925) was presented in the "Music Room, Boar's
Hill," both casts including Judith. The American edition of *Easter*
has a note that "Easter: A Play for Singers" was set to music
and was to be sung in Oxford in the spring of 1929. At the beginning of *Minnie Maylow's Story and Other Tales and Scenes*
(1931), Masefield thanks and names the "beautiful speakers
who, in the speaking of these tales and scenes, have deeply delighted me," while *A Tale of Troy* has a similar statement of
gratitude for the seven speakers "who first told this tale on Midsummer Night, 1932."

Several times the Poet Laureate participated in radio broad-
casts; on one occasion, "the first overseas broadcast ever made

by a poet," when he discussed a definition of poetry and read "Sea-Fever" and others of his poems; on another, in 1935, when he read his ode on the Silver Jubilee of King George.[80]

Masefield was generous to students and to the servicemen of his own country and of allied nations. American soldiers brought back with them memories of the white-haired poet laureate, "young in thought and action, graceful, brimful of charm and personality," who visited them in hospitals and camps. One American, recalling that Masefield's recital of his poems to a group of "about one hundred unwilling soldiers" quickly dispelled their apathy and was more effective than "hypnosis or an all-girl show," concluded "I thought that he was wonderful and so did everyone else in the mess hall that night."[81]

This is real service rendered to his art by a Poet Laureate. Over a period of years Masefield generously gave his time to Oxford undergraduates; on Sunday afternoons he would entertain them "with that kindness and old-world courtesy" which he extended alike to his "most distinguished guests and to the postman or the baker's boy."[82] The first pages of *A Macbeth Production* (1945) record the visit of a group of young men, ex-students and ex-soldiers, in search of advice on the starting of an amateur theater group; out of that visit and Masefield's serious consideration of the problem grew the book.

This was a new kind of Poet Laureate, one whose service to England and to the poetic art went beyond a selfish preoccupation with his work or a willingness to write appropriate odes for state occasions.

Masefield and His Country's Future

As England's Poet Laureate Masefield did not limit himself to the praising of her past glories or the consideration of topical events. He had long been concerned with his country's future. Frequently he lauded the former times when the arts were "a part of the national life"[83] in contrast to present days in which they are neglected and even scorned. He was not, however, a typical *laudator temporis acti se puero,* for he admitted that in many ways the present enjoys advantages denied to the past. Yet his chief concern was for the future, when England will live like Pavilastukay, the ideal city of the past that is the subject of one of his narrative poems (1942).

> I have a star for when the storm abates
> A cock that crows against the coming day
> England shall live like Pavilastukay.

In an introduction written for an anthology of Public School Verse in 1920, the poet recalls England's achievements in the past, her "great body of most delicate, tender, truthful and humorous art, that will answer for us when the nations are weighed." Calling a roll of English artists and achievements that includes Purcell, Turner, Gainsborough, Chaucer, Shakespeare, Wordsworth, Dickens, Trollope, and the China Clippers, he finds them products not of a "dull race, but of a race with delicate, profound capacities for lovely and ordered thinking." Masefield goes on to speak of a recent tendency "to think and speak slightingly of the arts and artists," a habit of doubtful origin against which powerful agents, including the schools, are working in what the poet believes to be a sort of postwar artistic revival.

Similarly, in his 1921 Foundation Day Address at the Bembridge School, he urges the boys to "bring back to this country so many of the glories that once belonged to this country and have been forgotten for so many less worthy things." In the 1920 anniversary essay on Ruskin, Masefield identifies these "less worthy things" and this antagonism toward the arts with the symbol of John Bull, "that image of grossness and obstruction, . . . who came to us with the German Kings."

> I have seen many images of John Bull, but none showing him as a person who would think, or pray, or be courteous, or chivalrous, or merciful, or practice any art, or sing, or be delightful, or make love, or do a decent day's work, or have an enlightened idea, or be tolerable company under any circumstances whatsoever. He is always a gross animal man, standing in the way.[84]

Ruskin is in Masefield's eyes a crusader for St. George, a warrior against " 'the blunt hand' marring the divine vision—John Bull waddling into the place of St. George."

It is such a crusade that Masefield began long before his appointment to the Laureateship and continued with even greater fervor in the years after 1930. One of his most eloquent appeals is in the four sonnets that appear at the beginning of E. Gordon Craig's book, *Scene* (1923). The sequence begins with a statement of England's achievement under the banner of her patron saint.

> Once we were masters of the arts of men.
>   Poetry, music, painting, building, all
> Beautiful noble arts were ours then,
>   Decking this England as for festival.
>
> A son of England could not lift his head
>   Then without knowing rapture of delight.
> The English hedgerow rose of beauty shed
>   Into all English hearts its red and white.
>
> Our current coins bore then the sacred stamp
>   Of style in the used thing. In the world's tower
> In space's darkness, England was a lamp.
>   Her lovely brain beheld, her hand had power
>
> In these two things alone, her spirit shows
> Her saint was then Saint George, her mark, a rose.

In every English village one may still find buildings, like the cathedrals, "Marvellous relics that an English hand/ Left as the tokens of an English mind." The third sonnet is a tribute to Shakespeare, and the fourth looks ahead to a better England after the darkness of the war years.[85] *Tribute to Ballet* (1938) includes an appeal to "The English Dancers" to participate in a revival of "that which has been" in a new England whose symbol will be not "a fat boor, whiskered and unwise" but "a St. George,/ Thrusting a trampled dragon through the gorge."

The coming of the Second World War intensified the Laureate's concern for the artistic future of his country. An American reporter, interviewing Masefield in 1940, found him hopeful, even in war time. He praised the work of the Board of Education in securing "a grant from the Pilgrim Trust for carrying music, pictorial art, and amateur drama to the industrial and munitions centers, where they are most needed." In the years of the blackout, reading increased, and Masefield believed that in time of war people both at home and in uniform were turning increasingly from "flimsy literature" to serious reading. War would probably retard the arts, Masefield felt, as in the years around 1918, but "this wartime care of the arts . . . will continue to grow through all the years to come."[86]

A Generation Risen (1943) includes Masefield's poem "Dame Myra Hess Playing to the Troops," in which are combined the evidence of wartime interest in art and a prophecy of the continuation of that interest in "the larger life," when "jackass and john bull are cast from us,/ And the Rose shines and we become a Nation." Here Masefield's scorn for the hated symbol of John Bull reaches its lowest depth: the names are not even capitalized, while the flower the poet associates with St. George as a loved symbol receives the distinction of a capital "R."

Among the poet's pleas for a new England are the closing lines of the autobiographical poem, *Wonderings* (1943), and the National Book Council lecture, *I Want! I Want!* (1944). The lecture, after a consideration of the damage done to the arts, and specifically of the loss of books, during the war, summarizes the poet's "wants" for the England of the future. He calls for attractive and well-stocked reading rooms, for places where the arts of the dance may flourish, for the establishment of theaters with theatrical workshops and libraries in all the universities, for increased study of the early history of Britain, for lovelier books and illustrations, and especially for the development of "a new art, not yet among us, but waiting to be brought to life." This new art is an art of story-telling that makes use of the related arts. England has all the requisite materials and skills for its development—her own stories and legends, speakers of verse and prose, musicians, dancers, mask-makers, "men with exquisite feeling for colour, . . . men with the power to coordinate lovely things." This "art of narrative not yet attempted" is a "new art of story-telling . . . so delightful that all will go to hear, and all come away exhausted, yet in brotherhood." In the following paragraphs Masefield further discusses his hopes and explains how they may be realized. The human will is the important thing: "You can have any kind of England you like, if you will it."

Wonderings is primarily a poem of recollection of the poet's childhood, a remembrance of things long past, but it closes with a plea for the future when "By England's children England is remade."

> And never think, that poets want the moon;
> They want an England better than the last,
> An England using to the full its skills,
> Not the dead England of our discontent
> Where life-long weariness just paid the rent
> And long dead custom set the dreary tune
> Forever thwarting the heroic wills
> And rivetting each daybreak to the past.
>
> Wake, for it sometimes happens that the change
> Must be profound as waking out of sleep
> At cockcrow from some rafter in the grange,
> When Spirit is unshackled and set free.
> Life is not milling dust in penny trade,
> But art to fashion or to be re-made,
> Such, that in every village there shall be
> Something that future men shall love to see;
> When mortals call, immortal thoughts invade.

This is the exhortation of England's poet to his country at the midpoint of the twentieth century, and this is the vision to which he consecrates her when destiny brings "a Saint George to loose the dragon's clutch," when "the storm abates," and England is a "valley with a million grass-blades blowing/ And a hill with clouds above it whither many larks are going/ Singing paeans as they climb."[87]

Notes to Chapter 8

1. See Edmund K. Broadus, *The Laureateship: A Study of the Office of Poet Laureate in England with some account of the Poets* (Oxford: Clarendon Press, 1921) (this account extends from the beginnings to Bridges).

2. *Ibid.*, "The Laureateship," *London Mercury* (June 1930), pp. 134–35.

3. Letter to Fraser Drew from the author of *John Masefield: A Critical Study* (1922), Feb. 23, 1951.

4. "Letters and the Arts," *Living Age* (June 15, 1930), p. 490.

5. Letter to Fraser Drew from J. M. B., Subscription Dept., *The Times* (London), Mar. 27, 1951.

6. *A Letter from Pontus and Other Verse* (London: William Heinemann, 1936).

7. Inconstant Reader, "Preferences," *Canadian Forum* (June 1930), pp. 328–29.

8. "The Trend of Events" (May 21, 1930), p. 95; "Editorial Paragraphs" (May 21, 1930), p. 587.

9. "The New Poet Laureate" (May 17, 1930), p. 2520.

10. "John Masefield" (June 1931), pp. 257–65.

11. "The New Poet Laureate" (May 28, 1930), pp. 688–89.

12. "Among the New Books" (July 1930), p. 47.

13. "John Masefield: Poet Laureate," *Bookman* (Aug. 1930), pp. 477–83.

14. *SRL* did, however, reprint in Masefield's honor on May 17, 1930, William Rose Benet's "O'Connor's Cafe," from *Moons of Grandeur*, p. 1044.

15. *New York Times*, May 10, 1930, pp. 9, 18.

16. "The New Laureate" and "An Uneven Writer," two subheadings under "Editorial Notes" (1930), pp. 100–101.

17. Letter dated May 12, 1930 in *My Brother, A. E. Housman* (New York: Charles Scribner's Sons, 1938), p. 183.

18. "Letters in the Arts," *Living Age* (June 15, 1930), p. 490.

19. *New York Times*, May 10, 1930, p. 9.

20. "A London Letter," *Saturday Review of Literature* (May 24, 1930), p. 1074.

21. "The Man of the Hour in English Letters" (Apr. 13, 1912), pp. 752–53, attributed to S. P. B. Mais by Charles H. Simmons, *A Bibliography of John Masefield* (New York: Columbia University Press, 1930), p. 147.

22. "A 'Rough-Cut Poet Laureate,'" *Literary Digest* (May 24, 1930), p. 20.

23. A. D. Godley, Honorary Fellow of Magdalen, Public Orator, Oxford University, June 28, 1922, when Masefield received the degree of D. Litt, quoted in letter to Fraser Drew from Dr. K. C. Turpin, Secretary of the Faculties, University Registry, Oxford, Mar. 13, 1951.

24. Prof. Stuart, Dean of the Faculty of Law, in presenting the candidates for honorary degrees (Masefield received the degree of LL.D. on Mar. 31, 1922), quoted in letter to Fraser Drew from Dr. W. Douglas Simpson, Librarian, University of Aberdeen, Apr. 2, 1951.

25. Catalogue for an exhibit of Water-Colour Drawings by Claude Muncaster, A.R.W.S., Barbizon House, London, April and May, 1933, foreword by Masefield, pp. 1–2.

26. "The Shadow of the Laureateship," *Poetry* (March 1933), pp. 332–35.

27. *A Letter from Pontus,* pp. 25–26.

28. *The Nine Days Wonder* (1941); *A Generation Risen* (1943); *Some Verses to Some Germans* (1939).

29. For typical critical reaction, see the following reviews of *A Letter from Pontus and Other Verse* (1936); Percy Hutchison, *New York Times Book Review* (June 21, 1936), p. 5; Edmund Blunden, *London Mercury* (July 1936), pp. 257–59; Winfield Townley Scott, *Poetry* (Sept. 1936).

30. "Queen's Poet," *Sat. Review* 36 (Dec. 26, 1953): 19.

31. *London Times* (May 5, 1966), p. 383; Handley-Taylor (London: Cranbrook Tower Press, 1960), pp. 9–11 and 76; Graves, "Chaucer's Man," *Poetry Review* 58 (London) (Autumn 1967): 241–46.

32. "Of Ships and Wonder," *Time* (Feb. 27, 1950), p. 108.

33. (1942); it is not to be confused with "The Workers on the Land," *A Generation Risen* (1942), pp. 68–71.

34. *London Times* (May 7, 1935).

35. *Ibid.,* n.d.

36. *Time* (Feb. 10, 1936), p. 53.

37. *London Times* (Jan. 29, 1936), p. 11.

38. *Ibid.* (Apr. 28, 1937), p. 10.

39. *Time* (Apr. 26, 1937), p. 18.

40. *London Times* (Jan. 31, 1947), p. 5.

41. *Ibid.* (May 12, 1947), p. 4.

42. *Ibid.* (Nov. 20, 1947), p. 5.

43. *Ibid.* (Apr. 26, 1948).

44. *Ibid.* (Nov. 16, 1948).

45. *Ibid.* (Mar. 30, 1949), p. 4.

46. Approved Souvenir Program, "The Coronation of Her Majesty

Queen Elizabeth II," June 2, 1953.
    47. *Virginia Gazette* (Oct. 25, 1957).
    48. *London Times* (May 6, 1950).
    49. *Ibid.* (Sept. 25, 1934).
    50. *Ibid.* (Sept. 12, 1938), p. 9.
    51. *Ibid.* (Sept. 14, 1938).
    52. *Ibid.* (Oct. 22, 1943), p. 2.
    53. *Ibid.* (May 8, 1945), p. 7.
    54. *Ibid.* (Nov. 23, 1946), p. 2.
    55. *Ibid.* (Oct. 17, 1946), p. 3.
    56. *Ibid.* (July 29, 1950), p. 5.
    57. *Ibid.* (Apr. 23, 1964).
    58. *Ibid.* (Jan. 23, 1936), p. 13.
    59. *Ibid.* (Mar. 25, 1944), p. 6.
    60. *Saturday Rev. of Lit.* (July 27, 1946), p. 10.
    61. *Ibid.* (July 21, 1956), p. 7.
    62. *Canterbury Cathedral Chronicle* 53 (Oct. 1958).
    63. *London Times* (Jan. 24, 1959).
    64. *Ibid.* (Mar. 26, 1959).
    65. *Ibid.* (Jan. 8, 1965).
    66. *Ibid.* (Nov. 19, 1934), p. 11.
    67. *Time* (Mar. 11, 1940), p. 23.
    68. *London Times* (Feb. 24, 1944), p. 2.
    69. *Ibid.* (June 14, 1944), p. 7.
    70. *Ibid.* (Apr. 12, 1948).
    71. Inconstant Reader, "Preferences," *Canadian Forum* (June 1930), pp. 328–29.
    72. Editorial, *Publisher's Weekly* (June 30, 1945), p. 2501.
    73. Letter to Fraser Drew from D. Kilham Roberts, Secretary-General, The Society of Authors, London, Mar. 20, 1951; the Council of the Society during Masefield's presidency included such members as Noel Coward, T. S. Eliot, Graham Greene, Laurence Housman, Walter de la Mare, W. Somerset Maugham, A. A. Milne, Alfred Noyes, Edith Sitwell, and R. Vaughan Williams.
    74. See also Masefield's plea for a small repertory theater for Oxford in the *Times* (May 30, 1919), and his 34-line prologue written for the opening of the Liverpool Repertory Theatre, Nov. 11, 1911.
    75. In June 1923, Masefield contributed an article to *The Spear,* called "The Speaking of Verse in Shakespeare's Time"; he reports on the first Oxford Recitations in articles in the *Manchester Guardian* (July 27, 1923 and Aug. 1, 1924).
    76. *The Oxford Recitations* (New York: The Macmillan Co., 1928), preface by Masefield, pp. 5–9.

77. For brief description and pictures, see "The Poet Laureate," *Bookman*, Christmas no. (Dec. 1930), pp. 161–65; see also Corliss Lamont, *Remembering John Masefield* (Rutherford: Fairleigh Dickinson University Press, 1970).

78. Gilbert Thomas, *John Masefield* (London: Thornton Butterworth, 1932), p. 214.

79. In a letter to Fraser Drew, Nov. 21, 1950, Lena Ashwell, to whose Lena Ashwell Players Masefield dedicated his *Sonnets of Good Cheer* (1926), writes of the sympathy and encouragement extended to her group during the nine years in which they "struggled to take good plays to the London Boroughs." The Lena Ashwell Players presented Masefield's *Tristan and Isolt* at the Century Theatre, Bayswater, in 1927, before its publication in book form.

80. Cesar Saerchinger, "Poetry is Made to be Spoken," an interview with Masefield, *Scholastic* (Mar. 11, 1939), p. 29–E.

81. Walter E. Glasser, in "Letters to the Editor," *Saturday Review of Literature* (July 22, 1950), p. 24.

82. Gilbert Thomas, p. 214.

83. *A Foundation Day Address* (Bembridge: Yellowsands Press, 1921), p. 6.

84. *John Ruskin* (an essay originally delivered by Masefield as a lecture at the Ruskin Centenary Exhibition held at the Royal Academy in 1919) (Bembridge: Yellowsands Press, 1920), p. 5.

85. See also Masefield's articles, "The Heart's Desire," *Review of Reviews* (Jan.–Feb., 1921), and "1919–1920: Signs of the Times," *Manchester Guardian* (Jan. 5, 1920).

86. Clair Price, "John Masefield Talks on Literature and the War," *New York Times Book Review* (Mar. 17, 1940), pp. 12, 26.

87. "Mornings and Aprils," *Old Raiger and Other Verse* (1965); "Pavilastukay" in *Natalie Maisie and Pavilastukay* (1942); and "The Hill," *On the Hill* (1949).

Conclusion

John Masefield began writing as the self-appointed poet of the common man. The first poem of his first book, *Salt-Water Ballads* (1902), is "A Consecration" of his work to the cause of the common soldier and the common sailor, of "the scorned—the rejected," of "the maimed, the halt and the blind in the rain and the cold."

Although the sailors and the yarns of *Salt-Water Ballads* and *Ballads* (1903) are often English seamen and English stories,[1] and although poems like "The West Wind" and "On Malvern Hill" are poems of the English landscape, there is no specific statement that the soldier and the sailor of "A Consecration" are English, or that "the man with too weighty a burden, too heavy a load" must be an Englishman.[2]

Masefield did not, then, begin his career with the avowed intention of being a national bard. It may be that the early prose studies, such as *Sea Life in Nelson's Time* (1905) and *On the Spanish Main* (1906), and the editorships of *A Sailor's Garland* (1906) and the Anson, Dampier, Hakluyt, and Nelson volumes (1906–1911) first gave impetus to a desire consciously and specifically to celebrate England and the English.

During the next decade, Masefield's work reveals his increasing preoccupation with English subjects. His first study of Shakespeare (1911) was followed by the four narrative poems, *The Everlasting Mercy* (1911), *The Widow in the Bye Street* (1912), *Dauber* (1912), and *The Daffodil Fields* (1913), in which his concern for the common man merged with his love for the English countryside and England at sea.

226

In the year following the appearance of *The Daffodil Fields,* England went to war, and the poet's first utterance out of that conflict, "August, 1914," "surely the best poem in English inspired by the war,"[3] was published. The war years produced Masefield's American addresses,[4] his studies of the campaigns in France,[5] and "the great book of the war,"[6] *Gallipoli*. Between 1919 and 1921 came the poetic trilogy of English portraits, English pastimes, and the English countryside—*Reynard the Fox, Right Royal,* and *King Cole.*

Thus, had Masefield died in 1921, he would have ranked, on the score of the previous eleven years' work, as one of the greatest interpreters of English life and landscape. The years that followed, however, were to be filled with further celebrations of England. In 1921 most of his novels of the English countryside and of Englishmen at sea were still to be written; the Arthurian tales and other British stories had not yet been retold; the poet had not fully acknowledged his debt to English poets of the past; another great war still lay ahead with English deeds to be recorded and English courage to be praised.

The appointment to the Laureateship in 1930 constituted no turning point in Masefield's career. It was only an incident in a logical course of events, a gratifying honor and a stimulating incentive toward the completion of what might be called an English cyclorama. All the major figures and scenes had been sketched, and many of them completed, before 1930, even before 1922. The Laureateship cannot therefore be said to have influenced appreciably the course of Masefield's writing; the work of the later years was but the work of ornamentation and of completion.

In the many fields of his literary endeavor, Masefield of course had competitors among the English writers. Some of these are well known for their peculiarly English themes, or scenes, or spirit, and naturally come to mind in a study such as this. Hardy is famous for his portrayal of English country life; Conrad, for being a "master of the fascination of the sea";[7] Charles Williams and other poets, for their retelling of Arthurian story; Surtees and Trollope, for the glorification of the English fox-hunt; Kipling, for his tales of the Englishman away from England; and Tennyson and Bridges, for their parallel experiences as Poets Laureate.

Masefield once said of Hardy: "He takes a tremendous strip of English country and life and makes it live for us."[8] Although Masefield's countryside never has the dramatic significance of an Egdon Heath, and although Masefield's country folk, even Charles Cothill and Baldy Hill, are not so memorable as the men and women of Hardy's Wessex, yet his countryside is vivid, and his countrymen are authentic. Hardy's eye, however, is always on characters and situations of rather more universal significance. Both men shared in "the gift of country life,"[9] and each has left abundant testimony to his love for England.

Conrad and Masefield were both sailors who frequently returned to the sea in their writing. Masefield's early reviews often praise the older writer's tales. Conrad's ships he found "strange" and "splendid," although no ship in Conrad's fiction has the significance that Masefield gives to the *Wanderer* or haunts Conrad's thoughts as that ill-fated barque haunts Masefield's. Conrad's sailors were to Masefield "profoundly significant studies, each realised in its minutest aspects"; Lord Jim is just such a study. Jim and Dauber are perhaps their creators' best-known sailors and each, in his search for fulfillment and peace, suffered a strange combination of failure and success. Lord Jim died "in a desperate reaching after an ideal of conduct which had eluded him in life,"[10] while Dauber, after winning the fight against his fear of the sea and the contempt of his fellow-sailors, died with his ideal as an artist still unachieved.

In their psychological impact on the reader, Conrad's complexities and Masefield's very English simplicities are far apart. A comparison of *The Taking of the Gry* and *The Secret Sharer*, two tales with many superficial similarities of setting, characters, and plot, reveals the essential differences between Masefield, the teller of a good yarn, and Conrad, the contriver of a subtle and haunting story.

In the Arthurian field many poets have turned to retellings of the legends. In the nineteenth century Tennyson produced his Victorian *Idylls of the King* and Morris his un-Victorian *Defense of Guenevere,* while Robert Stephen Hawker and Swinburne preceded Masefield in a return to the Celtic roots of Arthurian story. Among Masefield's contemporaries, the American E. A. Robinson differed in introducing a psychological dimension into the traditional Arthurian materials. Another contemporary, Charles Williams, was like Masefield in emphasizing the mythological and historical matrix of the Arthurian cycle. Williams, however, is difficult; even his enthusiastic critic C. S. Lewis admits that the unfinished Arthurian cycle of Williams may fail to gain a permanent place in English literature because of its "obscurity" and its "unshared background."[11] Masefield's direct and unsophisticated narrative method is far different from the method of Williams. Masefield's place among the modern Arthurians, in accordance with his primary interest in the story-telling art, is that of the story-teller and the student of early Britain.

Masefield is one of the most recent chroniclers of the fox-hunt in a long line that includes William Somerville, Peter Beckford, Thomas Smith, and Rowland Egerton-Warburton, as well as the more famous Robert Surtees and Anthony Trollope. Trollope loved the hunt and used it in novel after novel as setting, as a subsidiary part of his picture of the English social system; the books of Surtees are filled with the hearty, rough, masculine humor of the meet; but Masefield presents a picture of the hunt in which hunters, hangers-on, horses, hounds, and fox share with the "coloured countryside" the major roles in his English pageant. It is in this emphasis upon the pageantry of the hunt that Masefield differs from its other celebrators.

Kipling's work touches that of Masefield at many points, and among recent writers Kipling comes first to mind as a parallel figure. Both have been called "patriotic poets," and they were long ago named the unofficial laureates of British soldier and British sailor. Both are story-tellers of Englishmen away from home, and both have had large popular followings and varying reputations with the critics. As a patriotic poet, Kipling has generally been the poet of the British Empire, while Masefield has been rather the poet of England in the sense of the English land and the men who symbolize and embody England, at home and at sea. It is as story-tellers that these two writers may be longest remembered, and in Masefield's So Long to Learn (1952), his inner autobiography as an artist, he characterizes his own work as being "the finding, framing and telling of stories, in verse and prose, according to the tale and the power within me. I have done, and have enjoyed, much other work," he continues, "yet always with the love (and the hope) of story-telling deep within me, as a work beyond all other work, to which my nature called."

Masefield's place among the Poets Laureate is that of a poet well qualified, by practice and by temperament, for his post. His celebration of England, as has been shown above, began long before his appointment to an official post. He fulfilled the obligations of the Laureateship as conscientiously as Tennyson, more ably than Austin, and more generously than Bridges. Masefield's activities in behalf of the theater, the speaking of verse, and other arts were many; in his person the Poet Laureate changed from the incumbent of a nominal office to "a living symbol of the power and authority" of poetry.[12]

It is not the task of this study, however, to attempt judgment of Masefield's comparative success in these individual fields; it is, rather, to consider his overall significance as the interpreter of many varied phases of English character and English landscape and life.

The Englishness of Masefield's work is the heart of it. If the prose and poetry that are characteristically and openly English are separated from the rest of his work, little of major importance remains. The greater body of Masefield's work, and the finest part of it, is that in which he dedicates himself to the portrayal and the interpretation of English landscape and life. In this England of Masefield, John Bull sometimes makes an appearance, but always he is countered by St. George. And the spirit of St. George shines brightest in those longer poems and tales which are most likely to live—*The Everlasting Mercy, Dauber,* "August, 1914," *Gallipoli, Reynard the Fox, King Cole,* and the *Midsummer Night* stories.

There is no inconsistency in Masefield's apparent shift from a consecration to the common man to a consecration to England. His England is the England of the common man; and the beauties of that England of the future for which he calls repeatedly in his later work[13] are dedicated to the refreshment and the recreation of the common man in England and throughout the world. The new English theater for which he hopes in one of his later essays is but one of the agents Masefield invokes for the moving of "the

world with the glory of the English spirit that is now the one
thing left to us."[14]

Notes to Conclusion

1. Most of the names of the sailors are English names, with only
an occasional exception like Karlssen in "Cape Horn Gospel—I."
Place names used are often from the Spanish Main, although Liverpool and other British places are mentioned.

2. The nearest approaches to a specific statement are in "The
Yarn of the Loch Achray," where the men "are homeward bound/
With anchors hungry for English ground," and in "Cape Horn Gos-
pel—II" and "One of the Bo'sun's Yarns," where the phrase D. B. S.,
"Distressed British Sailor," is used.

3. *Saturday Review of Literature* (May 17, 1930), p. 1041.

4. "The War and the Future" and "St. George and the Dragon"
in *The War and the Future* (1918).

5. *The Old Front Line* (1917), *The Battle of the Somme* (1919),
and lesser essays.

6. "The Great Book of the War," *Bookman* (June 1925), pp. 389–
90.

7. Masefield in a review of *The Mirror of the Sea, Manchester
Guardian* (Oct. 16, 1906).

8. Quoted by Louise T. Nicholl, *John Masefield: English Poet,*
5: 6.

9. "Biography," *The Story of a Round-House* (New York: The
Macmillan Co., 1912), p. 191.

10. J. Donald Adams, Introd. to Conrad's *Lord Jim* (New York:
Modern Library, 1931), pp. vi–vii.

11. C. S. Lewis, "Williams and the Arthuriad," *Arthurian Torso*
(London: Oxford University Press, 1948), pp. 187–90.

12. Frederic G. Melcher, *Publisher's Weekly* (June 30, 1945),
p. 2501.

13. From the time of *The War and the Future* (1918); *Collected
Poems* (1918), preface, p. ix; and *A Foundation Day Address*
(1921); to such later books as *Wonderings* (London: William Heine-
mann, 1943), pp. 53–64; *I Want! I Want!* (London: National Book
Council, 1944), *passim; A Generation Risen* (London: Collins,
1943), introd., p. 7; "On England," *The Country Scene* (London:
Collins, 1937), pp. 9–10; "The English Dancers," *Tribute to Ballet*
(London: Collins, 1938), pp. 15–17; "Pavilastukay," *Natalie Maisie*

and Pavilastukay (London: William Heinemann, 1942), pp. 55–56; *So Long to Learn* (1952); "On Coming Towards Eighty," in *John Masefield, Aet. 80: An Exhibition* (1958); "The Bluebells," *The Bluebells and Other Verse* (1961); and "Mornings and Aprils," *Old Raiger and Other Verse* (1965).

14. *My Favourite English Poems* (London: William Heinemann, 1950), introduction, p. xix.

Selected Bibliography

I: Poems, Verse Plays, and Volumes of Poems by Masefield

Salt-Water Ballads. London: Grant Richards, 1902.

Ballads. London: Elkin Mathews, 1903.

Ballads and Poems. London: Elkin Mathews, 1910.

The Everlasting Mercy. London: Sidgwick and Jackson, 1911.

The Widow in the Bye Street. London: Sidgwick and Jackson, 1912.

The Story of a Round-House and Other Poems. New York: The Macmillan Company, 1912.

Dauber. London: William Heinemann, 1913.

The Daffodil Fields. New York: The Macmillan Company, 1913.

Philip the King and Other Poems. London: William Heinemann, 1914.

Good Friday and Other Poems. New York: The Macmillan Company, 1916.

Sonnets and Poems. Letchworth: Garden City Press, 1916.

Salt-Water Poems and Ballads. New York: The Macmillan Company, 1916.

Lollingdon Downs and Other Poems. New York: The Macmillan Company, 1917.

Rosas. New York: The Macmillan Company, 1918.

Reynard the Fox. New York: The Macmillan Company, 1919.

Reynard the Fox. New York: The Macmillan Company, 1920. First illustrated edition with the essay, "Fox-Hunting," as introduction.

Animula. London: The Chiswick Press, 1920.

Enslaved and Other Poems. London: William Heinemann, 1920.

Right Royal. New York: The Macmillan Company, 1920.

King Cole. London: William Heinemann, 1921.

The Dream. London: William Heinemann, 1922.

King Cole and Other Poems. London: William Heinemann, 1923.

Sonnets of Good Cheer. London: Mendip Press, 1926.

Tristan and Isolt. London: William Heinemann, 1927.

The Coming of Christ. New York: The Macmillan Company, 1928.

Midsummer Night and Other Tales in Verse. London: William Heinemann, 1928.

Easter. New York: The Macmillan Company, 1929.

The Wanderer of Liverpool. London: William Heinemann, 1930.

Minnie Maylow's Story and Other Tales and Scenes. London: William Heinemann, 1931.

A Tale of Troy. London: William Heinemann, 1932.

Poems. New and complete ed. with recent poems. Preface by the author. New York: The Macmillan Company, 1935. Reissued in 1953 with additional poems.

A Letter from Pontus and Other Verse. London: William Heinemann, 1936.

Lines Spoken at the Tercentenary of Harvard University. London: William Heinemann, 1937.

The Country Scene (Poems by John Masefield and Pictures by Edward Seago). London: Collins, 1937.

Tribute to Ballet (Poems by John Masefield and Pictures by Edward Seago). London: Collins, 1938.

Some Verses to Some Germans. London: William Heinemann, 1939.

Some Memories of W. B. Yeats. Dundrum: The Cuala Press, 1940.

Gautama the Enlightened and Other Verse. London: William Heinemann, 1941.

Land Workers. London: William Heinemann, 1942.

Natalie Maisie and Pavilastukay. London: William Heinemann, 1942.

A Generation Risen (Poems by John Masefield and Pictures by Edward Seago). London: Collins, 1943.

Wonderings. London: William Heinemann, 1943.

On the Hill. London: William Heinemann, 1949.

In Praise of Nurses. London: William Heinemann, 1950.

Selected Poems. New preface by the author. London: William Heinemann, 1950.

The Story of Ossian. New Rochelle: Spoken Arts, Inc., 1959. A record album that precedes any written publication of the poem.

The Bluebells and Other Verse. London: William Heinemann, 1961.

Old Raiger and Other Verse. London: William Heinemann, 1965.

In Glad Thanksgiving. London: William Heinemann, 1967.

Notes: *The Wanderer of Liverpool* and *Some Memories of W. B. Yeats,* listed above in the category of poetry, also have prose sequences. In listing Masefield publications prior to 1930, the first American edition is cited whenever its publication antedates the first English edition. Since exact dates of publication are not always available for first American editions since 1930, first English editions are generally cited.

II: *Novels by Masefield*

Captain Margaret. London: Grant Richards, 1908.

Multitude and Solitude. London: Grant Richards, 1909.

Martin Hyde. London: Wells Gardner, Darton and Company, 1910.

Lost Endeavour. London: Thomas Nelson and Sons, 1910.

The Street of Today. London: J. M. Dent and Sons, 1911.

Jim Davis. London: Wells Gardner, Darton and Company, 1911.

Sard Harker. London: William Heinemann, 1924.

ODTAA. New York: The Macmillan Company, 1926.

The Midnight Folk. London: William Heinemann, 1927.

The Hawbucks. New York: The Macmillan Company, 1929.

The Bird of Dawning. London: William Heinemann, 1933.

The Taking of the Gry. London: William Heinemann, 1934.
Victorious Troy. London: William Heinemann, 1935.
Eggs and Baker. London: William Heinemann, 1936.
The Square Peg. London: William Heinemann, 1937.
Dead Ned. London: William Heinemann, 1938.
Live and Kicking Ned. London: William Heinemann, 1939.
Basilissa. London: William Heinemann, 1940.
Conquer. London: William Heinemann, 1941.
Badon Parchments. London: William Heinemann, 1947.

III: *Prose Plays by Masefield*

The Tragedy of Nan and Other Plays. London: Grant Richards, 1909.
The Tragedy of Pompey the Great. London: Sidgwick and Jackson, 1910.
The Faithful. London: William Heinemann, 1915.
The Locked Chest; The Sweeps of '98. Letchworth: Garden City Press, 1916.
Melloney Holtspur. London: William Heinemann, 1922.
The Trial of Jesus. London: William Heinemann, 1925.
End and Beginning. London: William Heinemann, 1934.
A Play of St. George. London: William Heinemann, 1948.

Prose plays: Translations and Adaptations

Anne Pedersdotter. A Drama in Four Acts by H. Wiers-Jensen. English Version by John Masefield. Boston: Little Brown and Company, 1917.
Esther. A Tragedy Adapted and Partially Translated from the French of Jean Racine. London: William Heinemann, 1922.
Berenice. A Tragedy Translated from the French of Jean Racine. London: William Heinemann, 1922.

IV: *Miscellaneous Prose by Masefield*
(separate publications)

A Mainsail Haul. London: Elkin Mathews, 1905.

Sea Life in Nelson's Time. London: Methuen and Company, 1905.

On the Spanish Main. London: Methuen and Company, 1906.

A Tarpaulin Muster. London: Grant Richards, 1907.

My Faith in Woman Suffrage. London: The Woman's Press, 1910.

A Book of Discoveries. London: Wells Gardner, Darton and Company, 1910.

William Shakespeare. London: Williams and Norgate, 1911.

John M. Synge. Dundrum: The Cuala Press, 1915.

Gallipoli. London: William Heinemann, 1916.

The Old Front Line. New York: The Macmillan Company, 1917.

The War and the Future. New York: The Macmillan Company, 1918.

The Battle of the Somme. London: William Heinemann, 1919.

John Ruskin. Bembridge: Yellowsands Press, 1920.

A Foundation Day Address. Bembridge: Yellowsands Press, 1921.

The Taking of Helen. London: William Heinemann, 1923.

The Taking of Helen and Other Prose Selections. New York: The Macmillan Company, 1924.

Shakespeare and Spiritual Life. Oxford: Clarendon Press, 1924.

With the Living Voice. Cambridge: University Press, 1924.

Chaucer. Cambridge: University Press, 1931.

Poetry. London: William Heinemann, 1931.

The Conway. London: William Heinemann, 1933.

Recent Prose. Rev. ed. with new material. London: William Heinemann, 1932.

The Box of Delights. London: William Heinemann, 1935.

In the Mill. London: William Heinemann, 1941.

The Nine Days Wonder. London: William Heinemann, 1941.

I Want! I Want! London: National Book Council, 1944.

New Chum. London: William Heinemann, 1944.

A Macbeth Production. London: William Heinemann, 1945.

Thanks Before Going. London: William Heinemann, 1946.

University of Sheffield pamphlet. Speech by John Masefield. Sheffield, June 26, 1946.

The Ledbury Scene As I Have Used It in My Verse. Hereford: Jakemans Ltd., 1951.

St. Katherine of Ledbury and Other Ledbury Papers. London: William Heinemann, 1951.

So Long to Learn: Chapters of an Autobiography. London: William Heinemann, 1952.

Grace Before Ploughing: Fragments of Autobiography. New York: The Macmillan Co., 1966.

V: Prefaces, Forewords, Introductions, and Contributions by Masefield

Wolverhampton Art and Industrial Exhibition, 1902. Catalogue of the Exhibits in the Fine Art Section. Secretary: John E. Masefield. Wolverhampton: Whitehead Brothers, 1902.

Poems by John Keats, with an introduction by Laurence Binyon and notes by John Masefield. London: Methuen and Company, 1903.

Marlowe, Christopher. *Doctor Faustus*. Seen through the press by John Masefield. London: Hacon and Ricketts, 1903.

Reynolds, John H. *The Fancy*. Prefatory memoir and notes by John Masefield. London: Elkin Mathews, 1905.

Lyrists of the Restoration. Selected and edited by John and Constance Masefield. London: Grant Richards, 1905.

Essays Moral and Polite, 1660–1714. Selected and edited by John and Constance Masefield. London: Grant Richards, 1906.

A Sailor's Garland. Selected and edited by John Masefield. London: Methuen and Company, 1906.

The Poems of Robert Herrick. Edited with a Biographical Introduction by John Masefield. London: Grant Richards, 1906.

Dampier's Voyages. Edited by John Masefield. London: Grant Richards, 1906.

Lyrics of Ben Jonson, Beaumont and Fletcher. Edited by John Masefield. London: Grant Richards, 1906.

An English Prose Miscellany. Selected with an Introduction by John Masefield. London: Methuen and Company, 1907.

Hakluyt, Richard. *The Principal Navigations. . . .* Introduction by John Masefield. London: J. M. Dent and Company, 1907.

The Travels of Marco Polo the Venetian. Introduction and itinerary by John Masefield. London: J. M. Dent and Sons, 1907.

Masters of Literature: Defoe. Edited by John Masefield. London: George Bell and Sons, 1909.

Yeats, Jack B. *A Little Fleet* (anonymous verses written by Masefield). London: Elkin Mathews, 1909.

Visiak, E. H. *Buccaneer Ballads.* Introduction by John Masefield. London: Elkin Mathews, 1910.

Chronicles of the Pilgrim Fathers. Introduction by John Masefield. London: J. M. Dent and Sons, 1910.

Anson, George. *A Voyage Round the World in the Years 1740–1744.* Introduction by John Masefield. London: J. M. Dent and Sons, 1911.

Southey, Robert. *The Life of Nelson.* Introduction by John Masefield. London: Gibbings and Company, 1911.

Kauffman, R. W. *Daughters of Ishmael.* Preface by John Masefield. London: Stephen Swift and Company, 1911.

Mayor, F. M. *The Third Miss Symons.* Preface by John Masefield. London: Sidgwick and Jackson, 1913.

Phillimore, R. C. *Poems.* Introduction by John Masefield. London: Sidgwick and Jackson, 1913.

Liveing, E. G. D. *Attack.* Introduction by John Masefield. London: William Heinemann, 1918.

John Ruskin: Letters Written on the Occasion of the Centenary of His Birth. Edited by J. H. Whitehouse. With a letter from John Masefield. Oxford: University Press, 1919.

Public School Verse, 1919–1920. Introduction by John Masefield. London: William Heinemann, 1920.

Ruskin the Prophet and Other Centenary Studies. By John Masefield and Others. Edited by J. H. Whitehouse. London: George Allen and Unwin, 1920.

Roberts, Cecil E. M. *Poems.* Preface by John Masefield. New York: Frederick A. Stokes Company, 1920.

Catalogue of Pictures of the Belvoir Hunt and Other Scenes of English Country Life by A. J. Munnings. Foreword by John Masefield. 1921.

Craig, E. Gordon. *Scene.* Foreword and introductory poem by John Masefield. London: Oxford University Press, 1923.

Partington, Wilfred. *The War Against Malaria*. Foreword by John Masefield. London: Propaganda Committee of Ross Institute Fund, 1923.

Lubbock, Basil. *Adventures by Sea from Art of Old Time*. Preface by John Masefield. London: The Studio Limited, 1925.

The Oxford Recitations. Preface and contributions by John Masefield. New York: The Macmillan Company, 1928.

Catalogue of Exhibition of Water-Colour Drawings by Claude Muncaster. Foreword by John Masefield. London, 1933.

Seago, Edward. *Circus Company*. Introduction by John Masefield. London: Putnam, 1933.

Cameron, Captain Evan. *Goodbye Russia*. Foreword by John Masefield. London: Hodder and Stoughton, 1934.

Nevinson, H. W. *Fire of Life*. Preface by John Masefield. London: James Nisbet and Company, 1935.

Schreiber, George. *Portraits and Self-Portraits* (including autobiographical sketch by Masefield). Boston: Houghton Mifflin Company, 1936, pp. 89–90.

Novels of George Du Maurier. Introductions by John Masefield, O. M., and Daphne Du Maurier. London: The Pilot Press, 1947.

Masefield, Lewis C. *The Passion Left Behind*. Introduction by John Masefield. London: Faber and Faber, 1947.

Masefield, John, ed. *My Favorite English Poems*. Introduction by John Masefield. London: William Heinemann, 1950.

Lamont, Corliss, ed. *The Thomas Lamonts in America*. South Brunswick and New York: A. S. Barnes and Company, 1971. This contains a prose statement from the *London Times* of December 30, 1952, by John and Constance Masefield on the death of Florence C. Lamont, p. 133, a prose recollection of Thomas W. and Florence C. Lamont, pp. 137–44, and two poems in memory of the Lamonts, pp. 145–52.

VI: Contributions by Masefield to Periodicals (*not reprinted in book form*)

"Studies in Bed-Rock." Review of Bart Kennedy's *A Sailor Tramp*. *The Speaker*, April 5, 1902.

"A Measure of Shifting Sand." *The Speaker*, April 26, June 21, June 26, July 26, August 23, 1902.

"A Wanderer's Oddments." *The Speaker*, August 23, 1902.

"Old Starm Along." Review of Walter Runciman's *Windjammers and Sea Tramps*. *The Speaker*, February 14, 1903.

"Some Sea Dogs." Review of W. H. Fitchett's *Nelson and His Captains*. *The Speaker*, March 21, 1903.

"Voyages and Travels." *Manchester Guardian*, April 18, 1903.

"The Banner of Romance." *The Speaker*, December 12, 1903.

"Vallipo." *Manchester Guardian*, November 14, 1904.

"Trafalgar Day: Ship Life Under Nelson." *Manchester Guardian*, October 22, 1904.

"In Dock." *The Speaker*, November 5, 1904 and May 6, 1905.

"Gara Brook." *Manchester Guardian*, November 18, 1904.

Review of Sir Rennell Rodd's *Sir Walter Raleigh*. *Manchester Guardian*, December 20, 1904.

"A Trip to Nombre de Dios." *Manchester Guardian*, April 19, 1905.

Reviews of the several volumes of *Purchas His Pilgrimes*. *Manchester Guardian*, June 22, August 21, September 19, October 25, 1905; January 22, June 1, July 19, September 18, 1906; June 17, 1907.

"Chanties." *Manchester Guardian*, August 16, 1905.

"Whippet Racing." *Manchester Guardian*, August 19, 1905.

"Nelson's Guns." *Manchester Guardian*, November 21, 1905.

"Johnny Good." *Manchester Guardian*, November 21, 1905.

"Nelsonian Reminiscences." *Manchester Guardian*, December 15, 1905.

"On Folk Songs." Review of *Folk Songs from Somerset* by Cecil J. Sharp and Charles L. Marson. *The Speaker*, December 23, 1905.

"Sea Songs." *Temple Bar*, n.s. 1, January 1906, pp. 56–80.

"Brown." *Manchester Guardian*, January 16, 1906.

"In the Roost." *Manchester Guardian*, March 16, 1906.

"Old Sea Chanties." *Manchester Guardian*, March 27, 1906.

"A Steerage Steward." *Manchester Guardian*, June 21, 1906.

"Valparaiso." *Manchester Guardian*, August 25, 1906.

Review of Joseph Conrad's *The Mirror of the Sea. Manchester Guardian,* October 16, 1906.

Review of Hilaire Belloc's *Hills and the Sea. Manchester Guardian,* October 19, 1906.

"Lithgow's Travels." *Manchester Guardian,* October 26, 1906.

"Our Heritage of the Sea." *Manchester Guardian,* November 27, 1906.

"Sea Songs." *Manchester Guardian,* December 3, 1906.

"Ancient and Modern Ships." *Manchester Guardian,* December 28, 1906.

"The Passing of the Glory of the World." *Manchester Guardian,* February 14, 1907.

"A Duel with Davy Jones." *Manchester Guardian,* February 28, 1907.

"Liverpool, City of Ships." *The Pall Mall Magazine,* March 1907, pp. 273–81.

"A Great Adventure." Review of *General Historie and True Travels of Captain John Smith. Manchester Guardian,* March 25, 1907.

"Captain J. Cook." *Manchester Guardian,* May 28, 1907.

"Voyages of Elizabethan Seamen." *Manchester Guardian,* June 21, 1907.

"Encyclopedia of Ships." *Manchester Guardian,* October 23, 1907.

"The Royal Navy." *Manchester Guardian,* January 10, 1908.

"Naval Ballads." *Manchester Guardian,* April 28, 1908.

"Great Raleigh." *Manchester Guardian,* September 8, 1908.

"Inner Life of the Navy." *Manchester Guardian,* January 5, 1909.

"The British Tar." *Manchester Guardian,* February 22, 1909.

"Nelson and Other Studies." *Manchester Guardian,* July 2, 1909.

"The Nelson Whom Britons Love." *Manchester Guardian,* August 13, 1909.

"Sailing Ships and Their Story." *Manchester Guardian,* August 20, 1909.

"Buccaneer in the West Indies." *Manchester Guardian,* October 27, 1910.

"Letters of English Seamen." *Manchester Guardian,* November 8, 1910.

"Shakespeare's Sea Terms Explained." *Manchester Guardian,* January 5, 1911.

"Captain Cook." *Manchester Guardian,* March 10, 1911.

"A New Marine Magazine." *Manchester Guardian,* March 27, 1911.

"Famous Sea Fights." *Manchester Guardian,* May 1, 1911.

"The Drake Family." *Manchester Guardian,* May 12, 1911.

"Captain Kidd." Review of Sir Cornelius N. Dalton's *The Real Captain Kidd. Manchester Guardian,* June 26, 1911.

"A South Sea Buccaneer." *Manchester Guardian,* November 15, 1911.

"Pressgang Days." *Manchester Guardian,* November 17, 1911.

"Naval Miscellany." *Manchester Guardian,* August 13, 1912.

"Nelson in England." *Manchester Guardian,* March 14, 1913.

Reviews of Lieutenant H. S. Lecky's *The King's Ships. Manchester Guardian,* August 28, 1913, January 23, 1914; April 13, 1915.

"From Naval Cadet to Admiral." *Manchester Guardian,* October 24, 1913.

"The Sailors Nelson Led." *Manchester Guardian,* November 28, 1913.

"Shakespeare as Playwright." *Manchester Guardian,* January 26, 1914.

Review of Basil Lubbock's *The China Clippers. Manchester Guardian,* May 12, 1914.

"The Harvest of the Night." *Harper's Magazine,* May 1917, pp. 801–10.

"The Common Task." Address printed from stenographic notes in *The Yale Alumni Weekly,* July 5, 1918, pp. 1014–15.

"The Most Heroic Effort." *Manchester Guardian,* November 14, 1918.

(Three early poems of John Masefield, published for the first time in Louise Townsend Nicholl's article, "John Masefield in Yonkers." *The Bookman,* January 1919, pp. 544–49).

"1919–1920: Signs of the Times." *Manchester Guardian,* January 5, 1920.

"The Heart's Desire." *Review of Reviews,* January-February 1921.

"On Shakespeare." *The Spear* (Huddersfield), June 31 (sic), 1922.

"The Speaking of Verse in Shakespeare's Time." *The Spear,* June 1923.

"The Oxford Recitations." *Manchester Guardian,* July 27, 1923.

Review of David W. Bone's *The Lookout Man. Manchester Guardian,* September 19, 1923.

Review of E. Keble Chatterton's *Ship Models. Manchester Guardian,* October 12, 1923.

"A New Feeling for Poetry." *Manchester Guardian,* August 1, 1924.

"Melbourne." *London Times,* November 19, 1934, p. 11.

Untitled "prayer," poem of 12 lines. *London Times,* May 7, 1935.

"To Rudyard Kipling." *London Times,* January 23, 1936, p. 13.

"On the Passing of King George V." *London Times,* January 29, 1936, p. 11.

Untitled sonnet. Quoted in *Time,* February 10, 1936, p. 53.

Untitled sonnet. Quoted in *Time,* April 26, 1937, p. 18.

"A Prayer for the King's Reign." *London Times,* April 28, 1937, p. 10.

"The New Figurehead." *London Times,* September 12, 1938, p. 9.

"Neville Chamberlain." *London Times,* September 14, 1938.

"To the Australians Coming to Help Us." Quoted in *Time,* March 11, 1940, p. 23.

"Men of the Royal Navy." *London Times,* October 22, 1943, p. 2.

Untitled 12-line poem. *London Times,* February 24, 1944, p. 2.

Untitled 12-line "commemorative ode." *London Times,* March 25, 1944, p. 6.

Untitled 12-line poem. *London Times,* June 14, 1944, p. 7.

"A Moment Comes." *London Times,* May 8, 1945, p. 7.

"On the Ninetieth Birthday of Bernard Shaw." *Saturday Review of Literature,* July 27, 1946, p. 10.

Untitled 12-line "prologue." *London Times,* October 17, 1946.

Untitled 24-line poem. *London Times,* November 23, 1946.

"To His Most Excellent Majesty the King Upon the Sailing of the Royal Family for South Africa." *London Times,* January 31, 1947, p. 5.

"To His Most Excellent Majesty the King Upon His Return from South Africa." *London Times,* May 12, 1947, p. 4.

"Lines on the Occasion of the Wedding of Her Royal Highness the Princess Elizabeth." *London Times,* November 20, 1947, p. 5.

"Franklin Delano Roosevelt." *London Times,* April 12, 1948.

"Lines on the Occasion of the Silver Wedding of Our King and Queen." *London Times,* April 26, 1948.

"A Hope for the Newly Born." *London Times,* November 16, 1948.

"The Poet Laureate to His Cathedral Church, Liverpool Cathedral." *London Times,* March 30, 1949.

"My Library: Volume One." *Saturday Review of Literature,* May 20, 1950, p. 16.

"A Word of Hope." *London Times,* July 29, 1950, p. 5.

"On the Coronation of Our Gracious Sovereign." *London Times,* June 2, 1953.

"Lines for a One Hundredth Birthday: George Bernard Shaw." *Saturday Review of Literature,* July 21, 1956.

"On Coming Toward Eighty." *John Masefield: An Exhibition of Manuscripts and Books in Honor of his Eightieth Birthday, June 1, 1958.* London: The Times Bookshop, 1958.

"Lines Written in the Memory of Margaret Babington, A Friend of Canterbury Cathedral Who Died on August the 22nd, 1958." *Canterbury Cathedral Chronicle* 53, October 1958.

"Lines for the 25th January, 1959, being the 200th Anniversary of the Birth of Robert Burns." *London Times,* January 25, 1959.

"In Memory of Alfred Edward Housman, Born March 26, 1859." *London Times,* March 26, 1959.

"Lines for the Fourth Centenary of William Shakespeare." *London Times,* April 23, 1964.

"East Coker." *London Times,* January 8, 1965.

VII: *Bibliographies, Critical Studies, and Full-length Memoirs of Masefield*

Nicholl, Louise Townsend. *John Masefield, English Poet.* Unpublished manuscript written in 1919.

Williams, Iolo A. *Bibliographies of Modern Authors: No. 2. John Masefield.* London: Leslie Chaundy and Co., 1921.

Hamilton, W. H. *John Masefield: A Critical Study.* London: George Allen and Unwin, 1922. Rev. ed. 1925.

Biggane, Cecil. *John Masefield: A Study.* Cambridge: W. Heffer and Sons, 1924.

Simmons, Charles H. *A Bibliography of John Masefield.* New York: Columbia University Press, 1930.

Thomas, Gilbert. *John Masefield.* London: Thornton Butterworth, 1932.

Yu Da-Yuen. *John Masefield.* Peiping: San Yu Press, 1934.

Mason, John Edward. *John Masefield.* Exeter: Wheaton, 1938.

Drew, Fraser. *John Masefield: Interpreter of England and Englishmen.* Ann Arbor: University Microfilms 3929, 1952.

Strong, L. A. G. *John Masefield.* London: Longmans, Green and Co., 1952.

Spark, Muriel. *John Masefield.* London: Peter Nevill, 1953.

Drew, Fraser. *Some Contributions to the Bibliography of John Masefield.* New York: Papers of the Bibliographical Society of America, June and October 1959.

Handley-Taylor, Geoffrey. *John Masefield, O. M., The Queen's Poet Laureate: A Bibliography and Eighty-First Birthday Tribute.* London: The Cranbrook Tower Press, 1960.

Lamont, Corliss. *Remembering John Masefield.* Rutherford: Fairleigh Dickinson University Press, 1971.

VIII: *Articles about Masefield in Books and Periodicals* (in alphabetical rather than chronological order)

"An American Renaissance in Twenty Years." *Common Welfare Survey,* April 1, 1916, pp. 40–42.

Becker, May Lamberton. "John Masefield." *The Independent,* May 30, 1912, pp. 1158–61.

Beers, Henry A. Reviews of several Masefield books. *The Yale Review,* April 1913, pp. 560–63.

Blunden, Edmund. *The London Mercury,* July 1936, pp. 257–59.

Bogan, Louise. "The Shadow of the Laureateship." *Poetry,* March 1933, pp. 332–35.

Bregy, Katherine. "John Masefield." *The Catholic World,* June 1931, pp. 257–65.

Campbell, Gertrude H. "John Masefield of the Present Day." *The Bookman,* January 1921, p. 445.

Canby, Henry S. "Noyes and Masefield." *The Yale Review,* January 1916, pp. 287–302.

Chubb, Thomas C. "Some Recollections of John Masefield." *Mark Twain Journal,* Summer 1969, pp. 7–10.

Cournos, John. "A Visit to John Masefield." *The Independent,* September 1912.

Daniels, Diana P. "Without Fog Falling." *Christian Science Monitor,* September 18, 1968.

Davison, Edward. "The Poetry of John Masefield." *English Journal,* January 1926, pp. 5–13.

Drew, Fraser. "John Masefield's Dauber: Autobiography or Sailor's Tale Retold?" *Modern Language Notes,* February 1957, pp. 99–101.

————. "Those Singing Sailors." *Christian Science Monitor,* May 14, 1957.

————. "John Masefield and the *Manchester Guardian.*" *Philological Quarterly,* January 1958, pp. 126–28.

————. "John Masefield in New Haven." *Yale University Library Gazette,* April 1958, pp. 151–56.

————. "Poetry and Pugilism: John Masefield's Fights." *Canadian Forum,* October 1958, pp. 155–56.

————. "John Masefield's Ledbury." *In Britain.* October 1967, pp. 13–48.

————. "The Irish Allegiances of an English Laureate: John Masefield and Ireland." *Eire-Ireland,* Winter 1968, pp. 24–34.

"Editorial Paragraphs." *The Nation,* May 21, 1930, p. 587.

"Editorial." *The Publisher's Weekly,* June 30, 1945, p. 2501.

Firkins, O. W. "Mr. Masefield's Poetry." *The Nation,* March 15, 1919, pp. 389–90.

Fletcher, John Gould. "John Masefield: A Study." *North American Review,* October 1920, pp. 548–51.

Garrison, Winfred Ernest. "The New Poet Laureate." *The Christian Century,* May 28, 1930, pp. 688–89.

Glasser, Walter E. Letter to the Editor. *Saturday Review of Literature,* July 22, 1950, p. 24.

Gordon, Douglas. "Reynard the Fox." *Quarterly Review,* October 1922, pp. 265–78.

Gould, Gerald. "The Great Book of the War." *The Bookman,* June 1925, pp. 389–90.

Graves, Robert. "Chaucer's Man" (an extended version of address given at the memorial service for Masefield in Westminster Abbey, June 20, 1967). *Poetry Review,* Autumn 1967, pp. 241–46.

Housman, Laurence. *My Brother, A. E. Housman.* New York: Charles Scribner's Sons, 1938, p. 183.

Hutchison, Percy. *New York Times Book Review,* June 21, 1936, p. 5.

Inconstant Reader. "Preferences." *The Canadian Forum,* June 1930, pp. 328–29.

Kernahan, Coulson. *Six Living Poets.* London: Thornton Butterworth, 1922, p. 29.

Kunitz, Stanley J. and Haycraft, Howard. *Twentieth Century Authors.* New York: H. W. Wilson and Co., 1942, pp. 924–27.

"Letters and Arts." *The Living Age.* June 15, 1930, p. 490.

Lowell, Amy. *Poetry and Poets.* Cambridge: Houghton Mifflin Co., 1930, pp. 191–92.

"Man of the Hour in English Letters, The." *The Literary Digest,* April 13, 1912, pp. 752–53.

John Masefield, a pamphlet issued by The Macmillan Company. New York, *c.* 1927, p. 8.

Maynard, Theodore. "John Masefield." *The Catholic World,* April 1922, pp. 64–71.

Monroe, Harriet. Review of *Lollingdon Downs. Poetry,* September, 1917, pp. 320–23.

Murry, J. Middleton. "The Nostalgia of Mr. Masefield." *Athenaeum,* January 23, 1920, pp. 104–5.

"New Poet Laureate, The." *The Publisher's Weekly,* May 17, 1930, p. 2520.

Nicholl, Louise Townsend. "John Masefield in Yonkers." *The Bookman,* January, 1919, pp. 544–49.

"Of Ships and Wonder." *Time,* February 27, 1950, p. 108.

Outlook, The. January 26, 1916, p. 173.

"Poet Laureate, The." *The Bookman,* Christmas number, December, 1930, pp. 161–65.

Price, Clair. "Masefield Talks on Literature and the War." *New York Times Book Review,* March 17, 1940, p. 12.

Rascoe, Burton. "Among the New Books." *Arts and Decorations,* July, 1930, p. 47.

"Rough-Cut Poet Laureate, A." *Literary Digest,* May 24, 1930, p. 20.

Saerchinger, Cesar. "Poetry is Made to be Spoken." *Scholastic,* May 11, 1939, p. 29-E.

Salomon, I. L. "Queen's Poet." *Saturday Review,* December 26, 1953, p. 19.

Scott, Winfield Townley. "Prophet with Honor." *Poetry,* September 1936.

Scudder, Vida D. "Masefield's Arthurian Tales." *The Yale Review,* Spring 1929, pp. 592–93.

Shepard, Odell. "John Masefield: Poet Laureate." *The Bookman,* August 1930, pp. 477–83.

Sieller, William Vincent. "For John Masefield, Poet Laureate." *New York Times,* May 13, 1957.

Smith, Geddes. "Reynard the Fox." *New Republic,* January 7, 1920, pp. 174–75.

Squire, J. C. "The New Laureate, An Uneven Writer." *Editorial Notes, The London Mercury,* June 1930, pp. 100–101.

Squire, J. C. "Reynard the Fox." *The Living Age,* December 20, 1919, p. 729.

Stringer, Arthur. *Red Wine of Youth.* New York: The Bobbs-Merrill Company, 1948, *passim.*

Titterton, W. R. (excerpt from an article in *Daily Herald*). *The Living Age,* January 1931, pp. 537–38.

"Trend of Events, The." *The Outlook,* May 21, 1930, p. 95.

White, Newman I. "John Masefield, An Estimate." *South Atlantic Quarterly,* April 1927, pp. 189–200.

Willing, Ernest J. "John Masefield's 'The Everlasting Mercy'— A Study in Conversion." *The Homiletic Review,* October 1915, p. 262.

IX: *Letters and Miscellanea*

Ashwell, Lena. Letter to Fraser Drew, November 21, 1950.

Broadus, E. K. *The Laureateship: A Study of the Office of Poet Laureate in England with some account of the Poets.* Oxford: Clarendon Press, 1921.

Broadus, E. K. "The Laureateship." *The London Mercury,* June 1930, p. 134.

Hamilton, W. H. Letter to Fraser Drew, February 23, 1951.

Histories of the Kings of Britain by Geoffrey of Monmouth. Introduction by Lucy Allen Paton. Everyman's Library. London: J. M. Dent and Company, 1911, pp. viii–x.

J. M. B. (Subscription Department, *London Times*). Letter to Fraser Drew, March 27, 1951.

Kilham-Roberts, D. (Secretary-General, The Society of Authors, London). Letter to Fraser Drew, March 20, 1951.

Masefield, John. Letter to Louise Townsend Nicholl, April 9, 1919.

Masefield, John. Letter to W. H. Hamilton, n. d., *c.* 1920.

(Masefield, John). Nine post cards (not posted or dated) with views of Ledbury and surrounding country and annotations in Masefield's hand concerning *The Everlasting Mercy* and *The Widow in the Bye Street.*

O'Faolain, Sean. Letter to Fraser Drew, March 23, 1951.

Simpson, W. Douglas (Librarian, The University of Aberdeen). Letter to Fraser Drew, April 2, 1951.

Sir Thomas Malory: Le Morte D'Arthur. Introduction by Sir John Rhys. Everyman's Library. 2 vols. New York: E. P. Dutton and Company, 1906.

Turpin, K. C. (Secretary to the Faculties, University Registry, Oxford). Letter to Fraser Drew, March 13, 1951.

Yeats, Elizabeth C. Letter to L. G. Thornber, July 14, 1922.

Yeats, Jack B. Letters to Fraser Drew, July 13, 1950, and May 31, 1951.

Index

251